Secret Sky

The Ancient Tantras on Vajrasattva's Magnificent Sky

With Tibetan Text

Translations by

Christopher Wilkinson

Published by Christopher Wilkinson

Cambridge, MA, USA

ISBN: 1512373400
ISBN-13: 978-1512373400

DEDICATION

For my daughter, Arwyn.

ALSO TRANSLATED
BY CHRISTOPHER WILKINSON

The Great Tantra of Vajrasattva:
Equal to the End of the Sky

Secret Wisdom:
Three Root Tantras of the Great Perfection

Beyond Wisdom: The Upadesha of Vairochana on the
Practice of the Great Perfection

The Sakya Kongma Series:

Sakya Pandita's Poetic Wisdom

Jetsun Dragpa Gyaltsan: The Hermit King

Admission at Dharma's Gate by Sonam Tsemo

An Overview of Tantra and Related Works

Chogyal Phagpa: The Emperor's Guru

Advice to Kublai Khan: Letters by the Tibetan Monk
Chogyal Phagpa to Kublai Khan and his Court

Secret Sky

CONTENTS

The Tibetan Texts

ACKNOWLEDGMENTS

First and foremost, I wish to thank my root teacher Dezhung Rinpoche for constantly bringing out the best in me and encouraging me to pursue a comprehension of every branch of Buddhist learning. It was he who introduced me to Dilgo Kyentse Rinpoche, and through his recommendations enabled me to receive full empowerments, transmissions, and permissions in the areas of Mahā, Anu, and Ati Yogas. With the highest regard I wish to thank Dilgo Kyentse Rinpoche, Khetsun Zangpo Rinpoche, and Khenpo Palden Sherab for their kind instruction and encouragement in my effort to translate the literature of the rDzogs chen. There are many individuals, too many to name here, that have helped me over the years to become a qualified translator, in many ways. At this time I want to remember the kindness of Ngawang Kunga Trinlay Sakyapa, Jigdral Dagchen Sakya Rinpoche, Dhongthog Rinpoche, H.H. Karmapa Rangjung Rigpay Dorje, Kalu Rinpoche, Chogyam Trungpa Rinpoche, Geshe Ngawang Nornang, David Ruegg, Turrell Wylie, Gene Smith, Karen Lang, Richard Solomon, Jack Hawley, David Jackson, Cyrus Stearns, Herbert Guenther, Eva Neumeier-Dargyay, Leslie Kawamura, Robert Thurman, Paul Nietupski, Lou Lancaster, David Snellgrove, Jean-Luc Achard, Steve Landsberg, Moke Mokotoff, Tsultrim Alione, Carolyn Klein, Rob Mayer, Jonathan Silk, David White, Mark Tatz, Steve Goodman, and Kennard Lipman. I want to make special thanks to Sarah Moosvi and Otavio Lilla for proofing the manuscript. The many people who have contributed to my understanding and ability to do this work cannot be counted. I wish to thank everyone that has taken a kind interest in these translations, however slight, for your part in making this work a reality.

INTRODUCTION

The Tantras of Vajrasattva's Magnificent Sky, also known as the Unfailing Royal Insignia,[1] come to us in manuscript traditions, books copied through the centuries, from Tibet and Bhutan. The texts are translations attributed to Vairochana, a famous translator of the eighth century, a Tibetan who went to India in search of the literature on instantaneous enlightenment, found it, and brought it back to Tibet. The original Indian texts have been lost in time.

Vairochana's translations fill many volumes,[2] but he is most famous for translating the *Ngagyur Nga* (*snga 'gyur lnga*): The Five Early Translations. These are The Cuckoo of Awareness, Shaking off the Grand Search, The Soaring of the Magnificent Garuda, Meditating on the Bodhicitta, and the Unfailing Royal Insignia: The Magnificent Sky. I have already translated and published Vairochana's own teachings on these five Tantras.[3]

The teachings on the Magnificent Sky are said to be oceanic in proportion. What we have, in terms of surviving manuscript traditions, is fifteen individual titles.[4] Basically, there are three Root Tantras, five Embellished Tantras, two Tantras associated with the Heart of Secrets, the *Guhyagarbha*, and a set of fifty-five verses that are found under various titles, and which constitute chapter 30 of the *Kun byed rGyal po*. I have already published a translation of one Root Tantra in this set: The Unborn.[5] There remain two Root Tantras: Effulgent Vajra Light and Vajrasattva's Magnificent Sky. Both are translated here. The Embellished Tantras are: The Unwritten, For the King, For the Brahmins, For the Yogins, and for the Yoginis. The first three of these are translated in the book you now hold.[6] The two Tantras connected to the *Guhyagarbha* will be published in an upcoming volume.

How do these teachings fit into the Buddhist tradition? Generally speaking, the vast array of the Buddha's teachings is divided up in many different ways, depending on the objectives of different schools and individuals. We often hear of the division between the Hinayana and the Mahayana, where a concern for personal liberation characterizes the first and an enlightened attitude based on great compassion for all sentient beings characterizes the latter. We hear of a division between the approach of the Sutras and the approach of the Tantras, where the first represents the practical approach of a gradual search for enlightenment through the development of generosity, rules, patience, perseverance, meditation, and wisdom, while the approach of the Tantras is usually based on a deity yoga in which special methods are employed in the hope of rapid enlightenment. The Tantras of the Magnificent Sky belong to a special class of Tantra, the Great Perfection, which does not employ deity yoga, rejects practices of visualization, and recommends instantaneous enlightenment. For those who follow the Ancient Traditions of Tibetan Buddhism, the *Nyingma*, this is the highest and most profound Buddhist teaching. The schools of Buddhism in Tibet that are known as the New Schools, or *Sarma,* did not recognize the instantaneous approach as a true Buddhist teaching.[7] The primary difference in opinion is that the New Schools insist that our progress toward enlightenment is a gradual process, while the Great Perfection teaches that enlightenment is instantaneous. We might say that while all the other pathways offered by Buddhism teach about becoming enlightened, the Great Perfection teaches about being enlightened. The Tantras of the Magnificent Sky are profound expressions of this approach.

We have reason to believe that the authenticity of the Magnificent Sky Tantras was in doubt, even during Vairochana's lifetime. In the closing comments of The Sun of My Heart: A Hearty Elixir for Panditas and Siddhas, while speaking of the Magnificent Sky, Vairochana states:

> This has no resemblance to what Universal Monarchs or teachers like Śākyamuni have taught. An investigation that will approve of or refute the ocean of upadeśa on the Unfailing Royal Insignia, which is the heart transmission of the All Good Garab, does not disturb my mind. I hope this will be a lamp for those whose fortune it is to see things partially.[8]

As you read the present translations, you will have an opportunity to evaluate these teachings from twelve-hundred years ago for yourself.

During the early period of Buddhism in Tibet, the five Tantras that represent the Early Translations by Vairochana, including the Magnificent Sky, were said to address the concerns of the mind, *Sems phyogs*, while later on these Tantras were referred to as the Mind Section, or *Sems sde*, which is then differentiated from the Space Section (*kLong sde*) and the Upadeśa Section (*Man ngag sde*). These divisions are not found in the Tantras themselves, but represent the commentarial tradition that developed in Tibet.

These Tantras have been faithfully copied as manuscripts over the centuries, and are found today in either the Hundred Thousand Tantras of Vairochana[9] or in the collections known as the Hundred Thousand Tantras of the Ancient Ones, the *Nyingma Gyubum.* Collections called *Nyingma Gyubum* were kept in various monasteries and libraries, each with its own set of "Ancient Tantras." Several different versions of the *Nyingma Gyubum* are now available. The present translations were done based on witnesses found in the mTshams brag Manuscript.[10] I include images of the pages of the manuscript for those who may be interested and to help preserve these ancient writings.

Many people, both kind and wise, have helped me understand and learn to translate these Tantras. Any shortcomings there may be are entirely my own. It is my sincere hope that you find these translations to be enjoyable reading with enlightening content.

All the best,

Christopher Wilkinson
May 2015

EFFULGENT VAJRA LIGHT

In the Indian language:

Bodhicitta Vajra Prabha Tantra Nāma

In the Tibetan language:

Byang chub sems rdo rje 'od 'phro ba'i rgyud kyi rim pa zhes bya ba

In the English language:

The Progressions of the Tantra on Bodhicitta: Effulgent Vajra Light

FAILURE DOES NOT LEAD TO TERMINATION

I bow to the Blessed One,
Glory of glories,
The one who is beyond speech, thought, and utterance.

I heard these words at one time:

The Blessed One, the glorious Vajrasattva, was in a single company and gathering with the Bodhisattva Vajrasattva in the abode of the All Good, Akaniṣṭa, a palace of awareness, an inconceivable dominion that is called: "Promulgation of Miraculous Blessings."

At that time, Vajrasattva addressed the Blessed One, the All Good One, with these words:

Please give us a method
By which those who have failed in their samaya
May heal.

The Blessed One, the Lord of the Dharma, gave an oration:

O Mahasattva,
Now listen!
The god of the five Atiyogas[11]
Is a superior yoga
That is even better than yoga.
It is a nobility
That is even greater than nobility.
The vajra Victorious One

Is the ancestor of us all.
The most holy and revered one,
The All Good,
Is a refuge from fear
For king Vajradhara.

When it happens that we get cut off
Due to a failure,
There is no one else for us
Then this revered protector.

The protector of living beings has correctly stated
That samaya are just the mind.
The mind itself has no substance,
So what could cut it off?
What could discontinue our equanimity?

What did we fail at?
What is the failure?
How did we fail?
This is precisely what an attitude of failure is.
This is precisely what clinging to a downfall is.

When we wash our minds with the water of purity
There is nothing that will not become pure.
If we understand the meaning of isolated emptiness[12]
We will not have even a name for happiness and sorrow.

Happiness and sorrow,
Beauty and the unbeautiful,
Self and selflessness,
Emptiness and non-emptiness:
We can hold onto these things
As being the way that it is,
But there is no substance to their being.

It does not matter what conventionalities we designate them with.
How will they ever propel us to the top?
Uncontrived settling of ourselves
Is exemplified as being our awareness.
The time in which our being cut off will happen
Is when the sky comes to an end.

We see reality,
But it seems that when we feel something
With the tip of our finger,
That is when we see its reality.

So he spoke.

From the Tantra on the Holy and Revered Bodhicitta: Effulgent Vajra Light, this is chapter one: Failure Does Not Lead to Termination.

TEACHING THAT EVERYTHING IS THE MIND

O Mahasattva,

What is it that is called: "Failure"?
What is it that is called: "Termination"?
We may hold that there is failure and termination,
But nothing is evident that constitutes these things.
When we work toward a fruition and desire to succeed at it
We will not find it.
It is as if we were blind people scrutinizing the sky.

The nature of the Bodhicitta
Is difficult to analyze.
There is not even an atom to be said of it.
Just like the nations of the six classes of beings,
It does not exist.
The minds of ordinary people do not touch it.

What is enlightenment?
What is the mind?

The basis of all things,
Self-originating wisdom,
By its very character,
Is a magnificent absence of complications.
Its superior virtues are not to be sought out.
It is the mind.
It is the Bodhicitta.

In the same way that the tip of a fire
Totally burns up material substances,
But is unable to burn its own substance,
The Bodhicitta knows all things,
But it does not know self-awareness.

Knowledge itself does not know.
There is nothing to be done about this:
No search and no endeavor.
There is no duality between the pure and the impure.
To say about great self-originating purity:
"This does not exist"
Is just an attribution.

When we do not dwell on attributions,
We will dwell in the Bodhicitta.
There is no dwelling in this dwelling,
So we do not attribute any such conventionality as: "Dwelling."

The Buddhas of the three times
Have arisen from the mind.
So does the mind harbor conventionalities,
Or what?

Everything that emerges from the mind
Is all the mind.
The mind is unborn.
It is the way that it is.
It knows lucidly that everything is self-luminous.

This knowledge is also the mind.
You must understand this,
O Mahasattva.

From the Tantra on the Holy and Revered Bodhicitta: Effulgent Vajra Light, this is chapter two: Teaching that Everything is the Mind.

EVERYTHING COMES FROM THE MIND

O Mahasattva,

The totality of samsara
Emerges within the mind.
Nirvana is also like that.
It is whatever occurs within it.

By merely signifying it, saying: "It exists,"
We do not make it properly exist.
It is everything,
And it is nothing at all.

This is how I myself understand it correctly,
And this is how you fortunate ones must understand it.

Furthermore,
O Vajrasattva,
Emotional problems are, in fact, the pathway of enlightenment.
Reversions are, in fact, enlightenment.
Correctness is, in fact, reversion.
Everything was created by the mind.
The mind is something that exists for us.
Self-originating wisdom exists within ourselves.
If it did not exist within ourselves,
It would not be self-originating wisdom.

But if we seek it in something else,
And we have to work on it,
Then it depends on both causes and conditions,

And is not self-originating wisdom.

That which does not depend on causes and conditions
Is a solitary self-luminescence that is filthless.
It is not generated out of causes and conditions.
It is self-originating.

It is an unshadowed luminosity,
So it is wisdom.
From the primordial,
Our heart-essence has been enlightenment.
Our dominion is not to be shaken
By thoughts about a search.

This is taught in dependence on that.
We use the method of oiling things,
To make them endure.
This is why the people who work to accommodate us
Must be taught the meaning of awareness.

If they did not understand its meaning,
And they did not have the water of the Bodhicitta,
Even the Victorious Ones would be thirsty.

If a queen who desires milk,
Must look for it somewhere else,
Then a queen who milks a goat
Will get no milk from the goat.

Everything comes from this,
And goes back to this.
There is not even one thing
That does not come forth from this.

From the Tantra on the Holy and Revered Bodhicitta: Effulgent Vajra Light, this is chapter three: Everything Comes from the Mind.

TEACHING THE ESSENCE OF THE MIND

Then Vajrasattva addressed him:

O Blessed One,
What is the essence of the mind?

The Blessed One gave an oration:

Mahasattva,

The true nature of the mind
Is not any thing,
But may appear as anything.
It is immeasurable,
Unspeakable,
And inconceivable.
It is not to be exemplified by saying: "This."
I proclaim this to be the nature of the mind.

The sorrows of living beings appear,
But beings are themselves.
They do not come from anyone else.

It is said that with the exception of the dominion of the Dharma,
Not even an atom's part of happiness, freedom, and pleasure
Exists.
The wheels of our bodies and our adornments
Are also our own minds.
They are not anyone else's.

The Buddha, Dharma, and Sangha are ourselves.
They are nothing else.
For this reason,
There is no object for our devotions.

This is not to be protected,
Not to be worked on,
And not to be sought after.
It has no color, shape, place, or class.
There is no happiness and sorrow,
No cause and result.

It is not non-existent.
It is unspeakable.
It is not a self.
It is not an other.
It does not die or pass on.

It is not non-existent.
It is the source of everything.
It is not a source.
It is what it is.

The encompassing character of wisdom,
Where everything is one,
Is like drinking water that tastes like the sky.
There is a single significance,
But it is not clearly distinguishable.
This is the self-awareness of the Bodhicitta.
It is not to be taught by saying: "This."
Anything at all may appear from nothing at all.

This self-originating heart-essence
Is of the highest significance.
In its appearance,
Nothing appears.
It is made visible
By using the way of invisibility.

To say: "It does not exist"
Is just a grasping.
We must not dwell

Even on this.
If we dwell on it,
It becomes a ground for deviation.

Who is it that deviates?
How do they deviate?
These are the appearances of deviation.
They are also without substance.
This is why we must not dwell on them.
If we dwell on them,
We are holding on to something.

So he spoke, and Vajrasattva began to dwell on himself.

From the Tantra on the Holy and Revered Bodhicitta: Effulgent Vajra Light, this is chapter four: Teaching the Essence of the Mind.

TEACHING THE VIRTUE OF THE MIND

O Mahasattva,
You, O Hero of the Mind,
Must listen,
For I will explain the virtues of the mind.

Regarding the magnificent virtues of the mind,
Buddhas equal in number to the atoms of the three thousand worlds
May speak out for ten million eons,
But they will not be able to speak on this.

This is a total luminosity that is not shadowed.
This is, in fact, the heart-essence of everything.
We may be tormented by ten million sorrows,
But there is not even an atom of this that is moved.

The entire totality of happiness and sorrow,
Is great pleasure for this,
But we do not hold onto this in its time.

The embodiment of the Dharma,
Which is not to be visualized as anything,
Delights in this magical nature,
But this is not delight.
It is what it is.

It does not expand.
It does not contract.
It is not written.

It is beyond reckoning.
It is a spontaneously realized embodiment.

We flow in it.
The clouds of offerings for this
Are there by the river.
This is the method by which we succeed.[13]
It is a siddhi that is naturally irreversible.
Its objective is a perfect *mudra.*

A person who understands the meaning of this
Does no service,
And maintains no recitations or chants.
He has no practice,
And has no meditation.
He has nothing to protect,
And nothing to think about,
Nothing to give up,
And nothing to take on.

There is nothing that we do
To relinquish the Bodhicitta.
Everything is perfect.
This is the self-arising king.
This is the true identity[14] of all the Buddhas.

It is a condensed elixir of all our fruits.
It is naturally luminous,
And has no darkness.
Everything that appears,
With no exceptions,
Comes from this,
And returns to this.

Faults and virtues are not a duality.
There is nothing to take up.
There is nothing to cast off.
There is no change by passing on.
We achieve everything
Without having done anything.
Everything is revealed to us
Without our going anywhere.
We understand everything

Without being taught.

This is called: "The virtue of the mind."
The Blessed One, the All Good One, has proclaimed it.

From the Tantra on the Holy and Revered Bodhicitta: Effulgent Vajra Light, this is chapter five: Teaching the Virtue of the Mind.

THE UNTHINKABLE
IS NOT TO BE TAKEN INTO OUR EXPERIENCE

Then Vajrasattva said:

O Blessed One,
Please explain the method
By which we are to take this into our experience.

The teacher gave an oration:

O Mahasattva,
There is nothing to be taken into our experience,
So use the way where there is no taking in
To take this in.

Do not reject appearances.
There is nothing to think about.
Do not dwell on an absence of ideas.

The absence of ideas is a lucidity.
This lucidity is also an absence of ideas.
It is the basis for a true essence
That is not a designation.
We remain within a river of awareness,
Just as it is.

The space of awareness
Is a clear light that is beyond our ideas.

It is primordially pervaded by luminosity,
Just as it is.

It has no thought.
It has no memory.
It has no motion.

The dhyāna meditation of greatest virtue
Is to use your dhyāna
Toward an absence of thought,
But we do not dwell on this absence,
And we do not hinder our ideas.
This is called: "The king of ideas."
The Victorious Ones have explained it correctly.

We must know that the way things are,
Without thought or analysis,
Is like water in water.
To dwell on non-duality
Is said to be a magnificent dwelling.
The All Good Hero of the Mind[15]
Has explained this correctly.

The meaning of this is not to be explained.
It has not been explained by the Victorious Ones.
Victorious ones of the future
Will also not explain it.
Even in the present,
It is not being explained.

From the Tantra on the Holy and Revered Bodhicitta: Effulgent Vajra Light, this is chapter six: The Unthinkable is Not to be Taken into Our Experience.

TEACHINGS ON THE TRUE NATURE OF THE BODHICITTA

Then again Vajrasattva addressed him:

O Blessed One,
What is the Bodhicitta?

He gave an oration:

Mahasattva, listen!

The definition of the Bodhicitta
Is that it is everything
And it is not anything whatever.

Even the four great elements, or the five,
Are, in fact, described to be the Bodhicitta.
It does not appear to be
On the outside or in the inside,
A position or a side,
Samsara or nirvana,
Cause or result,
Buddha or sentient being,
Male or female,
A color, shape, place, or lineage.

Any definition or defining feature
That may appear in the transmission,
Or among the people,
Whatever it may be,

Is, in fact, the Bodhicitta.

It does not come from anything else,
And is not to be sought after.
All things are essentially existent,
But when they are mixed up,
They become indefinite.

I do not proclaim that things are multiple.
Everything appears to us without hindrance.
But I also do not say that there is a one.
I am liberated from unity and plurality.

The definitions for this are without certitude.
This is, in fact, the embodiment of the Dharma of enlightenment.
We realize the essence of all things spontaneously,
Without any search.
We are primordial Buddhas.
We arrive everywhere without going anywhere.
Everything comes together without being compiled.
We are free from all obstructions
Without rejecting anything.

On the path to enlightenment there will appear
Samsara and nirvana,
The Buddha and sentient beings,
And the six classes of living things,
But even though we might organize all these things
Into essential definitions,
Using hundreds of thousands of: "This came from that,"
We will not exemplify it,
For it is what it is.

We exemplify it by saying:
"It is exemplified just by saying: 'It is',"
But while we may say things in words,
There is nothing to exemplify,
And no act of exemplification.

This is to be exemplified
Using the way of no exemplifications.
This is the greatest exemplification.
When you know that the meaning of this

Is the totality of your awareness,
All the wheels of samsara and sorrow's delusions
Will, in fact, be your Bodhicitta.
This is what I have explained.

From the Tantra on the Holy and Revered Bodhicitta: Effulgent Vajra Light, this is chapter seven: Teachings on the True Nature of the Bodhicitta.

REMOVING OBSTACLES

Then the Blessed One Great Bliss gave the entourage an oration in words:

O Mahasattvas,

The thing that we think of as equanimity
Is an obstruction to both problems and virtues.
To desire to be attached to happiness
And to reject sorrow
Is like a person who was born blind
Tying a knot in the sky.

If you do not clearly understand the real meaning,
The meaning of uncontrived equanimity,
Then even though the bodies of the Victorious Ones
Might fill the three thousand worlds,
They would be of no use.
If they did not fill them
It would do no harm.

Enlightenment and emotional problems are not a duality.
In the vastness of the basis of all things,
They are one.
For this reason,
There is nothing to take up or to reject.
This is, itself, not something that is made,
For it is self-evident.

Depression and wildness,
Hopes and worries,
Clarity and lack of clarity,
The spaces of origins and applications,
Experience, thought, and contrived cessations,
The evidence of defining attributes,
And the abundance of feelings:
From the primordial,
All of these things
Are perfected in their own lack of clarity.

Without making attributions,
This is the primordial embodiment of the Dharma.
Our true self[16] is ornamented
With playfulness that does not abandon anything.

Those who do not perceive their true selves
Are the ones who were born blind.
The meaning that they will not find
Is that there is nothing to be taken up or cast off.

When you understand that problems, in themselves,
Are oriented toward equanimity,
That is what is called: "The All Good."

In the same way that clouds, tornadoes, rainbows, and lightening
Are evident in the emptiness of the luminescent sky
Without being mixed up with the stars,
Or the sun and the moon,
In the essence of the luminescent sky,
They are, from the beginning,
One.

Faults and virtues will appear
In the sky-space of a yogin's mind,
But there is nothing to be taken up,
Or to be cast off.
All of the details on the vehicles,
None excepted,
Are fully perfected without confusion
In this freedom from rejecting things,
And taking things on.

The essence of omniscience,
An inconceivable absence of clarity,
Is not to be visualized.

From the Tantra on the Holy and Revered Bodhicitta: Effulgent Vajra Light, this is chapter eight: Removing Obstacles.

SETTLING INTO EQUANIMITY

Then the Tathagata
Entered the equanimity of samadhi
In the magnificent purity of the unspoken,
And Vajrasattva said:

Blessed One,
What is the meaning of leaving things unspoken?
How will you give me an oration on this?

O Mahasattva,

You will understand this through contemplating
That everything appears at the same time.
That which we do not conceptualize in any way whatever
Does not move away from this essential significance.

When we do not understand
The meaning of that which is not spoken,
Then everyone and everything we conceptualize to be equal
Will be, in fact, a gathering of the blind.

The Blessed One, the Tathagata, proclaimed this.
It is not confused with anything.
It is an unhindered clarity.
In brief,
Our heart is just enlightenment.

This is not an idea.
It is apart from taking things up and casting them off.
All the inquiry into this primordial pervasion
That encompasses all things
Uses names, words, and symbols,
But does not exemplify this.
Wisdom that is not exemplified
Is the best of embodiments.

It is clear without being written,
A speech that is understood.
The clear light of non-conceptualization
Is the best of hearts.

It is not to be sought.
It is spontaneously realized.
It is present from the beginning.
This is a magnificent and trouble-free objective.
It is an objective that is not anything at all.
Our cognition does not think about anything,
And this is beyond conception.

This kind of thought is a magnificent thought.
It is just like a *kalabingka* bird.
All our wishes come true without a search.
For this reason,
Living spontaneously without seeking
Is the best of objectives.

From the Tantra on the Holy and Revered Bodhicitta: Effulgent Vajra Light, this is chapter nine: Settling into Equanimity.

TEACHING THE PATH OF PRACTICE

O Mahasattva,

Non-existence and the stomach,
The solitary and the spontaneously perfected,
Those gathered unto me and those without a side,
Appear to me,
And are spontaneously formed in me.

The primordial protection that is not to be sought
Is the best of samayas.
It is protected from the beginning,
So there is nothing to protect.
To be competent without protection
Is the best of samayas.

The great spirit[17] is everything.
There is nothing whatever to seek for
Anywhere else.
It is not an idea.
It is not a thought.
Nothing stops it.

A path of practice like this
Is free from rejection and acquisition.
We do not leave the state of equanimity.
I state that this is the only samaya of the great perfection.

We achieve our purposes without thought or effort.
This is a spontaneously realized samaya.
If we do meditations on our hands,
And contemplations of what we have heard,
Offerings, singing melodies, and distributing alms,
Without the power of the unattached great perfection,
Then all these things will be causes for our entrapment.

When we do not take anything seriously,
Our practice is a magnificent absence of practice.

I practice myself.
I grant empowerment to myself.
The king of awareness
Is beyond words and thoughts.
There is no one whosoever that teaches it.

From the Tantra on the Holy and Revered Bodhicitta: Effulgent Vajra Light, this is chapter ten: Teaching the Path of Practice.

THE GREAT ETERNITY OF BODY, SPEECH, AND MIND

O Mahasattva,

Self-originating wisdom,
The Bodhicitta,
The great spirit,
The supreme embodiment of the Dharma,
The pacifier of both exaggerations and degradations,
The meaning of equanimity,
The magnificent attribution of all time:
The vajra body,
By its very nature,
Is unable to define what it is.

How could it be that wisdom is a transmission?
You may say anything in words
About a permanent transmission,
But I myself,
The king of awareness,
Am free from passing on and changing.
From permanence and impermanence.

Ordinary wisdom has a birth and an end,
But it does not have the ability to do things meaningfully.
When we have nothing to take on or cast off,
We are free from meanings.

The past, future, and present
Are incapable of being forever,
And for this reason,
This essence that is primordially permanent
Is beyond speech.

It is not fitting that anyone define it.
In the past, future, and the present,
There will be a time,
The arrival of which is indeterminate,
An instant in which we know
Unconfused clarity.

I do not say that this is a permanence or a knowledge.
It certainly is these things,
But I am free from attachments and ideas.

This, in fact, abides primordially throughout the three times.
A snake in a dark house
And a delusion
Are not the same.

We may have abided in this through beginningless time,
But the purity there is in not abandoning things
Is the level of the Buddha.
To work towards our purpose without effort
Is the best of good works.

From the Tantra on the Holy and Revered Bodhicitta: Effulgent Vajra Light, this is chapter eleven: The Great Eternity of Body, Speech, and Mind.

PRAISES AND ENDOWMENT

Then, from out of the emptiness, these words echoed forth, without making a sound:

E Ma Ho!
The wisdom of the all good is an organizer.
It is the origin of everything.
It fulfills our wishes.
It is an embodiment of wish-fulfilling jewels.
Conception-free omniscience
Does effortless good work.
I bow to the totally pure Bodhicitta.

E Ma!
I am spontaneously realized without a search,
So I do not teach those who are gathered unto me
About an essence,
For this is not compounded.
This is beyond words.
Its heart is the Bodhicitta.
I bow to that which is beyond speech, thought, and words.

E Ma Ho!

I am a magician who overcomes demons,
Which are not permanent.
The works of my body, speech, and mind
May appear as anything.
They are all subsumed within me,

So I am the great spirit.
My works will appear to be anything.
I bow to them.
A Ho!

Then the Tathagata gave an oration to Vajrasattva:

Kye!
This is beyond exaggeration and denigration.
It is an elixir of meaning.
It shows things without thinking of them,
Like a mirror.
The teaching that maintains no giving up or taking on
Is the best of vehicles.

The one who makes everything his
Is the true king.
He is forever without thoughts.
The center of his heart does not fail,
And is not diffused.
The tenth level is its objective.
It is a supreme study of fearlessness.
It is the highest summit
Of the meaning of the Mahayana,
Which remains superior.

May those of brilliant senses melt into it,
And may its wheels always spin.

So he spoke.

Vajrasattva and the inestimably large entourage of Bodhisattvas, along with the palace and everything else, converged into his body. Then even his body melted into the heart-essence of the Bodhicitta, and became invisible.

From the Tantra on the Effulgent Light of the Holy Lord-King Bodhicitta,[18] this is chapter twelve: Praises and Endowment.

The Tantra of the Effulgent Vajra Light of the Holy Lord-King, the King of Tantras on the Unfailing Royal Insignia,[19] is finished.

THE UNWRITTEN

THE TANTRA OF VAJRASATTVA'S MAGNIFICENT SKY EMBELLISHED AS THE UNWRITTEN

rDo rje sems dpa' nam mkha' che rgyas pa'i yi ge med pa'i rgyud

THE BASIC SCENE

It is stated in the Tantra for the King that when the Unwritten was proclaimed, those who are no different than myself heard something that they had not heard before, and were terrified.

Then Vajrasattva and the rest of the assembly, heroes of the mind and heroines of the mind, male and female door keepers, the holy protectors of the doors beginning with the Slayer of the Lord of the Dead, the Blessed One Unmoving and the other Blessed Ones, along with their ladies, filled the place up as if it was a pack full of sesame seeds.

Then the entourage presented a request:

Most Direct One,[20]
Please explain the supreme significance
Of the only thing
That the Tathagatas take to heart.
Please explain the holy and supreme method
To relinquish definitions.
Please explain the Unwritten.

From the Unwritten, this is chapter one: The Basic Scene.

PLEASING THE MASTER

Then he took the form of the Supreme Master, the Maker of All Appearance,[21] and without stopping, made a smile. He took the objectives of the entourage to heart, and proclaimed:

Children of Heritage,
If you wish to listen well,
I will speak on what you ask.

This Tantra is extremely difficult to analyze.
It has no defining characteristics.
A great hero's conquest is most difficult to reverse,
But is to be studied in the ways of its success.
We may develop a longing at first,
But it will be extremely difficult to control it.

Then the entourage, with a single voice, asked the meaning of this:

This is an understanding
Of what it means to move in bliss.
It is of supreme import.
It has no defining characteristics.

We do not seek out the meaning of the Unwritten,
For motion through bliss is unwritten,
And writings are made use of by criminals.

We have turned away from definitions.
We seek to be liberated from the five kinds of attributions.

Then the omniscient one did not turn away
From speaking out on this holy objective:
His oration of the Unwritten.

To begin,
We brighten our intellects with the Tantra.
In the interim,
We determine our thoughts,
Or we make an intellectual search
For what is most excellent.
We comprehend the significance of what is said
In our heads,
And study methods that are not mistaken.

This appears under the identity of Ta.
The mouth that illuminates it
Brings together our spirits[22] and our minds.
For students who are stumbling toward the ultimate truth,
The identity of liberation
Is a heritage of jewels.

This is chapter two: Pleasing the Master.

THE STAGES OF WISDOM

Then the Supreme Master spoke on the stages of wisdom:

Wisdom is not generated.
Its dominion is not generated.
When you see your own mind by yourself
You are defining it.
This is not the holy truth.

The development of a negation or an end
Is a mental contrivance.
You must be aware of this.

The practice is a dominion of Dharma
That has no depletion.
We do not stop using the Three Baskets,
Even though they do not have an essence
That is a single Dharma.

If we were to find samadhi
Through the appearance of a definition,
We would attain both ignorance and liberation.
The special quality of this samadhi
Would be both a path to enlightenment
And a visualization.

From the Sugata's Unwritten, this is chapter three: The Stages of Wisdom.

TEACHING THAT WISDOM IS NOT TO BE VISUALIZED

Then that entourage of Sugatas asked the Supreme Master:

Kye Ma!
Leader of those who move in bliss!
The holy Unwritten has never been restricted,
But today it is restricted.
The narrow places are shaking open into wideness.
The entourage has not heard these things before,
And is terrified.
What is special about the knowledge
Of the meaning of the Unwritten?

The holy leader gave an oration:

The knowledge of the Unwritten
Is a wisdom that cannot be visualized.
It does not contrive the dominion of the Dharma
To be a material thing.

The vase of wisdom
Uses self-originating awareness
To instantaneously cut through.
We encounter our wisdom and its dominion
Face to face.

From the supreme Tantra of the Unwritten, which is the true nature of all the Tathagatas, this is the fourth chapter: Teaching that Wisdom is not to be Visualized.

LIVING NATURALLY

Then they asked something specific:

This is an excellent oration on the Unwritten,
Which is unspoken and is not to be visualized.
We pray that the Blessed One will give an oration
So that we may be done with words and letters.

Again he gave an oration, an intentional statement:

The definition of living naturally
Is that it is a peace in which there is nothing to take up,
And nothing to cast off.

The true nature of the Dharma is emptiness.
Even the Buddha does not see it,
So how could it be seen through direct perception?

Not to see anything at all
Is a magnificent seeing.
The pure *kāya*[23] is the dominion of the Dharma.
We may turn the wheel of the Dharma,
But we are doing nothing,
Even for an instant.

There is no visualization
For the understanding of what this means.
This supreme Tantra,
The Unwritten,

Is, as an analogy,
Like a king.

From the King of Tantras, the Unwritten, this is chapter five: Living Naturally.

PLEASING THE MASTER

Then the supreme leader of the Unwritten took the questions of the entourage to heart:

This great vehicle is worthy of our honor,
For it is the magnificent heart-essence of enlightenment,
But those who are endowed with a heritage of jewels
Must learn of it from their guru's mouth.

Among the pathways there are,
This is the short road.
It is a most excellent method,
And is famed as the Unwritten.

If we do not know its way,
We will not discern that it is unwritten.
One who gets the meaning of this
Will attain the fruits of the great vehicle.

From the magnificently embellished Unwritten, this is chapter six: Pleasing the Master.

YOGA IS NOT SEEN

Then that entourage, let by the Bodhisattva Blissful,[24] questioned the Supreme Master in a single voice:

Great Hero,
You have overcome delusional ideas!
Please give us an unsurpassed explanation
Of this most excellent freedom
From the demons of gloom,
This solitary and holy truth
That you hold in your heart.

Then he understood the thinking of the Bodhisattva Blissful[25] and the others, and he gave an oration:

If you would all like to listen well,
I will explain the solitary contemplation of my heart.
You must remain mindful.

The sky is indivisible,
But at the first moment we determine
That the totality of the sky is a thought,
And at the final moment,
We negate the existence of any sky other than this one,
For this is not to be visualized.

In the holy truth,
The sky is indivisible,
So there is nothing to negate.

This is a validation that is not to be negated.

If there is existence in this,
We move toward negation.
If there is non-existence,
It is like a flower from the sky.
The ends of my contemplation have no negation.

From the Unwritten Tantra, this is chapter seven: Yoga is not Seen.

BEQUEST TO THE ENTOURAGE

Then again they asked the Supreme Master:

Is there not a contradiction
In believing that these defining characteristics have a name?
You, O Lord, have knowledge of this,
So please give an oration,
So that we may cleanse our intellects.

Those of you who have debased thinking
Must listen to this king of the profound Tantras,
The Unwritten,
With respect,
But at the moment of dawn you must stop.
Then you must apply it,
Immerse yourselves in it.
These are the avenues of the Unwritten.

I have demarcated what is to be done with it,
And sealed it with a bequest:
It is for those with a heritage of jewels.
The vessel for my orations is consciousness.
This Tantra is granted in stages.

From the magnificently embellished Unwritten, this is chapter eight: Bequest to the Entourage.

CONCLUSION

Then he gave some practical advice to the entourage:

This is a samadhi that has no meditation or practice.
It does not seek.
Its initial unity is beyond doubt.
Our contemplation over the interim is definitive.
In the end,
We understand the contrivances of our minds.
Those who live without visualizations
Have nothing to seek.

With the seal of bequest by the Sugata,
This is the conclusion.

It was translated by the Tibetan monk Vairochana and the Indian wise man Jñānagarbha, then edited and published.

THE TANTRA OF VAJRASATTVA'S MAGNIFICENT SKY

EMBELLISHED FOR THE BRAHMINS

In the Indian language:

Vajrasatva Samaya Khe Mahādeha Puṣṭigara Tantra

In the Tibetan language:

rDo rje sems dpa' nam mkha' che bram ze rgyas pa'i rgyud

In the English language:

The Tantra of Vajrasattva's Magnificent Sky
Embellished for the Brahmins

THE BASIC SCENE

I bow to the Blessed One, All Good.

These things were once discussed:

In a crystal palace in the abode of Akaniṣṭa,
The sky of reality,
The sphere of our true domain,
The abode of the mind itself:
Wisdom that has no shadows,
There is the manifest entourage of my own true nature,
My own essence,
And my own compassion.

The entourage of my true nature is called:
"The embodiment of the Dharma."
The entourage of my own essence is called:
"The embodiment of perfect pleasure."
The entourage of my great compassion is called:
"The manifest embodiment."
They dwell in a single congress
With that indivisible entourage that includes Vajrasattva.

Then the Blessed One, All Good, convened them all,
And they sat in a single great circle.[26]

Then Vajrasattva,
Who was sitting in the one great circle,

His own true nature,
Got up from it.
He got up with a glowing radiance,
With a mind of joy for the Blessed One,
The All Good,
Then he presented himself.

Then the Blessed One All Good spoke to Vajrasattva:

Vajrasattva,
E Ma'o!
You have given birth to a mind of joy!
E Ma'o!
You emit a glowing radiance!
E Ma'o!
You have arisen from me!
E Ma'o!
You enjoy bowing!
E Ma'o!

So he spoke.

Vajrasattva asked him:

Teacher of teachers,
All Good One,
You are truly a teacher,
But the circle is not complicated.

The whole of the entourage
Is an uncomplicated circle.
The whole of the teaching
Is also an uncomplicated circle.
The time and the place
Are also an uncomplicated circle.
The whole of everything
Is also an uncomplicated circle.

Teacher of teachers,
What will you teach?
What will the retinue surrounding you in an entourage
Surround?
You will teach this entourage.

So what will you teach them?
How is it that the time and the place
Are one?

Then the All Good One proclaimed these words:

I will explain everything,
Without exception,
In a language.
Work it out in your minds!

The mind itself is me,
The All Good.
The teacher, teaching, entourage, time, and place
Come from me.
I am the primordial circle.

My true nature is presented to be a circle,
A circle whose portent has been uncomplicated
From the beginning.
This circle is an uncomplicated heart,
From the very beginning.

From the Tantra of Vajrasattva's Magnificent Sky Embellished for the Brahmins, this is chapter one: The Basic Scene.

TEACHING THAT THE HEART IS THE ROOT

Then again Vajrasattva asked him:

Blessed One,
Great Bliss,
All Good One,
Please explain your roots.

All Good gave an oration:

Listen!
I will teach my true nature
To the entourage that is gathered unto me.

This place is the abode where reality abides
In its own dominion.
This clarity is the luminescence in the sky of awareness.
Its pervasion is that it encompasses the whole
Of the vessel and its contents.
Its origin is that it appears
Everywhere in the apparent world.
Its being is that it is the Bodhicitta.
Its teaching is taught as the nine vehicles.
Its summation is its coalescence
Into the great perfection.

This teaching does not have any defined substance.
It is not some object that we do not see.
There are no statements made of words

By which to understand it.
This heart-essence does not come from a cause.
It exists.
There is only one.
It is elaborated so that these elaborations
Encompass the many things.

We do not see it through investigation.
It may appear to be anything.
Regardless of how we meditate,
It does not change.
It is elaborated into differences,
But the circle is one.

It is totally free.
It is unified.
It does not go anywhere.
It is the basis for all the many things
That there are to see.
It is exemplified and taught
As something not to be visualized.
If you want to understand the meaning of this,
With certainty,
Use it to enquire into the way that
It is like the sky.

Its meaning is an unborn reality.
Its investigation is the unstoppability of the mind.
The reality that is like the sky
Is exemplified through the analogy
Of being like the sky.
The reality that is not to be visualized
Is exemplified and taught
Without visualizations.

There is nothing to discuss in words,
So I say words that are not to be discussed.
I teach the essence of the meaning of non-visualization.
Through its great significance,
You will come to understand.

If you do not understand this great significance,
Then no matter which words with meaningful sounds

You are taught,
You will not meet up with the essential meaning.

So he spoke.

From the Tantra of Vajrasattva's Magnificent Sky Embellished for the Brahmins, this is chapter two: Teaching that the Heart is the Root.

PRESENTING THE TEACHER, TEACHINGS, AND ENTOURAGE

Then again Vajrasattva asked him:

Blessed One,
Great Bliss,
All Good One,
Please explain the teacher and the teaching,
Along with the assembled entourage.

All Good gave an oration:

Listen,
You who are an assembled entourage!
The teacher has three aspects.
The teaching also has three aspects.
The entourage that hold to it
Are also described as being three-fold.

The three for the teacher are as follows:
Teachers of the true nature of the Dharma,
Teachers of the essence of the Dharma,
And teachers of words that are meaningful sounds.

Teachers who teach its true nature
Work to teach the way that it is
Through the blessings of the unborn
That Dharmas appear the way they do.

Teachers who teach the essence
Teach that all Dharmas,
Just as they appear,
Come forth as embodiments of emptiness,
And there is nothing that is other than this essence.

Teachers who teach the sounds of words
Subsume the meanings of the Dharmas into words,
Then write down verbal wordings of these meanings
For sentient beings who are not aware,
And do not understand.

The three kinds of teachings are as follows:
The teachings on the embodiment of the Dharma
Teach my true nature.
There are no divisions in my true nature.
The totality of all the Dharmas that appear
Is the essence of the mind,
And that is how it is.

Those who distort these things,
And use them for meditations,
Will not understand the teachings
On the embodiment of the Dharma.

The Bodhicitta is an invisible reality.
They do not have an unmistaken understanding
Of the way that this is.
Those who distort these things,
And use them for meditations,
Do not understand that their own minds
Are not to be contrived.

The dharmas of the apparent world,
And the Bodhicitta of the apparent world,
Reveal the way things are for our minds.
In the way that it is,
We see separate things without analyzing them.
The way things are,
Those who work on searches through dominions,
Even on the quests of the Victorious Ones of the three times,
Do not find anything.

The teachings of perfect pleasure are to be enjoyed.
The five pleasures are one
In the pleasure of reality.
The pleasure of all the Buddhas,
And of all sentient beings,
Is a level of perfect pleasure,
And there is nothing to be done but this.

The five kinds of pleasure.
Beginning with our bodies,
Are one,
But five fives is twenty-five.
The pleasures of the five channels[27]
Are the ways for the five embodiments.[28]
This is described to be the true essence
Of the true meaning
Of the true Dharma.

The teachings of the manifest embodiment
Enact the significance of compassion.
The sentient beings of the three realms
Have differing thoughts,
But by these three:
Their bodies, speech, and minds,
They use their bodies, speech, and minds
To turn all their thoughts around.

The entourage who hold this
Is taught to be of three kinds.
The *Atiyoga* is an entourage that is beyond seeking
And does not work on things.
They have entered the door of conviction,
And abide on the level of the Buddha.
They surround the level of the vision keepers,[29]
And the first ten levels.
They abide on the level of the meditators,
Those who have not yet attained it,
But have almost touched it.

The entourage that practices reverence
For the generation of the Bodhicitta
Abides where virtuous causes

Overpower their own fruition.
They are taught to be the entourages
For the three kinds of teachers.

From the Tantra of Vajrasattva's Magnificent Sky Embellished for the Brahmins, this is chapter three: Presenting the Teacher, Teachings, and Entourage.

EFFORTLESSNESS

Again Vajrasattva asked:

Blessed One,
Great Bless,
All Good One,
Please explain your lack of effort.

The All Good One gave an oration:

Listen,
O entourage that is gathered unto me!
This is the meaning of effortlessness.
It is the true nature of me,
The All Good.
My true nature does not change.
If you meditate on it or contrive it,
It is changed.
It has been spontaneously realized from the beginning,
So to work on it is to contrive it.

I have been finished with working from the beginning.
This is a reality that has no tasks:
The reality of my true nature.
There is nothing to be done about this true nature.

Vajrasattva,
You must not contrive my true nature,
For it is uncontrived.

Vajrasattva,
If you contrive it,
You are contriving the All Good.

The totality of all the dharmas that appear
Is also my true nature.
It is not static.
It is not an object to be visualized.
It is not complicated.
It is not to be thought on.
It is beyond objects.
Anyone who works to reject or terminate it
Will have difficulty finding it,
Even if he searches for an eon.

You will not achieve anything
By looking for me.
You will not learn anything
By studying about me.
There are no subjects
That do not refer to me.
There are no pathways
That do not lead to me.
There are no obstructions
Through not learning about me.
There is no going
That travels to me.

The embodiment of the Dharma of great bliss
Is single in our minds,
So there is no former and latter.
There are no three times.
There are no differences.

Self-originating wisdom is not to be conceived of
As an object.
It is unnecessary to use objects
To seek out the wisdom of awareness.
Without our searching for it,
We have achieved it spontaneously
From the beginning.

So from the beginning,
The good work of a quest,
Has been unnecessary.

From the beginning,
Everyone has lived on the level of enlightenment,
So it is not necessary to study
On the level of the vision keepers,
Or on the ten levels.

From the beginning,
Our work is over.
It is not necessary to meditate on a view.

From the beginning,
We are pure.
It is not necessary to protect samaya.
We do not abide.
We do not have ideas.
We do not contemplate anything at all.
We live naturally in the land of non-conceptual equanimity.

From the Tantra of Vajrasattva's Magnificent Sky Embellished for the Brahmins, this is chapter four: Effortlessness.

THE BODHICITTA IS UNCONTRIVED

Again Vajrasattva asked:

Blessed One,
Great Bliss,
All Good One,
It being that everything is nothing but the Bodhicitta,
Please explain the meaning of Buddhahood.

The All Good One gave an oration:

Listen,
O entourage that is gathered unto me!

The embodiment of the Dharma is the Bodhicitta.
No one whosoever has contrived even an atom
Regarding the embodiment of the Dharma
Arising from the Bodhicitta.
This being so,
There is no Buddha in our minds.

The embodiment of perfect pleasure is the Bodhicitta.
There is a perfect pleasure
In the forms that emerge from our minds.
It has no other embodiment than this.

The manifest embodiment is the Bodhicitta.
The Bodhicitta is a manifest act.
For working to help living beings,

There is no other.

This is none other than the Bodhicitta
Of the Buddhas of the three times.
The Buddhas from of yore,
Who have passed away,
Had already seen their own minds
With no contrivance,
Then they understood.

The Buddhas who live in the present
Have come to understand their true nature,
A true nature that is uncontrived,
Just as it is.
They also work to help living beings
In the present.

The Buddhas that will come later on
Are contriving this self-occurring sentience
To have a past,
So their coming has not been foretold.

Right now,
Do not contrive your mind of samadhi.
After you have entered the path of no contrivance,
You will have arrived.

As you do not understand
That the Bodhicitta is within the dharmas of appearance,
You contrive and work on them,
But you will not succeed.

You may count out the enumerations
Of a multitude of eons,
But you will not meet up with unsought bliss.
The three embodiments are not contrived
From out of our minds,
So teachers who distort the way it is,
Saying that the three embodiments come from
The excellent embodiment of our teacher,
May teach any style of truth,
But they are teaching my own true nature.

From the Tantra of Vajrasattva's Magnificent Sky Embellished for the Brahmins, this is chapter five: The Bodhicitta is Uncontrived.

THERE IS NO VIEW OR MEDITATION

Again Vajrasattva asked:

Blessed One,
Great Bliss,
All Good One,
Please explain your view and meditation.

The All Good One gave an oration:

Listen,
O entourage that is gathered unto me!

The view of the great perfection
Is not to be meditated on.
It is a wonder
That is the mind of the All Good.

It is not necessary to use
The greatness of the virtues of the Bodhicitta
To search for or practice things
That are difficult to work on.
This has no causes or conditions,
So it is not necessary to seek it.
We have finished with any true nature in our results,
So it will not be necessary to work on them.

It is not necessary to use meditation
On the true nature of reality

To do anything.
Not doing anything is not a remedy for destruction.
Our meditation does not refer to anything else,
So it is not necessary to seek it.

It is not necessary to work on a meditation
To protect our samaya.
It is not necessary to work on a meditation
To seek to do good works.
Do not travel on a path!
Do not study the levels!

The Dharma comes from myself.
It is not to be sought elsewhere.
I am beyond every field of practice.
I am not to be penetrated by words.
I am beyond the domains of the senses.

I convene my true nature,
And dwell in a circle.
It is not complicated.
It is non-dual.
It is presented as being primordially one.

Self-originating wisdom is not to be understood.
It does not move.
It is beyond cause and result.
Do not work on it or seek for it!.
You will not find it,
So do not meditate on substantial things.
It is unborn,
So it is not necessary to stop it.

It does not appear
At the center of the space
Of magnificent pervasive great bliss.
It is not an object to be visualized.
It abides naturally
In the invisible true nature of reality,
As a magnificent non-conceptual equanimity.
Awareness does not understand
The uncomplicated true nature of reality.

Do not do samadhi!
One who meditates on a state
Will, due to the meditation itself,
Fail to encounter this state.

I am the true originator of reality.
Do not foster sorrow!
It is not necessary to give things up.
This is self-originating.
It has no birth or ending.
It is unnecessary to stop up your senses
On the dependencies and connections
Of ignorance.

My spirit[30] is pure.
It is not necessary to cleanse reality.
It has been pure from the beginning.
It is not necessary to work to purify or adorn it.
It is spontaneously achieved, always.
It is not necessary to work on seeking or acquiring it.

My essence is something that everyone sees.
The Dharmas that I have truly brought forth
Are teachings about me,
For I have a multitude of senses.
This being so,
Everyone must understand my true nature!
If there are those who do not see my true nature,
Do not teach them my true nature,
For it is All Good.

Those who do not have the fortune
Of the great perfection,
Or its meaning,
Are stuck within the interpretable transmissions
Of the vehicles of cause and result.

From the Tantra of Vajrasattva's Magnificent Sky Embellished for the Brahmins, this is chapter six: There is no View or Meditation.

SAMAYA ARE NOT TO BE PROTECTED

Again Vajrasattva asked:

Blessed One,
Great Bliss,
All Good One,
Please explain your samaya.

The All Good One gave an oration:

Listen,
O entourage that is gathered unto me!

A true nature that is unborn and uncomplicated
Brings forth a multitude of objects
Through the miracle of birth,
But there are no objects.
So I say: "I am my own true nature."

This is not to be conceptualized.
It is beyond the objects of our ideas.
Without holding onto an object
There is no relinquishment or taking on.
This absence is the same as our own stomachs:
We achieve them spontaneously.

This is different from all the rules of the way
That must be guarded.
There are no samaya that protect me.

I am All Good.
I have no causes or conditions.
It is unnecessary to seek or work towards me.
I am spontaneously realized.
It is unnecessary to work at doing anything.

I have existed from the beginning.
It is unnecessary to work toward understanding me.
I am self-originating,
So causes and conditions are not needed.
There is no good or bad,
So it is not necessary to work at
Taking things up and casting them off.

I have no substance,
So I am described as being non-existent.
I do not actually arrive,
But my wisdom is unstoppable.
It is attributed to be my stomach.

All things are one in the mind,
So I am attributed to be unique.
All the Dharmas,
However they may appear,
Maintain a conviction that is perfected in the Bodhicitta,
So I describe them to be "spontaneously perfected."

The true nature of reality
Does not transform into anything at all,
So I do not predict that there will be success
Through a search.

The realities of hunger and thirst,
Heat and cold,
Muteness and stupidity,
Frighten the retinue of the three embodiments,
So they have six rituals to escape from them.
These come about by themselves,
So it is unnecessary to seek them or work on them.
This is because their cause is, itself,
Self-originating wisdom.

Do not fall under the power
Of the conditions of karma!
Self-originating wisdom is not like anything else,
So we cannot prove that there is any self-origination
To the causes and conditions of karma.

One thing is sure,
But there are two kinds of truth.
Because of these two truths,
Nothing is published.
Where is there taught even one certain thing
In the transmissions of the unsure,
Those who harbor doubts?

The three kinds of teachers depend on the transmissions
Of cause and result,
Then they moisten people who are yogins
With the Dharma.
They need two truths and four validations.

In the Dharma I create
Two truths are not necessary.
In the Dharma I create
Who needs two truths?

Everything I have created
Was created in the Bodhicitta.
The Bodhicitta has no ultimate or relative reality.

So he spoke.

From the Tantra of Vajrasattva's Magnificent Sky Embellished for the Brahmins, this is chapter seven: Samaya Are Not to Be Protected.

GOOD WORKS ARE NOT TO BE SOUGHT OUT

Again Vajrasattva asked:

Blessed One,
Great Bliss,
All Good One,
Please explain your good works.

The All Good One gave an oration:

Listen,
O entourage that is gathered unto me!

From the beginning,
The great perfection has been beyond causes and results.
For this reason,
You will have no success with the effortless
Through seeking it or working on it.

When you understand the meaning of this,
You will not create karma,
And by not creating karma
You will abide in the way that it is.
Those who abide in the way that it is
Will succeed,
For this is not contrived and is not mistaken,
And just as it is unmistaken,
It is also uncontrived.

My nature is made out to be
An unmistaken true essence.
The Buddha was not contrived out of
The way things are.
The Bodhicitta is unborn.
For these reasons,
There never was a cause or a result
In our minds.

Once we use the analogy of a Dharma
That is born in the world,
There will be something that is born,
Which will in turn end.
Do not exaggerate like this!

Those who have not discriminated
That self-origination is beyond causes and results
Are stuck in measuring the Dharmas that demark the world,
And say:
"After we have sought out the cause,
The result will emerge."
This is an interpretable transmission
From the vehicles of cause and result.

The teaching in which wisdom is called: "Wisdom"
Is that the unstoppability of self-originating wisdom
Is the same for everyone.
This unparalleled wisdom does not come from a cause,
But it generates all things.
There is no foundation for the Dharma
Other than this.

You set up measures for the Dharmas
Of the causes and results in the world,
But when you seek after them,
The results do not come to pass.

The Bodhicitta has no causes or conditions.
It is unborn.
Do not get stuck on measuring
The Dharmas that are born and end in the world.

The Bodhicitta is not born under any conditions.
Do not use analogies based on Dharmas
That come forth due to conditions in the world.

Do not meditate on a samadhi in your mind.
Do not make up ideas
About wisdom being in an object.

It is not necessary to chant with your voice,
Or to mutter essential mantras.
It is not necessary to stamp
The things we gather with our hands
With a seal.
Do not work on samadhis
In which you expand and contract your mind.

Those that there are
Come from me.
Without moving,
They attain this spontaneously.
This is living in the way it is.
No one has contrived it.

The state of non-searching,
Just as it is,
Is not to be contrived.
It is taught to be the supreme work
Of having nothing to do.

Those who want something greater
Seek for quests and practices,
But just because they are seeking for
Meditations and things to work on,
They do not succeed in this greatness.

The greatness of self-originating wisdom
Has been great from the beginning.
If you meditate on it,
You distort the contemplation of the Buddha,
And by force of this,
Will be abandoned by all the Buddhas.
Through doing this,
You abandon your own Bodhicitta.

Even in an eon,
You will not meet up with your own true nature.

From the Tantra of Vajrasattva's Magnificent Sky Embellished for the Brahmins, this is chapter eight: Good Works are Not to Be Sought Out.

TEACHING THAT THE LEVELS ARE NOT TO BE STUDIED

Again Vajrasattva asked:

Blessed One,
Great Bliss,
All Good One,
Please teach on the true nature of the levels.

The All Good One gave an oration:

Listen,
O entourage that is gathered unto me!

My own level,
That of the All Good,
Is to live in the heart
Of everyone's enlightenment.

The true nature of the Bodhicitta
Is a palace for the dominion of the Dharma.
It is the magnificent space
That is an abode for the minds
Of all the Buddhas of the three times,
And all the sentient beings of the three realms.
There is nothing whatsoever that does not dwell within it.

It is an abode and level for everyone.
We dwell in it,
Without joining it or leaving it.
It is not necessary to study it,
Or to travel on it.
If you were to study it or travel over it,
You would distort your own mind in it.
It is not necessary to use contrivances
To purify your own mind.

This is a popular level.
It is an abode for everyone.
The three embodiments that emerge from out of me
Teach three kinds of uniform levels
To an entourage of those who are beyond causes and results.

They are taught to be these three:
The level of generation,
The level of practice,
And the level of attainment.

If we generate the Bodhicitta
On the level of generation,
We will not have the Bodhicitta
Of the dominion of the Dharma,
Of the sky.

The granting of empowerments
As interpretations on the karmas of virtue and evil
Is a rejection of the reality of external objects,
And even though self-originating awareness is unobstructed,
They obstruct it.

While self-originating wisdom is not to be thought of
As an object,
They say:
"There is a subject and an object."
You must overcome them.

This being so,
While the Bodhicitta is unborn,
You work on ten enlightenments
On the level of practice.

There are no Dharmas whatsoever,
However it may appear,
That move away from the Bodhicitta.
The reality that is like the sky
Is the exhaustion of appearances.

There is not even one atom
That moves about in the sky.
In this same way,
There is no movement in the Bodhicitta.

Those who wish to work toward enlightenment
On the stages of practice
Also give names to the levels
On which they work toward enlightenment.
These are the levels of Total Light and the Unattached Lotus,
Vajra Holder[31] and Dense Array,
The Great Mass of the Wheel and Vajradhara.[32]

These six are no different than causes and results
For the All Good.
The true nature of the mind has no causes or conditions,
So I do not teach that a result will be achieved
By working toward it.
That is a teaching of those for whom
The true nature of the mind appears to be six-fold.

The six true natures of the mind are as follows:
When there are signs of the unstoppability
Of self-originating wisdom
That are totally luminous in the five doors of our senses,
It is given the name: "Total Light."

To have no attachment for,
And not conceptualize any object
Is called: "The Eye of the Unattached Lotus."

I have named the unborn and unceasing Bodhicitta:
"The Vajra Holder."

While the reality of my own self nature is unfathomable,
Self-originating wisdom is displayed in non-conceptual equanimity.
This is named: "Dense Array."

The Dharmas of enlightenment
In which the mandala of the true nature of the Bodhicitta
Abides within us
Are named: "The Great Mass of Letter Wheels."

Our bodies, speech, and minds
Have no birth or ending.
So I have described: "The Level of Vajradhara."

The Bodhicitta has neither causes nor results.
It has never taken up or rejected
Any goodness or badness
In any of the Dharmas that emerge from our minds.
I have therefore described it as: "The Level of Indivisibility."

This being so,
The dominion of the Dharma of the Bodhicitta
Is where all the Buddhas of the three times
And all the sentient beings of the three realms
Come from,
And it is where we abide.
The dominion of the Dharma of the Bodhicitta is,
Therefore,
The level of Eyes Everywhere.[33]
It is called: "The level of the achievement of Buddhahood."

There is no other true nature for the Bodhicitta
Than this.

From the Tantra of Vajrasattva's Magnificent Sky Embellished for the Brahmins, this is chapter nine: Teaching that the Levels are Not to Be Studied.

THE PATH IS NOT TO BE TRAVELLED UPON

Again Vajrasattva asked:

Blessed One,
Great Bliss,
All Good One,
Please explain your magnificent pathway.

The All Good One gave an oration:

Listen,
O entourage that is gathered unto me!

The Bodhicitta is a magnificent vehicle
For everyone.
It has something others do not have.
In it, we live naturally.

These three:
The place, the object, and the level of Buddhahood,
Abide in the dominion of the Dharma,
And in this reality.
They abide in the dominion of the sky,
And in this palace.

Real Buddhahood is our objective,
The Bodhicitta.
We do not dwell on pathways that go anywhere else.
We do not go on the pathway of the sky by travelling over it.

Our own minds are an uncomplicated dominion of the Dharma.
All the Buddhas dwell
In the absence of contemplations.
This being so,
Do not travel on a path!

Our own minds are not shadowed.
They shine out as the true nature of the sky.
All the Buddhas of the three times dwell in this.
This being so,
Do not travel on a path!

As our minds are an uncontrived reality,
The Buddhas of the three times are spontaneously realized.
This being so,
Do not travel on a path!

The Buddha is our own mind,
And is not an idea.
You do not get to your own mind's freedom from ideas
By travelling.

If you should travel
On the path of ignorance,
There will be no time
In which you go,
And there will be no level
On which you understand.
There is no going to the level of Buddhahood
By travelling.

The Buddha is our own mind,
And is not an idea.
Through meditating on a view
We lose the object of our samadhi.
We lose non-conceptual equanimity.

Due to guarding samaya,
We live in an undiminishing clinging.
Due to this undiminishing clinging,
We lose non-conceptual equanimity.
Due to seeking for good works,

We work on samadhis that will succeed.
Due to samadhis that will succeed,
We lose non-conceptual equanimity.

Through studying on the levels,
We work on a samadhi of abiding.
With the samadhi of studying
We lose non-conceptual equanimity.

Through investigating reality,
We work on a samadhi of luminosity.
Due to luminous samadhi
We lose non-conceptual equanimity.

Through luminous wisdom
We work on a samadhi of understanding,
But we lose the equanimity
Of understanding things clearly.

The way in which the samadhi of desire is luminous
Is that it does not get any happiness
That it does not want.

It is because we do not do samadhi
Or gather habitual tendencies
That self-originating wisdom does not fall
Under the control of karma.

Self-originating wisdom is the heart-essence
Of the embodiment of the Dharma.
We will not get it by searching for it.
We will get it by living naturally.

Our success is not based on anything that we work on.
A so-called: "Meaning"
Is just a name that has been attached to something.

Those who work to give a name to the Buddha
Do not have a definitive transmission.
This is something taught in the interpretable transmissions.

So he spoke.

From the Tantra of Vajrasattva's Magnificent Sky Embellished for the Brahmins, this is chapter nine: The Path is Not to Be Travelled Upon.

TEACHING SELF-ORIGINATING WISDOM

Again Vajrasattva asked:

Blessed One,
Great Bliss,
All Good One,
Please explain self-originating wisdom.

The All Good One gave an oration:

Listen,
O entourage that is gathered unto me!

The wisdom of the teacher of this entourage
Is a wisdom that enquires into objects.
Those who make up ideas about objects
Take this to be the wisdom of the Vedas.

It is a topic that we are made to understand,
For it has come forth from the Bodhicitta.
It is a wisdom that conceptualizes the Bodhicitta,
Which is not an object,
As an object.

It emerges from an object,
So it is not self-originating.
The simple absence of an object
Makes this unclear.

The thing that is called:
"Self-originating wisdom"
Is a wisdom that is a primordial knowledge.
Self-originating wisdom is primordial knowledge.

For this reason,
Self-originating wisdom is a wisdom
That is a primordial knowledge.
To call something "Wisdom"
Is to make an attribution for this.

Wisdom comes from itself.
So do not meditate on a samadhi for it.
Those who do not meditate on samadhi
Do not accumulate habitual tendencies toward samadhi.

A reality where there are no habitual tendencies
Is described to be the contemplation
Of the Buddhas of the three times.

We do not conceptualize the object
Of the contemplations of all the Buddhas of the three times.
We have dwelt in equanimity from the beginning.
From the beginning,
There has no conceptualization
In the self-originating heart of wisdom
Of all the Buddhas of the three times.
For this reason,
The Buddhas do not work on contemplations,
For this is different than any of the objects we may conceptualize.

Self-originating wisdom
Makes up the contemplation of the Buddha.
Self-originating wisdom
Is not to be thought of as being in an object.

Our conceptualizations do not wear
The habitual tendencies of our ideas.
Karma is the habitual tendency to scrutinize samadhi.
I have never claimed
That non-conceptualization is an habitual tendency.

Non-conceptualization is self-originating wisdom.
The nature of the mind
Is described as being the five doors of the senses,
But self-originating wisdom does not stop with them.
The essence of the Bodhicitta appears to everyone,
And this unstoppability of self-originating wisdom
Is clear to us as individuals.

It appears under its own conditions.
We do not cast it off or reject it.
Non-conceptual samadhi will not gather habitual tendencies.
This subsumes the contemplations
Of the Buddhas of the three times.

In the experience of our awareness
We understand this directly,
And we elucidate self-originating wisdom
As being in an object.

We do not believe that five objects exist
On account of there being five wisdoms.
The five kinds of desired objects
Appear to the five wisdoms.
This is because these objects have been wisdoms
From the beginning.

I do not teach that the objects and the wisdoms
Are two things.
This being so,
I explain that even objects
Are self-originating wisdom.

Self-originating wisdom is not anything at all,
So the teacher of this entourage
That I have brought forth
Attributes names to wisdom,
Basing them on the objects.

The occurrence of a wisdom that is to be enumerated
Is that a single wisdom that is under scrutiny
Appears to be a single object,
But appears in discrete true natures.
The subject is given the name of the object.

There is no certitude in this.
These attributions are delusional.

So he spoke.

From the Tantra of Vajrasattva's Magnificent Sky Embellished for the Brahmins, this is chapter eleven: Teaching Self-originating Wisdom.

SPONTANEOUS PERFECTION WITHOUT EFFORT

Again Vajrasattva asked:

Blessed One,
Great Bliss,
All Good One,
What is it to be without desire for effortless perfection?

The All Good One gave an oration:

Listen,
O entourage that is gathered unto me!

If you want to succeed in every Dharma,
Do not work toward the level you desire.
The mind that is working with desire
Rejects everything that it does not accept.

This is beyond cause and result,
For this reason,
The desire for a result does not constitute a cause.

We succeed at living naturally,
Without conceptualizing it.
Reject all the samadhis of desire!
Take up all the ones that are desireless!

Through holding onto samadhi
We hold onto desire.

This desire is not pure.
There is nothing that is pure that we apprehend.

We will have accomplished
The totality of all the works that we do,
Without seeking to,
Spontaneously.

We achieve this spontaneously, without a search.
There will be no success through our efforts.
This is effortless:
We have already achieved it spontaneously, from the beginning.

To abandon the totality of our desires
Is a major obstruction in our effort to succeed.
The samadhi of desire is an habitual tendency.
The habit is that we hold on to our minds.
Through holding on, we reject happiness.
Through not holding on, we receive every happiness.
This is the nature of the way it is.

To visualize something that does not exist
Is not a samadhi of non-conceptualization.
It's non-existence is the essence of its meaning.
When we have no desire for something
We will get it.

This is uncontrived, just as it is.
It is the single contemplation of all the Buddhas.
With the exception of great bliss,
What is there to desire or hold onto?

The samadhi that does not hold on,
And is not attached,
Is the finest holding on.
It holds everything,
And we have already succeed in it,
Since the beginning.
Settling into equanimity
Is the king of non-conceptual success.

So he spoke.

From the Tantra of Vajrasattva's Magnificent Sky Embellished for the Brahmins, this is chapter twelve: Spontaneous Perfection without Effort.

UNMOVING AND FREE FROM SEARCHING

Then again Vajrasattva asked:

Blessed One,
Great Bliss,
All Good One,
What is the desirelessness
That does not shift and is not sought?

The All Good One gave an oration:

Reality is primordially unchanging.
Not even an atom that is moved by changes exists.

Happiness and sorrow are one
In enlightenment.
Buddhas and sentient beings are one
In the mind.
The apparent world:
Both container and contained,
Are one in reality.
Even truths and lies are equal
In their reality.

When we are attached to happiness,
That is sorrow.
When we live naturally
We succeed in everything.

In this total luminescence there are no ideas.
This is self-originating wisdom.
Wisdom does not accumulate habitual tendencies,
So how could it be stained by karma?

When we do a variety of meditations,
Their unity is not obvious.
Those who work on samadhis for clarity
Do not have samadhi.

There is unity in the way that it is,
But we divide Buddhas from sentient beings.
Once we have divided happiness and sorrow
Into a duality,
We are taught to be serious about virtue.
We are taught to throw our evil behind us.
These things are in contradiction
To the significance of what is sure.

In the natural Dharma there is no shifting.
The nature of the Buddha does not shift.
For the Victorious Ones of the three times,
This is reality.

The Buddha is not set apart from this.
Without the Bodhicitta
There would be neither Buddhas nor sentient beings.

The mind itself, without our conceptualizing it,
Is the Buddha.
The mind itself
Is recommended to all the Buddhas.
The mind itself does not move.
It does not search.
This lack of search is not a contrivance.

So he spoke.

From the Tantra of Vajrasattva's Magnificent Sky Embellished for the Brahmins, this is chapter thirteen: Unmoving and Free from Searching.

THE SELF-LUMINOSITY OF AWARENESS

Again Vajrasattva asked:

Blessed One,
Great Bliss,
All Good One,
How is it that your awareness is luminous?

The All Good One gave an oration:

Listen,
O entourage that is gathered unto me!

Awareness is luminous
In a magnificent vase.
Awareness is luminous
In being without thought or action.
The unthinkable is luminous
In the state of having no thoughts.

Awareness is luminous
In being without ideas or graspings.
Not to engage in thoughts
Is luminous in being direct.
Awareness is luminous
In being without visualizations or designations.
The unthinkable is luminous
In the state of equanimity.

Awareness is luminous
In being without tasks or searches.
The dominion of the sky is luminous
In the space of great bliss.
Awareness is luminous
In being without memories or traces.
Knowing awareness is luminous
In being beyond thoughts or actions.

Awareness is luminous
In being without graspings or ideas.
The unmoving is luminous
In the state of equanimity.
Awareness is luminous
In not being placed on anything whatever.
It is luminous
In being without the limitations of our actions.
Awareness is luminous
In being my own magnificent way.
It is luminous
In being beyond any effort or search.

Awareness is luminous
In being direct and unimpeded.
The unthinkable is luminous
In the state of equanimity.
Awareness is luminous
In being without clingings or traces.
The unthinkable is luminous
In being free from complications.

Awareness is luminous
In being without thought or action.
Knowledge is luminous
In being without intellectual designations.

When our thoughts are not engaged
In anything at all,
Our awareness is luminous
Without any recognition.

Awareness is luminous
In being an unceasing vastness.
Awareness is luminous
In its never falling into a position.
Awareness is luminous
In its connectedness to everything.
It is luminous
In being the basis for all things.

So he spoke.

From the Tantra of Vajrasattva's Magnificent Sky Embellished for the Brahmins, this is chapter fourteen: The Self-luminosity of Awareness.

SETTLING INTO UNTHINKABLE EQUANIMITY

Again Vajrasattva asked:

Blessed One,
Great Bliss,
All Good One,
When we settle ourselves into equanimity
How should we settle ourselves?

The All Good One gave an oration:

Listen,
O entourage that is gathered unto me!

The All Good One is indefinite,
Like the sky.
We settle ourselves in a state of inconceivable luminescence.
We do not stop up the five doors of the senses,
We settle ourselves into our own place.

We settle ourselves in our own unsought magnificent way.
We settle ourselves in a state of unshakable equanimity.
We settle ourselves in an uncomplicated absence of thought.
We settle ourselves where we do not recognize anything.
We settle ourselves where we like,
Without blocking appearances.
We settle ourselves in a state of unthinkable luminescence.
We settle ourselves in a state of non-dual equanimity.

We settle ourselves at ease,
In our bodies, speech, and minds.
We also settle ourselves into our own uncontrived place.
We settle ourselves into non-attachment,
And freedom from cravings.
We settle ourselves where knowledge has no recognition.
We settle ourselves without engaging in any thought whatever.
We settle ourselves where knowledge has no thought or action.

So he spoke.

From the Tantra of Vajrasattva's Magnificent Sky Embellished for the Brahmins, this is chapter fifteen: Settling into Unthinkable Equanimity.

CONCLUSION

Then the All Good One brought together the entourage that included Vajrasattva, and explained the meaning of this Tantra:

The root of all the Tathagatas of the ten directions and the three times,
And the root of all the sentient beings of the three realms
Is the heart of the All Good One,
Self-originating wisdom.

This heart of self-originating wisdom
Is, in fact, the Embellished for the Brahmins.
This Tantra is, in fact, the All Good One.
It is my own Bodhicitta.
It is the body, speech, and mind
Of all the Buddhas.

The one who is holding this Tantra
Is, in fact, a Buddha.
So samsara is pure right from the start.
The one who is holding this
Is the All Good One,
For everything is self-originating wisdom.

In the same way that rocks and dirt are not visible
On the islands of precious gold,
Samsara is primordially pure.
It is, in fact, self-originating wisdom.

From the Tantra Embellished for the Brahmins, this is the sixteenth chapter: The Endowment of the Tantra.

The Embellished for the Brahmins is finished.

THE TANTRA OF VAJRASATTVA'S MAGNIFICENT SKY

EMBELLISHED FOR THE KING

In the Indian language:

Vajrasatva Khasa Mahārāja Puṣṭiṃi Tantra

In the Tibetan language:

rDo rje sems dpa' nam mkha' che rgyal po rgyas pa'i rgyud

In the English language:

The Tantra of Vajrasattva's Magnificent Sky Embellished for the King

THE BASIC SCENE

I bow to the Blessed One, the glorious All Good One, Great Bliss.

I heard these words on one occasion:

The Blessed One, the Tathagata, the fully perfected Buddha All Good settled himself into the equanimity of an inconceivable samadhi:

The supreme abode of Akaniṣṭa is spread out
In the unshadowed palace of wisdom,
The castle of the dominion of the Dharma.
My own true nature
Is the embodiment of the Dharma.
My own essence
Is the embodiment of pleasure.
My own compassion
Is the embodiment that manifests.
Vajrasattva and the others,
An indivisible entourage,
Are present in a single great circle.

Then Vajrasattva asked:

O Teacher of Teachers,
All Good One,
The teacher himself is an uncomplicated circle.[34]
All the teachings are also an uncomplicated circle.
Time and place are also an uncomplicated circle.
Each and every thing is an uncomplicated circle.

So what will the teacher of teachers teach?
What will the entourage that you have organized here
Revolve around?
How is it that the time and the place are one?

And for the special retinue
Of Vajrasattva and the rest,
The tip of the Blessed One's tongue
Brilliantly promulgated this secret:

I myself,
The All Good One,
Am the teacher,
The teaching,
The retinue,
The time,
And the place.
They are a circle that comes from me.

My own true nature is a circle.
A circle is never complicated.
An uncomplicated heart is a circle.
It is the most important thing of all.
Its magnificent virtues are the highest perfection.

This is a heart transmission
Of the highest heart-essence,
The way it is with every dharma.
An exclusive audience will maintain it accordingly.

No matter where we may look for
The heart-essence of true intent,
We will not find it.
Self-awareness has no shadows.
It is pure.

When we immerse ourselves in a rigorous analysis of it,
This is a holy approach.
This is an unmistaken path.
It is highly recommended
By the All Good One.

The sorrows of living beings
Are entirely cleansed
By an enlightened attitude.
So we play in them,
And while we do not move about in them,
We abide in an equanimity
That is like the end of the sky.

This heart of an undying vajra
Does not depart.
It is the finest heart-essence.
One who abides in this ineffable state
Will have the supreme hardness
Of the heart of a vajra,
The mandala of vajra wisdom.

That yogin is fortunate.
He is totally encompassed by an embodiment of the Dharma,
The finest embodiment,
One with every form,
The equal of all the Buddhas,
Which nothing whatever will divide.

So he will play in the land
Of spontaneously formed nature.
Through seeing, hearing, touching, and remembering,
He will be totally liberated
From all the evils he has done.

The path of total liberation
Has dwelt naturally within every living being
Since the primordial.
We may make reverted attributions,
But there is nothing else
Other than self-originated liberation.

This heart essence of pure intent
Is spontaneously realized
By the wisdom of omniscience,
Without any doing or making.
Its fruition is the embodiment of the All Good.

So he spoke.

From the Tantra of the Magnificent Sky of Vajrasattva Embellished for the King, this is chapter one: The Basic Scene.

SPONTANEOUSLY REALIZED FREEDOM FROM SEARCHING

Then the Blessed One entered the equanimity of the samadhi of the heart of a vajra, and made this intentional statement:

This is a great bliss that is spontaneously present,
But for direct perception,
It is not there.
It encompasses everything.
Self-originating wisdom does not search.
It is beyond the intentions of dominion and wisdom.

The mind that searches has an unsurpassed happiness,
But is obstructed by it.
This is a big problem.
It is because this is not a conventionality made of words
That we are liberated from virtue and evil.

This spontaneously perfected essence
Does not use practices, views, or consequences
To seek.
Self-originating wisdom is not divided by anything,
So it does not search.
It is beyond the intentions of dominion and wisdom.

There is no evidence
That a fruition of virtue
Comes from a magnificent non-conceptual wisdom.

This is different from the paths
That we travel over or study.
On careful investigation,
There is no real object that is there.

This view is not a disposition,
Or even an essence.
For the name of the sky,
We get nothing.

The finest embodiment
Is formed spontaneously,
Without effort.
It does not make way for conventionalities.
It is a unified state.
It is not made of anything.
When it is not clear,
Nothing will be accomplished.
It is like that.

So it is that in this way,
And for this reason,
This is taught to them,
And this is what they attain.
This is the essence,
And because of this,
This comes from this.
It is very amazing.

The previous this,
And the present this,
And likewise the continuity of this,
Are like pathways for this,
And this has the true nature
Of being this.

This is the sort of comprehensive pathway
That comes from the moon.
It may appear to be a mudra,
With a body that has a support structure,
But it is not made of anything at all.

So he spoke.

From the Tantra of the Magnificent Sky of Vajrasattva Embellished for the King, this is chapter two: Spontaneously Realized Freedom from Searching.

THE ACTUAL PRESENTATION OF THE SECRET

Then the Blessed One entered the equanimity of the most profound samadhi, and made this intentional statement:

This abides in the fullness
Of what is most certainly a great secret.
The Blessed One naturally abides
In all living beings.
We may make attributions about this,
Through reverted thinking,
But there is nothing that is other than
Self-originating liberation.

This heart-essence is not to be sought after.
The Bodhicitta totally encompasses
The sorrows of living beings,
So it plays in them,
And while it does not move in them,
It abides in an equanimity
That is like the end of the sky.

The embodiment of the Dharma
Is not to be visualized as anything.
The Dharmas of samsara and nirvana
Are a space that has no bottom or sides.
On careful examination,
It is not anything at all.

Sentient beings have ideas about it.
These are accommodated,
So the source of all things
Is a wish-fulfilling jewel for everyone.
All things are equal.
There is no duality.

When we would condense
The dominion of the magnificently inseparable
Equality and dominion,
There is nothing to be condensed.

The embodiment of the Dharma
Is not to be visualized as anything at all.
It is not born and does not cease.
It does not contemplate anything.
It is a magnificent equanimity
That does not divide anything.

A wish-fulfilling jewel brings us what we want,
Without hindering its origin or applications.
It may appear to us as anything.

The unerring intent of this supreme heart essence
Is holy.
It is not complicated,
And while nothing can hinder it,
It blazes like a heap of jewels
That brings forth all things.

The space of totality,
The summation of all things,
The space for all that there is,
The summation of the vajra,
The embodiment of great bliss,
The state in which a shared equanimity comes together,
The excellence of the great wisdom
Of the dominion of equanimity,
Is not to be visualized.

It was not born.
It is invisible.
This heart-essence of excellence is holy.

In the way things truly are,
There is no middle way.
Non-visualization does not uphold two truths.
Even Bodhisattvas who are on the eighth level
Do not have two truths.

So he spoke.

From the Tantra of the Magnificent Sky of Vajrasattva Embellished for the King, this is chapter three: The Actual Presentation of the Secret.

MAKING THE HIDDEN SECRET EVIDENT

Then the Blessed One entered the samadhi of the essential meaning, and made this intentional statement:

There are no entities in meditation.
This path is not exemplified by words.
The wisdom that has no dominion
Has been gathered here.

The statements that we speak are all obstructions.
The heart-essence is not to be viewed,
Not to be practiced,
Not to be protected,
And not to be meditated upon.
There is nothing whatsoever to do,
And there is nothing to be visualized.
There is no objective to study or to search for.

The three realms are primordially cleansed.
They are primordial Buddhahood.
This is not something that is in the domain of the senses,
So how would it be exemplified by words?
All the things that we talk about in our speech
Are collected into our dominion and our wisdom.
This is a big problem.
It is an obstruction.

All dharmas are empty by nature,
And by their true essence they maintain a force,

A perfectly pure soul.[35]
It is not contrived out of a path,
But the ideas and cravings of the inferior vehicles
Are traditions that believe in a personal continuum,[36]
And are reverted.

We may divide things up individually,
And classify them,
But the holiness of this supreme wisdom,
Which coalesces the leaves and roots,
Is not to be worked toward.
There is no other way to be liberated
Than through this spontaneous perfection.

The samaya are a precious jewel.
The ground structure, the ocean, and the vajra boat
Are the same for our stomachs.
They are perfected in emptiness.
Of all the things that have the character of the sky,
Moving through the domains of the various worlds,
And all the actual occurrences of a Victorious One,
There are none in the four times and ten directions
That are not in the domain of the sky.

Princes, fathers, mothers, and all the rest,
All melt into the dominion of the sky.
Know this.
Do not leave it.
Unsurpassed wisdom is a great miracle.

The Blessed One,
The great originator,[37]
Abides in fullness,
And so is a Blessed One.
He dwells naturally in all living beings.

Through our reversions we make attributions,
But to be brief,
There is no other self-originating liberation
Than the totality of holiness.
This unchanging circle of wisdom
Is the origin of supreme, non-dual enlightenment.
It abides pervasively.

It is one.
It is perfected in emptiness.
It is an inexhaustible treasure of jewels.
It encompasses everything,
And matures as many things.
This is the true Blessed One.

It is the heart-essence of sentient beings,
So it dwells naturally in all living things.

So he spoke.

From the Tantra of the Magnificent Sky of Vajrasattva Embellished for the King, this is chapter four: Making the Hidden Secret Evident.

THE UNSURPASSED VEHICLE THAT TURNS THE WHEEL OF EVIL

Then the Blessed One entered the equanimity of the samadhi that is unstained by problems, and made this intentional statement:

The superiority of the unsurpassed vehicle
Is that those who have the five kinds of emotional problems,
Who are content to care for their bodies,
Will have something special to work on.

This is the best there is.
It is unsurpassed at bringing us success.
When we do not have a clean or dirty mind,
That is the best vehicle
For those who are wise in views.

They will not be disoriented by problems.
Regardless of whatever bad karma they have done,
They will be praised as fit recipients
For the unsurpassed vehicle.

Once they have understood their own Bodhicitta,
Their abode will transform into total purity.
They may join with girls who are not their sisters,
And go to a place that is unsurpassed.
They will eat food without regard to its being clean or dirty.
They will fight with monks,
And ridicule them.

They will join up in a land where there is no Buddha.
They will burn the chapels and the Sutras.
Those who practice these blazing evils
May be experts on the significance of the vehicles,
But if their minds are stable and pure,
They will not be stained by the problems there are in these actions.

They will delight the Buddhas,
And hold to the Dharma,
For they will have dwelt on the unsurpassed vehicle
Since the beginning.
There is nothing fit to measure or calculate
The true embodiment of the victorious Sugata,
So there is nothing that would stain them with a problem.

This is a heart-essence that is not compounded.
It is from the Buddhas,
And from primordial Buddhahood.
It is not to be worked on,
But it has been proclaimed to be something to work on.

As soon as we have achieved an understanding of this
We will be inseparable from all the Victorious Ones.
Even the five inexpiables will not be able to obstruct us.
We will practice the significance of every Dharma.

This is the objective of the highest happiness.
It is the way things are with the supremely correct Dharma.
We do everything without regard to purity or filth,
While those who have no compassion
Kill everyone.

This is the best of the best,
The highest embodiment,
The embodiment of all the Tathagatas.

So he spoke.

From the Tantra of the Magnificent Sky of Vajrasattva Embellished for the King, this is chapter five: The Unsurpassed Vehicle that Turns the Wheel of Evil.

TEACHING THAT OFFERINGS ARE NOT TO BE VISUALIZED

Then again the Blessed One entered the equanimity of the samadhi in which one who offers bodily fluids and urine to all the mandalas is a king, and made this intentional statement:

Once you understand your own Bodhicitta,
Self-originating wisdom will occur to you by itself.
When you understand that there is no mandala
Other than the soul,[38]
You will not offer the smells of sandalwood
To me,
The lord of the mandala.

You must make offerings
With the five objects of your desires,
And use urine as an implement
To succeed at equanimity.

Eat my body,
And use it for offerings.
This will be a delight for all those who have heritage.

Wise ones, who have intelligence,
Will fill up a random vessel,
A new vessel or an old vessel,
With urine, feces, bodily fluids, and blood,
And use it to make offerings,

Every day and every night,
To me,
To the great mandala of the soul.

The dominion of the sky is not to be visualized.
It is entirely pure.
Self-originating wisdom moves through space.
It appears by its own nature,
And likewise manifests.

The wise will pour a variety of impure things
Into a new vessel or an old vessel,
And a soul will make offerings to a soul.
This will please all the mandalas of the Victorious Ones.

For those who are great experts in methods,
The mandala of self-awareness is one's own mind.
It is spontaneously realized from the primordial.
This is the mandala of the soul.

We must make offerings to it
With impure things.
This is an offering of a hundred hundred thousand mandalas.
Total success and real success
Are in our own minds.
This is a miraculously great siddhi.

And by the specific qualities
Of offering mandalas to the soul,
The great wrathful lord
Of this exquisitely blazing mandala
Will take on a body,
And just as was written in the ancient scriptures,
Will appear to us,
Right before our senses,
But we will see the embodiment of the Dharma
That is an uncontrived peace
And does not shift or change.

This Dharma that is not compounded
Is not to be exemplified by saying: "This."
It is beyond words.
The *mudra* of this embodiment is obviously perfect.

The five emotional problems are themselves
Fields for the Victorious Ones.
Things like emotional problems
Are nirvana.

Buddhahood does not come from any other act of accomplishment.
The mandalas of desire, and all the rest,
Are magnificent mandalas.
The best of the best.
Those who enter into them
Will achieve a variety of pleasures in their minds,
As if it was a jewel at the center of their hearts.

Secret mantras do not change our minds.
The ground of all things
Arises as a sun of awareness.
The lord of the mandala may appear
As anyone at all,
But is perfected
In an unborn and invisible domain.

So he spoke.

From the Tantra of the Magnificent Sky of Vajrasattva Embellished for the King, this is chapter six: Teaching that Offerings are not to be Visualized.

BEING WITHOUT THOUGHT AND MEDITATION

Then the Blessed One entered the equanimity of the samadhi that has no meditations, and made this intentional statement:

Those who would work toward the Buddha's enlightenment
Must observe the intention of the Unwritten,[39]
And apply it to the speech that has no essence.
When we place ourselves into this invisible reality,
Without searching,
That is meditation.

If we search everywhere for this and this,
This will not come about from this,
And we will have a long road to perfect Buddhahood.
Likewise, the dominion of the sky,
While not appearing to be anything,
Is a great bliss that is not complicated.

In the invisible reality that we do not visualize,
A meditator does not occur in our minds.
When we settle ourselves into non-searching,
We are meditators.

Living without desires
In the true significance of what is internal
And what is external:
That is the work of great happiness.
One who stops doing things
Will be on the supreme path of freedom.

The essence of what is stated by
All the Buddhas and those in their fields,
The heart of all the vajra teachers,
The essence of essences that holds five wisdoms,
Is sure.
Its fruition is a path for everyone.

Vajra wisdom is like the sky,
But due to an ignorance that is nowhere to be envisioned,
The Buddhas of the four times,
All of them,
May seek for three eons,
But even these Buddhas will not see it.

Once we have found the center,
Which resembles the unvisualized sky,
Without visualizing it,
We will be mature.
We will contemplate a significance
That even the Buddhas and Bodhisattvas
Do not contemplate.
We will work at an objective
That is not an attribution.
We will use an indestructible essence
To destruct.
We will think of things that are not to be thought of.
When we settle ourselves naturally
In a state where we are not searching for anything,
This is called: "Meditation."

It is unborn and does not stop.
It is entirely pure.
It has been ineffable from the very beginning.
It is beyond the conglomerations of words and names.
This is why there is nothing to show
As the essence of a soul.

Through the skull-jump[40] of primordial fearlessness
We reach the unexcelled level of a heroic person,
But it is not necessary to learn this.

This is the vehicle of the unchanging vajra,
In which the soul is essentially without substance.
It is the best of vehicles.
It is unsurpassed.

It does not proclaim a teaching
That the reality of primordial emptiness
Is a substance.
A Victorious One has arisen
Who does not deny this.

We do not dwell on an attachment
To the taste of samadhi,
For we are not attached,
We do not understand,
And we do not dwell.

The ambrosia of the Bodhicitta
Has no thoughts.
It is not to be thought of.
There is nothing to meditate on.
It is beyond the words that there are
For wisdom and methods.

For this reason,
There is no Buddha in our minds.

E Ma'o!
There is not even an atom of conventionality
To this!
It is not to be exaggerated or denigrated.
There is no object
To listen to or to visualize.
There is nothing that needs to be learned.

The Bodhicitta has no depth or measure.
It is beyond all the topics of conversation,
However many there may be.
There is no structure on which to attribute
A name for it.
We penetrate the door without delusions.
This is the highest holiness.

It is not necessary to perpetrate
The two kind of truth.
There is not even an atom here
That is to be exemplified in writing.

This is difficult to investigate.
It is not something that exists.
This unthinkable circle is not exaggerated on,
Even in the thoughts of the Rishis.
It is not appropriate to think of it,
Saying: "This is enlightenment."

So he spoke.

From the Tantra of the Magnificent Sky of Vajrasattva Embellished for the King, this is chapter seven: Being without Thoughts and Meditation.

BEING WITH THOUGHT AND MEDITATION

Then the Blessed One entered the equanimity of the samadhi in which there are thoughts and meditations, and made this intentional statement:

The unborn Bodhicitta
Is the foundation for the many things.
It is not to be exemplified by saying: "This."
It is the embodiment of the Buddha.

The best path
Is not to practice philosophical conclusions.
The deluxe contemplation
Has no thoughts of any kind.
The foundation for the appearance
Of the totality of self-origination
As the many things
Is a basis that is not to be exemplified
By saying: "This."

It has no measure.
It is a space of holiness.
The Bodhicitta is nothing at all,
But appears endlessly.
The best path
Is not to wish for a level of ascertainment,
Or to succeed.
We do not have to think about
The meaning of the unthinkable.
This contemplation has no thoughts,

And has no motion.

The self-occurring Bodhicitta
Is the spontaneously made holiness of the Buddha,
And manifests as the many things.

As we read we will have a variety of quick ideas.
Watch how they move and appear without contrivance.
To settle oneself in simply not thinking
Is the heart of the Buddha.

This is easy because it is difficult,
And difficult because it is easy.
It is not to be contemplated,
Even by the Sugata.
This is the contemplation of the Victorious One,
It is the Sugata's heart.

Sentient awareness that is not disturbed
Is the heart of the Victorious One.
We do not think about it,
And we do not dwell on it.
It is not to be sought out.

When we are completely sure
That self-awareness is Buddhahood,
We do not think about what is best,
And we do not work toward
The best attainment,
For even this attainment cannot be indicated
By saying: "This."

Thinking and non-thinking
Are things to think about.
There is no essence to these thoughts whatsoever.
We do not seek this in an object,
So we also do not dwell on it.
The essence of self-awareness is to be sought
In our own space.

As soon as we dwell in certitude
Within this self-awareness,
We transcend the words

That have been made up about this dwelling.

Nobody needs to work on Dharmas that already exist.
As for Dharmas that do not exist,
We will not find them
No matter where we look for them.
It is not appropriate to jump over this
By the use of analytics.

Chasing along the trails of analytics
Is an impediment to freedom.
There is no object that we would find
Through searching.
Desiring to be free by searching
Is the work of children.

This is the magnificent reality of the All Good,
A teaching of the heart-essence of the Dharma.
It is not an object,
So even the thoughts
Of the quickest of our mind's consciousness
Will have extreme difficulty chasing after it.

The heart-essence of the Dharma
Is not any real thing at all,
But from it there naturally arises
A mudra and the apparel of desire.
This is not in some other place.
This is the highest place of our heart's essence.
It is difficult to teach,
Or to talk about.
There is not even an atom of it to be visualized.

We have no attachment to anything.
There is nothing to be attached to.
The body of our mudra
Blazes forth from this.
There is no further description of this
Beyond saying: "This is the holy Buddha."

The idea that the earth was made
By exemplifying the earth
Is a primordial delusion.

This heart-essence is not an object.
It is not to be associated with any philosophical conclusions.
The desire to be free through searching
Is the work of children.

In the magnificent reality of the All Good
Chasing the trails that use analytics
Is an obstruction to freedom.
This is entirely without meaning or non-meaning,
Happiness or unhappiness.
We do not meditate on it.

We settle ourselves without thinking,
Without being distracted,
Without a perspective,
And without a meditation,
As if we were in a circle of no contrivance.

So he spoke.

From the Tantra of the Magnificent Sky of Vajrasattva Embellished for the King, this is chapter eight: Being with Thought and Meditation.

BEING BEYOND THOUGHT AND PRACTICE

Then the Blessed One entered the equanimity of the samadhi that is the best, and made this intentional statement:

E Ma'o!
There is not even an atom of conventionality in this.
It is not to be exaggerated or depreciated.
There is nothing to hear about,
Nor any object to be visualized.
So there is nothing to learn.

The Bodhicitta has no depth or measure.
There is no structure on which to attribute a name.
This is beyond the topics of our conversation,
However many there may be.

This is not to be exemplified by words and letters.
It will not happen that our minds penetrate
This subject that has not been taught.
This is an unsurpassed heart-essence
That does not make us leave behind
The space of holiness.

Wisdom does not appear as a mudra,
So it will not be apprehended through wisdom and methods.
There are no contemplations on this.

The best contemplation is simply no contemplation.
Dwelling in equanimity from the primordial

Is the best contemplation.

The unthought circle is not an exaggeration.
It is difficult to investigate it.
It is not something that exists.
Even the Rishis
Never think about it.

The views of others on existence and non-existence
Do not work as views for saying: "This,"
And even if we would succeed in them,
We would not want them.
This is how we achieve the supreme heart-essence.

E Ma'o!
This dominion of the mind
Is what we have sought
For a hundred hundred-thousand eons.
In the clear equanimity of the circle of wisdom
We instantly achieve this heart-essence.
The Bodhicitta has not moved.

Death in samsara is an ambrosia to enjoy.
There is nothing here to think about,
So we do not even think about our bodies,
And we have no meditation either.
For these reasons,
There is no Buddha elsewhere
Than in our minds.

It does not dwell either on the outside or on the inside.
It has never been a place that we would search for.
The ambrosia is the Bodhicitta.
It glistens,
And is not to be thought on.

We do not think about not thinking.
There is no meditation.
This is beyond our dominion and our wisdom,
And so it is that there is nothing whatever to think about

This unthinkable heart-essence
Is an abiding in the way things are.

There is no thought in this.
It is the highest heart-essence.

There is nothing whatever to think about.
Emptiness and the dominion of the Dharma,
The essence of self-awareness and the way that things are
Are sought out in a space
In which they do not disturb us at all.

This is a magnificent method
For those who desire enlightenment.
It is not found in the scriptures,
And has not been taught.

The perfect Buddha,
Who is the one who has manifested
From out of the center,
Is the Buddha who is present.

Those who interpret and are not holy
Also maintain this heart-essence of the Dharma.
The noble path is not long.
It is a shining path.
It lives in the hearts of the noble.
It is beyond working on or seeking,
Beyond taking in and holding on.

This is the method preferred by the unsurpassed Buddha,
The level of the magnificent vastness of the space of wisdom.
It is praised as being the best of all the vehicles.

So he spoke.

From the Tantra of the Magnificent Sky of Vajrasattva Embellished for the King, this is chapter nine: Being Beyond Thought and Practice.

ALL DHARMAS ARE PURE

Then again the Blessed One entered the equanimity of the samadhi in which all dharmas are naturally pure, and made this intentional statement:

Here,
We do not have to deal with
The suffering there is in austerities.
The gathering of accumulations
Is done in reference to a cause.
It is a pathway of delusion.

The things we get for explaining this in other ways
Are Dharmas of delusion.
The things we get from the other Buddhas
Are mistaken pathways.

Those who play with words about relative reality
Have a river of understandings,
But the ones who hold onto these kinds of topics
Will not see the Buddha.

The perfect Sugata is not to be visualized
As anything at all.
It is a mistake to attribute a name
To designate a Buddha.
Our teacher did not find enlightenment
By talking about it.
The meaning of non-abiding,
Non-visualization,

And the absence of birth or ending,
Is unspeakable and immeasurable,
So it is not to be discussed.

To say: "This is what my teacher said to me, face to face"
Is a contradiction.

E Ma!
Those whose cause it is to travel toward high status
Will not find the path to enlightenment.
If we do not make a magnificent medicine
By living naturally, without distraction,
The illnesses of the three poisons
Will give us nothing to read for our lives.

Hoping that delusional understandings will dry away
Is a river of delusion.
This idea is founded on a belief
That enlightenment comes from a search.

The highest bliss is not ascertained through any object,
Anything we think about or anything that we perfect.
Delusional enlightenment is always ravenous.
It feeds on the Dharma.
Those who hold onto these kinds of objectives
Do not see the Buddha.

There is no exhaustion.
This is inexhaustible.
It is a limitless exhaustion.

Not to say anything,
No matter what is happening,
As presented in the Vinaya of the Sutra traditions,
Is wrong from the beginning.

From their very depths,
The stages of the vehicles present nothing to work on.

There are no Three Jewels!

This is not in the domain of the senses.
The embodiment of the Dharma has no form.

Its explanation has no depth,
But like the moon in a mirror of water,
The hosts of gods appear to explain it.
This is the vehicle of inconceivability.

It is not appropriate to be attached
To the tastes of dhyāna meditation and samadhi.
This is the true nature of the primordially perfect Bodhicitta.
Primordial Buddhahood is our own mind.
Ravenous delusional enlightenment
Feeds on the Dharma.

When our awareness will not rise up out of
The camphor pit,[41]
We will have a river of writings and ideas
About teachers and their teachings.

Vajrasattva is our own Bodhicitta.
This is the pathway that the Victorious Ones travel on.
We absolutely do not practice
Anything that is internal or external.

You will not find a name
For our teacher's teachings.
This is not to be associated with any teaching
That says: "This."

There is nothing to understand from this teaching.
There are no words that it proclaims.
There are no Dharmas that are born or that pass on.

This appears as a unity.
The natural abiding of our heart's essence
Is the embodiment of the Dharma.

So he spoke.

From the Tantra of the Magnificent Sky of Vajrasattva Embellished for the King, this is chapter ten: All Dharmas are Pure.

SPONTANEOUS PERFECTION WITHOUT WORK

Then the Blessed One entered the equanimity of the samadhi that is effortless, and made this intentional statement:

In this spacious heart-essence,
There is no objective to apprehend.
Direct perception has no idea at all about it.
There is no abode for the mind.

The embodiment of the Dharma encompasses all dharmas.
There are no dharmas that it does not surmount.
It abides as it is in visualized objects that appear by themselves.
There is no object that we perceive to be amazing.
Not even a piece of a piece of an eye that sees this exists.
There is also no object that retains this heart-essence.

Its embodiment does not appear to be an embodiment.
It is a body that has no limits.
It cannot be exemplified through our conclusions.
It is not written down in any dominion.

It is difficult to teach this Dharma
So that its taste will penetrate our experience.
There is nothing to say about it.

The dominion of the Dharma is like the sky.
It has no dominion.
It is not some kind of wisdom.
It is empty of emptiness.

It is also not emptiness.

There is nothing to apprehend in our minds,
Through meditation.
There is no object.
There is nothing to think about.
Being disturbed about the trails of our practice
Is an impediment to freedom.

The desire for freedom through seeking
Is the work of children.
There is no substantial heart-essence of the Dharma whatever.
The mudra and the apparel of desire
Occur to us naturally.

From the primordial,
Nirvana and all the many samsaras
Are indivisible,
But they are subsumed into three mandalas.

In the way that bees prosper in consort with bright flowers,
The non-dual embodiment of the Dharma never shifts,
But from it there grow two very good things:
The two physical embodiments.

We meditate that the multitude of Dharmas,
Nirvana and samsara,
Are in the form of a magnificent mandala.
The nature of all dharmas
Is that they are illusory.
We abide in this,
Without visualizing any appearance or emptiness,
In the way of the moon on water.

When we visualize non-visualization,
Many things appear.
The Tathagata has been totally equanimous from the beginning,
And from the beginning,
Killing a sentient being is just the sky.
The three realms tremble,
And the killer goes off in the sky.

In the field of the Buddha,
The unmoving source of all things,
The finest of families
Is an entirely pure self-nature.

There is no doubt that the highest king
Will achieve a vajra body,
A lordship over body, speech, and mind,
The true essence of the Sugatas
Which has no purity or pollution.

This is not some other place.
This is the highest place of the heart.
It is difficult to teach,
Or to talk about.
There is not even an atom of it to be visualized.
It is the sky.
There is nowhere to place it with our thoughts.
It is difficult to fathom it,
Even with the very quickest of thoughts.

From the beginning,
The five emotional problems have been
The Dharmas of the heart.
This is the heart of hearts.
It is the embodiment of the Dharma.
We live naturally
In the primordial absence of a true nature.
We keep no garbage whatever.
We are removed from all the ten directions.

We do not believe that there is an atom
That enters into a single minute atom,
Or that there are lumps of atoms,
Or that there are collections of atoms.

To perceive things in terms of four times
Is also a delusion.

This is amazing.
It brings everything together,
And maintains it all.
There is no object that we see.

Accounts of the forms that appear
To the eye that sees
Are many.

The place of the heart is not a god.
It is the embodiment of the Dharma.
It is nothing at all.
It is difficult to describe its flavor.
Topics such as this one
Go beyond speaking, contemplation, and conversation.

So he spoke.

From the Tantra of the Magnificent Sky of Vajrasattva Embellished for the King, this is chapter eleven: Spontaneous Perfection Without Work.

DEMONSTRATING LIBERATION

Then the Blessed One entered the equanimity of the samadhi that does not tremble, and made this intentional statement:

This is vast.
It is magnificent.
We have dwelt from the beginning
In a space of unchanging bliss,
And no one can overcome this.

It is entirely pure.
It is not shadowed by anything.
We have been pure from the primordial,
So what remedies are we to study?

There is no Dharma
Other that our own minds,
And because our minds are primordially pure,
The son of a king who has killed a most supreme Auditor,
Or even one who has killed a hundred hundred-thousand Buddhas,
Will play in a hundred thousand self-arising wisdoms,
Not visualizing a path to enlightenment.
His unchanging heart will play in the dominion of the sky.

The Auditors do not trespass here.
It is a supreme happiness.

The path of freedom does not accept or reject anything.
The dominion of the Dharma does not reject grasping or ideas.

In the space of magnificent self-awareness
We are pure from the beginning.

By totally killing this sentient being,
This supreme Auditor,
We will not be liberated,
But when the path of freedom shines,
It will be none other than an illuminator
Of our unchanging hearts.

The indivisibility of Buddhas and sentient beings
Is entirely pure.
In this indivisible heart,
We do not fail,
For we have had this heart's unchanging transmission
Since the primordial.

To kill a Supreme Benefit
That is not supreme
Is the supreme happiness.

The body of the king has arisen
From purity itself.
His two hands blaze in the light
Of his mudra's body of self-awareness.
All the mandalas blaze through his head,
And when his heart is disturbed
By talking about things,
Or gathering things up with his hands,
It is just then that he is totally pure.
No matter what there may be
In the three supremacies of the apparent world
That he would travel over,
There is not even an atom of a thing to be traveled over.
The sky travels in the sky.

All the sentient beings in the three realms travel,
But they reach an embodiment
As Vajrasattva himself.
From the beginning,
This has been the supreme path of total liberation.

So he spoke.

From the Tantra of the Magnificent Sky of Vajrasattva Embellished for the King, this is the twelfth chapter: Demonstrating Liberation.

EVERYTHING TURNS INTO SPACE

Then again the Blessed One entered the equanimity of the samadhi that has no measure, and made this intentional statement:

My mind is not changed
By the natures of secret mantras.
The sun of awareness shines out
From the bottom of the basis of all things.

The lord of all the mandalas
May appear as anyone,
But while he may appear as anyone,
He is invisible, unborn,
And perfect within his own dominion.

This is a samaya for mantras
That is not to be broken
Through our views or through our practices.
For those who are expert in the significance of perspectives
This is the short path.

Use your mind to see the significance
Of the Unwritten.[42]
Use your awareness to investigate
This mind that has no essence.

Speech that is without awareness
Has not been born,
So it is natural that we settle our awareness

Into the natural state
Of the significance of the Unborn.[43]

The manifestation of awareness and wisdom
As a multitude of things
Dwells in our minds
With a vajra-like portent.

This scripture does not divide the perfect Buddha
Between a cause and a result.
It has come forth from a Dharma that has not been exemplified.
For this reason,
The appearance of a multitude of manifestations
As people,
While their manifest positions are surely not visible,
But for the purpose of training those who live,
The multitude of things
May appear as anything.
The cause for the occurrence of these invisible manifestations
Is not to be fathomed.

The origins and applications for the expansion and contraction of letters
Do not occur in the origins and applications of our thoughts.
In the same way,
There are no thoughts that we bring together
In our dhyāna meditation.

Even the embodiments of the five families,
Beginning with Vairochana,
Are, in the magnificently pure space
Of the sky realm of the five embodiments,
Truly the same as the five Buddhas.

The holy and supreme abode of the supreme Buddha
Is the wide open space of *Bhaga* totality.
By meditating on just one embodiment,
Our dominion becomes luminous.

The unchanging, undying, vajra sky space,
The turner of every wheel,
The Buddha's body,
Blazes forth from this magnificent mandala
In which everything is spontaneously perfected.

Those who dwell in a state of equanimity,
In which unchanging self-awareness
Does not change into anything at all,
And place themselves into a state
In which the space of unvisualized equanimity
Is the same as self-awareness,
Resemble the Buddha's supreme and perfectly great perfection.
Our teacher said this.

So he spoke.

From the Tantra of the Magnificent Sky of Vajrasattva Embellished for the King, this is the thirteenth chapter: Everything Turns into Space.

FREEDOM FROM SEARCHING

Then the Blessed One entered the equanimity of the samadhi that does not seek, and made this intentional statement:

The true essence of the sky
Is a clarity that does not appear anywhere.
So it is that this true essence of the sky
Is an uncomplicated great bliss.

In an invisible reality
That we do not visualize to be anything,
Meditation will not occur in our minds.
When we settle into not searching,
That is meditation.

The Auditors and Private Victors,
Who believe in the material appearance
Of the Sutras and of shrines,
As well as those who believe
They will get total liberation
Through generation and realization
In yogas like the *Kriya* and the *Anu*,
Those who hope that the views
That are the doorway we enter,
Will bring results that are pure,
Are all seeking for something.

From this seeking it will follow
That they do not get the meaning

Of the perfection in living naturally.

Perfect self-origination does not hinder anything,
But perfect Buddhahood is very far
On that road.

Those who believe that after seeking their objective
With long-term hardships:
Having no knowledge or methods,
Developing peaceful abiding,
Higher perception,
And equanimity,
That they will touch upon it,
Are Bodhisattvas who are seeking to be Auditors.
They will fail.

To believe that four kinds of secrets
Are generated into a body,
And a mudra will appear,
Is a supreme error.

This is a supreme bliss.
We are not attached to anything at all.
To live in a desire for the way it is,
Playing in everything:
That is the path of happiness.

This heart of excellence
Is the supreme pathway of freedom.
All the three realms have been liberated from the primordial.
The apparent world is stamped with the seal
Of spontaneously perfected Buddhahood.

The uncompounded nature of the unchanging All Good One
Plays forever in the wisdom of the dominion of the Dharma.
Even samsara is something to play with.
So from the beginning,
The All Good One is without measure,
The basis for both what is stable and what is shifting.
We are not attached to anything.
We do not dwell on the flavor of our samadhi.

No ideas,
No attachment,
And no dwelling
This is liberation.

The heart of what this means
Is like the repeated melting of butter.
It has not been exemplified.
If the camphor does not rise up
Out of the space of self-awareness,
You will not find the meaning
By words or by exemplifications in writing.

We do not cut through to this
By listening with our ears,
Or by cognizing it.
The organ of the tongue does not have
Even an atom to say about it.

No matter where we seek
This precious jewel that transcends the three worlds,
We will not find it.
Not even a part of this
Is dedicated to words.
So there is not even an atom of it
To be taught as a meditation
By saying: "This."

So he spoke.

From the Tantra of the Magnificent Sky of Vajrasattva Embellished for the King, this is chapter fourteen: Freedom from Searching.

ALL DHARMAS ARE UNMOVING

Then the Blessed One entered the equanimity of the samadhi that does not shift, and made this intentional statement:

The true nature of the reality
That is the apparent world,
The vessel and its contents,
Is within the All Good nature
Of the Bodhicitta.

It does not fade.
It is not a pacification.
It is naturally without peace.
Because there are no Dharmas
That fade or that are pacified,
This is naturally luminous.
Its essence does not shift.
The uncomplicated peace of natural reality
Does not fade,
And is not a pacification.
It is naturally uncomplicated.

Self-originating wisdom is not shadowed.
It is luminous.
It does not fade and it is not a pacification.
It has no peace.

I am the teacher,
The All Good One.

I do not move away from
The totality of the Bodhicitta.

Self-originating wisdom
Has no causes or conditions.
It is totally victorious
Over all causes and results.
The unhindered mind is victorious
Over the dominion of the sky.
Do not tell the keepers of causes and conditions about this.
It is very secret.

The five apparitions
Of the sky, the earth,
Water, fire, and wind,
Are completely victorious
In the essence of the Bodhicitta.
Do not tell the keepers of causes and conditions about this.
It is very secret.

The three realms and the three times
Are victorious in our bodies, speech, and minds.
Do not tell the keepers of causes and conditions about this.
It is very secret.

It is naturally luminous.
Its essence does not shift.
They turn the unmoving Dharma
Into something that proves causes and results.
That is not my transmission.
It is a transmission of desire.

I have no desire,
So I am totally successful.
Non-desire is the natural success
Of having no desires.

I have not spoken about anything,
Saying: "It is proven."
That is what is in the words
Of those who believe in proving causes and results.

They exaggerate me and depreciate me.
They are the greatest of my enemies.
Existence and non-existence,
Proof and disproof:
We abide in an equanimity regarding
All these attributions that exaggerate and depreciate,
For we do not think of them.

I am the ancestor of all the Buddhas.
I have not proclaimed any contemplation
Other than that of equanimity.

So he spoke.

From the Tantra of the Magnificent Sky of Vajrasattva Embellished for the King, this is chapter fifteen: All Dharmas are Unmoving.

EQUANIMITY

Then the Blessed One entered the equanimity of the samadhi of non-visualization, and made this intentional statement:

I have never said that there is a difference,
Good and bad or great and small,
Between the bodies, speech, and minds
Of all the Buddhas,
And the bodies, speech, and minds
Of sentient beings.

I have not said this because
None of the Buddhas' contemplations teach it.
All the Orations are orations on my essence.
My essence is in all the dharmas.

This king of naturally pure equanimity
Has an unchanging true nature,
Free from all attachments.
There is no object to apprehend.
There is also no place for the mind.

Our own minds have the nature of the sky.
They do not touch on any limits.
They are not written down in any dominion.

It is not reasonable that our own minds
Would find the nature of the sky.
The nature of all dharmas is just the same.

Nothing moves from what it is.

We may work with any samadhi
To play with the Dharma,
But in the way that it is,
Our essence does not change.

If there were a greater power,
Something higher than the unchanging,
Then with a single samadhi
Samsara would be no more.

We may talk about this,
But the way it is does not change.
We live naturally,
In the land of great naturalness.
This is a name
For our uncontrived true nature.
Its greatness is not contrived.,
But we say: "It is great."

Those who believe there is something
To be perceived directly
Are in a place of attachment
Due to this belief.
I have no idea about this.
It is not a contemplation on equanimity.
I have dwelt from the beginning
In the true nature of reality.

Those who work to prove positions,
Thinking that they are seeking me,
Are seeking their own minds
In some other place.
They may investigate the dominion of the Dharma,
And the dominions of the sky,
The abodes in the three realms,
And the Dharmas of the world,
But they will not find
The natural abiding of their own minds.

Reality that is not conceptualized
Evens out into equanimity.

Because of the evenness,
There is no one thing that is a dharma,
Or that is not a dharma.

There is no cause that is a sentient being.
There is no result that is Buddhahood.
The transmissions of the teachers
Who are teachers of causes and results
Are mistaken.

This is why the Dharma that comes from me is even.
What comes from me is neither good nor bad.
It is a unified equanimity.

So he spoke.

From the Tantra of the Magnificent Sky of Vajrasattva Embellished for the King, this is chapter sixteen: Equanimity.

TEACHING THAT THE ALL GOOD ONE IS THE BASE

Then the Blessed One entered the equanimity of the samadhi that is unchanging, and made this intentional statement:

My reality and the way things are are one.
Its basis is not made
By a method that we must understand.
Do not use the reality of a view
As a basis for seeing.
This is a method by which we are made to see.
The unborn is not an object that we must visualize.
We do not see the way things are
By looking at them.

Do not create a basis
For the removal of faults in samaya.
That is a method by which we are made to have no obstructions.
In the way things are,
There is no object to be protected.
When we are protecting,
We are unable to control the way things are.

Do not create a basis
On which to establish karma.
That is a method to establish things
Through a search.
In the way things are,

There is no object to seek out,
So in the way things are,
There is nothing that constitutes karma.

Do not create a basis
For using a path to travel over.
That is a method for travelling to a place.
In the way things are,
We use no path to travel,
So going by travelling
Is not the way that it is.

Do not create a basis
That will make you dwell on a level.
That is a method for unnecessary travel.
In the way thing are,
Everything dwells in everything,
So there is no level that is to be dwelt on,
Or for us to learn.

Do not create a basis
That will make you understand wisdom.
That is a method in which you must understand reality.
In the way things are,
There is no object to be understood.
Self-originating wisdom
Does not think about an object.

The Bodhicitta is the basis of this Dharma.
The individual vehicles use six different views,
And six different practices,
To make a search for six bases for these views and practices.
In the way that it is,
There is no object to be searched for.
Through searching,
We distort the way that things are,
And because of this,
We do not encounter the uncontrived basis
Of our own minds.

So he spoke.

From the Tantra of the Magnificent Sky of Vajrasattva Embellished for the King, this is the seventeenth chapter: Teaching that the All Good One is the Base.

TEACHING NON-CONTRIVANCE

Then the Blessed One entered the equanimity of the samadhi of effortlessness, and made this intentional statement:

The teaching that says:
"The view is not to be meditated on"
Is not a teaching that I teach myself,
For there is no root for any Dharma
Other than the mind.
I do not teach that our minds are objects.
That is why this is a view that is not to be meditated on.

The teaching that samaya are not to be protected
Goes beyond the words that would protect
This spontaneously realized totality.
We do not control anything by protecting it.
Our minds do not stop.
This is a self-originating wisdom.
It is not to be protected.
So it is that samaya are not to be protected.

The teaching that good works are not to be sought out
Is that the great perfection
Has transcended causes and results
From the beginning.

Those who believe that after we have worked on good deeds,
As a cause,
We will get a result,

Do not believe that the great perfection is a result.
This is why there is the teaching that says:
"Good works are not to be sought."

The teaching that the path is not to be travelled over
Is that the Buddhas of the three times
Travel through the three realms of sentient beings,
And so they travel the road of the Bodhicitta.

In our minds there are nothing but these two:
Buddhas and sentient beings.
This being so,
The mind does not travel
On the pathway of the mind.

The teaching that the levels are not to be studied
Is that those who believe they will attain
The level of the Bodhicitta's reality
Through study,
Are the keepers of causes and results.

This is the level of the dominion of the Dharma,
The Bodhicitta.
I do not teach that there is success
Through study and contrivance.

The teaching that says that
Wisdom is not to be thought of as an object
Is that objects are, from the beginning,
Self-originating wisdom.
From the beginning,
Self-originating wisdom is devoid of objects.
From the beginning,
Objects do not turn into wisdom.

Of all the Buddhas of the three times,
And all the sentient beings of the three realms,
There is not a single one
That does not abide in the abode
Of the magnificent space of the mind.
It is the abode of everyone,
And is their level.
We dwell in this without joining with it or leaving it.

It is not necessary to study or travel over this.
If we study or travel over it,
Our own minds will be distorted.
We will not cleanse our minds
With contrivances.

So he spoke.

From the Tantra of the Magnificent Sky of Vajrasattva Embellished for the King, this is chapter eighteen: Teaching Non-contrivance.

EFFORTLESS PERFECTION HAS NO PLACE

Then the Blessed One entered the equanimity of the samadhi of effortless perfection, and made this intentional statement:

An effortless objective
Is like a sky that does not abide.
Non-abiding is not an object to be visualized.

Non-conceptualization is the path of the Dharma.
It comes from an objective that is
A minute particle of dedication.
Contemplation and meditation
Are of no special significance
To the embodiment of the Dharma.

Self-originating wisdom abides in everything,
Just as it is.
It does not dwell in an objective
That is effortless.
It is not to be contrived as a remedy.

The limbs of the lord of the Dharma
Seek the land of the heart.
We use a method in which we do not think of anything
To play in it.
The heart manifests naturally.
The embodiment of the Dharma
Is nowhere else.

We care for one minute atom,
And we are lost from all the ten directions.
The true meaning on non-duality
Is the self-origination
Of the wisdom of the good.

It is a heart of goodness
That absolutely does not concern itself
With direct perception.
Once we have embarked on this road of purity,
We will achieve the king of equanimities.

It is unchanging,
And does not change.
There is nothing to be attached to.
Just so,
There is no object to be apprehended,
And there is no place for the mind.

Those who believe in seeing with direct perception
Are always meditating on a cause.
They get the bliss of attachment to meditation,
But do not get the meaning of equanimity.

A single body encompasses all things,
So there are no Dharmas to be surmounted.
It does not touch on any limits,
So it is not written down in any dominion.

The play of the Dharma
Has no higher place than this
To experience.
Self-origination is a magnificent topic.
It abides in all things,
Just as they are.

There is no amazing object to see.
This is the eye that sees them.
It is not proper that everyone should hear of this.
There is nothing to report.

Dharmas and non-dharmas are forever mixed.
They are indivisible and equal.

There is no explanation that says:
"This is the ultimate Dharma."
Or: "This is a higher place."

Through thinking about delusions,
And the path to enlightenment,
We will not get there.

Self-originating wisdom
Is beyond the limitations of words.
The soul of primordial Buddhahood[44]
Is right there before you.

Use the analogy of a shadow and a form.
You will get an idea from that.

This does not exist,
And it is not something that does not exist.
It is the occurrence of an essence of an absence.
It is empty,
But it is not something that is empty.
It abides in the object that is empty.

Memories are born,
From out of the natural state of the sky.
We accept the bliss
Of being done with freedom from labor,
Without any desire.

This is not something to eat,
But through it you will begin to understand wisdom.
Consider in your mind
Those who are attached to the trails
Of the Rishis of yore.
Through the torture of strenuous searches
They finally finished.
When we embark on the path of our true nature
We will not become omniscient.
We will have an idea that says:
"This is how it is,"
And for this reason
We will be meditating on ideas.

From our desire for great happiness
We get the disease of attachment.
When we do not contrive anything that is called:
"The medicine of dwelling in undisturbed equanimity,"
The result will be in our travelling in high status,
And the elimination of our emotional problems.

This is the great illness
Of those who have no path,
But embark on a path.
They want to go somewhere.
They are like the deer,
Chasing after optical illusions.

There is no place to find.
This is not to be found in the three worlds,
Or the places we refer to in the ten directions.
They are obstructions to enlightenment.

The quickest wisdom is free from every thought.
It is like a precious jewel
That comes to us through our dear companions.
It is not to be visualized,
And does not exist in reference to some changing abode.

The goodness in our own nature
Fulfills all our wishes.
This is not due to any investigation.
When we let go,
The emergence of goodness
Will be manifest.

It is actually invisible,
But it is revealed
In all the costumes of desire.

The revealer who has no self or other
Is a treasure of precious jewels.
That which is called:
"The objective of total success"
Is taught to be selfless compassion.

It does not move from within us.
There is no place to seek out
For our natural abode.

We become attached on account of objects,
But this is not a visualization,
Or a dedication to some object.

Without origination,
And without applications,
Selfless compassion does not bring forth
A deprivation of the wealth of others.
We have dwelt in it from the beginning.

When we desire happiness,
We are putting happiness behind us.
When we are finished with happiness,
Happiness will seek out happiness.

The primordial ravenousness
Of delusional enlightenment
Feeds on the Dharma.

Those who hold onto these objects
Do not see the Buddha.

There is no Buddha!
Even a name for the Buddha does not exist!

The Buddha is a teacher,
But to attribute a name to him
Is a mistake.

To work on attaining a Buddhahood
That is somewhere else
Is a mistaken pathway.

The formless embodiment of the Dharma
Does not have even an atom to be said about it.

To be finished,
To be attached,
To be free,

To have peace,
To be no entity,
And to give it all up:
The nature of these is a magnificent ambrosia.

This does not depend on
The way that we eat.
It is a great vastness.
It is a magnificent Dharma.
It is a compassion for the little ones.
It is equal to the things that they imagine to be great.
They will become free of visualizing anything,
Great or small.

The visualization and appearance
Of the Orations and their embellishment
Are like the drawings of illusionists.
Origins and applications
Are a dense darkening of wisdom,
And through its powers come to be.

This is the king of all the vehicles.
It is the depth.
It is still.
It is natural.
It has no desire,
And it accepts nothing.
Not even an atom of its flavor
Is to be generated.
It is like a magnificent garuda
Soaring in the sky.

It does not expand,
And it does not contract.
It does not worry about emptiness.
It has nothing to eat.

It has been here from the beginning,
Like the ocean.
It makes the multitude of Dharmas appear.
Its virtues are equal to the end of the sky.

There is nothing definite
About where it will coalesce,
But at the very moment
That we are at the heart of enlightenment,
The magnificent king of samadhi
Will appear to us.

His appearance is that of the vast ocean.
He is wide open,
Like the ends of the unthought sky.
In the practice field of the All Good One,
There are no dharmas of birth or passing on.

The twelve branches of causes and conditions
Are described as being blameworthy.
They are attributions.
The wise must understand
That this is only a door to delusion.

Living beings may appear to be in six classes,
But this is something that must be understood
On the pathways of faith.

When our practice of desire
Is moistened with compassion,
Anything that pleases us
Is a practice of enlightenment.

For butchers, prostitutes,
Those who have done unforgivable things,
Those who have done unspeakable things,
And those rejected by the world,
This is the entirely perfect elixir of the Dharma.

There is no great happiness,
Other than this.
All the Dharmas of prosperity are here,
For this is the true nature of the Dharma.

Seeking for the true Dharma in the Dharma,
Searching for the sky within the sky,
And the Dharmas that refer to other things,
Are like fires that kill fires.

They do an extremely difficult job.

This heart is not an idea.
It is not hidden within the comprehensive Tantras.
Those who practice enlightenment
Without holding onto it
Live naturally in every way.

So he spoke.

From the Tantra of the Magnificent Sky of Vajrasattva Embellished for the King, this is chapter nineteen: Effortless Perfection has no Place.

WORKS AND DOINGS ARE A PURE DOMINION

Then the Blessed One entered the equanimity of the samadhi that is effortless, and made this intentional statement:

All dharmas occur naturally.
So it is that all the dharmas that appear
Have been shown to be in a state of dominion,
Formed from the beginning.

From the beginning,
Everything that is outside us or inside us
Is a dominion of the Dharma,
A practice field that has been pure
From the beginning.

Buddhas and sentient beings are not a duality.
How could this be contrived
To be a path or to be a remedy?
This is not to be worked on.
Shake off the search!
We do not have a prayer.

The spontaneous perfection that is effortless
Is what I have taught you before.
In the dominion of the Dharma,
Where the practice of ideas,
And of conceptualizations,
Are not a duality,
Who will be deceived

By the practices of fools,
And their reverted ideas?

They are delusional,
So they are taught a mistaken pathway,
But this is not in duality
With the magnificent path I have taught above.

The knowledge of equanimity
Is the lord of all the Buddhas.
Teachings of a self or of a soul
Are delusional pathways used by the Tirthakaras.

There is no place to go to.
There is no time in which we understand this.
If reality sought out the Dharma,
What would it find?

Masters who have not been validated
Have transmissions that are like little monkeys.
Their teachings are pathways that are mistaken.
I hope they will finish with their ideas,
For it is worth it to trade something of inestimable value
For the precious jewel of a master who is a perfect teacher,
Someone who is gold veneered with alum.

So he spoke.

From the Tantra of the Magnificent Sky of Vajrasattva Embellished for the King, this is chapter twenty: Works and Doings are a Pure Dominion.

EFFORTLESS PERFECTION IS SPONTANEOUSLY REALIZED

Then the Blessed One entered the equanimity of the samadhi of spontaneously realized perfection, and made this intentional statement:

The true nature of the many things
Is not dual,
While in their separate parts
There are no complications.

There is no idea that says:
"This is what it is,"
But the Maker of All Appearance,[45]
The All Good One,
Has finished with and has expunged
The disease of seeking.
We remain spontaneous,
And settle into it.

So he spoke.

From the Tantra of the Magnificent Sky of Vajrasattva Embellished for the King, this is chapter twenty-one: Effortless Perfection is Spontaneously Realized.

PERFECT WORKS AND DOINGS ARE NOT TO BE MEDITATED UPON

Then the Blessed One entered the equanimity of the samadhi of the unborn, and made this intentional statement:

The unspeakable Bodhicitta is beyond our thoughts.
It is our teacher's lantern,
And is highly praised by everyone.
It is the heart-essence of the Dharma.
It is the youthful Mañjuśrī himself.
It abides in the fullness of bliss
Of effortless and spontaneous perfection.
It is a basis for oceanic practices,
Beginning with the rule of the way.

The teachings of the path of liberation,
However many there may be,
Are practice fields for the Sugatas,
And are equivalent pathways.
Without them there is no change.
For these reasons,
I am the supreme path of liberation!

This is subtle,
And difficult to understand.
It is a path for everyone.

Non-conceptualization is beyond our ideas.
It does not abide.
It is not to be visualized.
It is not complicated.
It is free from all our thoughts.
Words do not penetrate it.
It has no shape or color.
It has no sphere of influence.
It is difficult to teach or to investigate.
There is not even an atom
To be said of it.

I hope that those who embark on the pathways
Of the Rishis of yore
Will end the disease
Of the paths on which we are attached to our meditation.
When they see that the transmissions of our teacher
Are pathways on which we work with the limitations of words,
And that they are following a transmission of ideas,
As if they were chasing optical illusions.

The correct pathway
Is not to be exemplified through words.
In true correctness,
I have distorted the teachings.

Purity and impurity are non-dual.
They are mixed.
They are the same.
The wisdom that does not discriminate anything at all
Is ignorance.
The oil lamp of unhindered luminescence
Is not a part of any of our thoughts.

Being immovable by nature is a darkness.
We abide in the king of samadhis.
The thing that sees things directly
Is an eye that sees directly.
For this reason we call it:
"The eye of omniscience."

It has no boundary or center.
It is a natural and spacious knowledge.

Without taking things on or casting them off,
We abide in the king of equanimities.

Our minds and our habitual patterns
Are non-dual.
They are mixed.
They are the same.
The Dharmas that appear,
Those that we investigate by holding onto them,
Appear on account of their own conditions,
So we do not cast them off or reject them.
We use the method of not contemplating anything at all
To play in them.

We engage in Dharmas that are rejected by everyone,
And do not agree with anyone:
The five emotional problems,
And the five unforgivable acts,
As a path of purity,
And attain the king of equanimities.

Those who never play with girls or anything
Put the meanings of the stories
Into a mind of validations.
They investigate their three samadhis,
And work with the established philosophical conclusions.

To say:
"Through the effortless transmission we deviate"
Is a delusion.
To abide in a land of happiness,
A spontaneous perfection that is effortless:
This is the magnificent heart
Of self-originating wisdom.

It does not shift.
It does not change.
It is beyond all explanation.
We dwell in a land
Where we have finished with effortlessness,
Just as we are.

Everything has,
From the beginning,
The nature of a great circle.
It does not expand.
It does not contract.
It is unborn.
It does not cease.
We abide in this unceasingness,
Just as it is.

This heart-essence is not an idea.
It abides forever,
Like the sky.
It is beyond the topics
For discussions on ideas.

So he spoke.

From the Tantra of the Magnificent Sky of Vajrasattva Embellished for the King, this is chapter twenty-two: Perfect Works and Doings are not to be Meditated Upon.

THE EMPOWERMENT OF FOUR SPOKEN WORDS AND THE ABSENCE OF AN OBJECT TO VIEW

Then the Blessed One entered the equanimity of the samadhi that does not visualize an object, and made this intentional statement:

The dharmas that appear as they do
Are our own Bodhicitta.
There is no place to look for them.
When we do not conceptualize,
That is equanimity.

So it is with the contemplation of the sky.
This is what is called: "Yoga."
The things that appear to the faces of our senses
Are self-luminescent,
So we do not think about them.

Furthermore,
The contemplations of the sky
Are yogas for living with the way it is.
Through understanding the meanings of words and letters,
We get a non-conceptual equanimity about
The way that it is.

Further,
Abiding in the contemplation of the sky
Is an uncontrived yoga.
We settle into thoughtlessness.

The significance of this is not to be thought on.

Appearances are a great ocean,
Wide like the ends of the unthought sky.
They remain forever,
As does the sky.

So he spoke.

From the Tantra of the Magnificent Sky of Vajrasattva Embellished for the King, this is the twenty-third chapter: The Empowerment of Four Spoken Words and the Absence of an Object to View.

FOUR DEFINITE WORDS

Then the Blessed One entered the equanimity of the samadhi that achieves its purpose without doing anything, and made this intentional statement:

As things appear,
They are one in the way that they are.
No one is to distort the one.
In this king of uncontrived equanimity,
We abide in the contemplation
Of a non-conceptual embodiment of the Dharma.

So he spoke.

From the Tantra of the Magnificent Sky of Vajrasattva Embellished for the King, this is chapter twenty-four: Four Definite Words.

THE ENDOWMENT OF THE TANTRA

Then Vajrasattva addressed the Blessed One with these words:

E Ma Ho!
This is amazing!

This Tantra Embellished for the King
Does not exist in words.
Do sentient beings not have little fortune?
This Mahasattva Tantra[46] is beyond words,
And beyond being written in letters.

It is possible that the end of time occur.
It is also possible that it not occur.
Even if it occurs,
It will occur for only one person,
And nothing will be lost.

When it happens,
Unvisualized power,
Unvisualized wisdom,
Unvisualized equanimity,
And unvisualized awareness
Will shine out by themselves.

None of the nations of humans has,
By its own nature,
Transcended this unborn reality,

But by their natures they do not decline,
And it naturally comes to pass
That they have no place.

All those sentient beings who have this Tantra
Will transform into their own true natures,
As being the All Good One,
And will become Buddhas that do not pass away.

The mind that hears this Tantra
Will transform into self-originating wisdom,
And then become a circle of non-duality
That does not seek.

Then Vajrasattva and the rest of the retinue rejoiced.

This is the twenty-fifth chapter: The Endowment of the Tantra.

The Tantra Embellished for the King was translated for Nyingpo.[47]

It is completed.

THE TANTRA ON VAJRASATTVA'S MAGNIFICENT SKY

In the Indian language:

Vajrasatva Gagasame Mahātantra Nāma

In the Tibetan language:

rDo rje sems dpa' nam mkha' che'i rgyud ces bya ba

In the English language:

The Tantra on Vajrasattva's Magnificent Sky

THE BASIC SCENE

I bow to the glorious Vajrasattva.

On one occasion, I heard these words:

The Blessed One, the Tathagata, the All Good One, whose body has neither front nor back, who has the three heads of total freedom, who holds an eight-sided precious jewel of blazing light in his six hands, was in non-duality with his consort, the All Good Mother, in the abode of Akaniṣṭa, which has no border or center, in the magnificent palace of his consort.

On thrones constructed above elephants and other animals, thrones with a lotus, sun, and moon, there sat Vajrasattva and the rest of the Tathagatas: Maker of All Vision, Origin of Jewels, Bounteous Appearance, Success Without a Doubt, and the others, along with their queens.

There was an entourage of Bodhisattvas that included Earth Heart, Sky Heart, the Lord of the World, and Vajra in Hand, along with their queens. There were the Bodhisattvas Maitreya, All Good One, Remover of Shadows, Mañjuśrī, and the rest, along with their queens.

There were also the great wrathful ones: Killer of the Lord of the Dead, Great Mighty One, Horse-necked One, Swirling Ambrosia, and the rest, along with their queens.

They were there on a single initiative.

This is the first chapter: The Basic Scene.

TAKING UP THE TOPIC

Then Vajrasattva and all the rest of those other Tathagatas addressed the Blessed One, the Tathagata, the All Good One, with these words:

Blessed One,
All Good One,
How should we generate the spontaneously formed mandala
Of the great spirit?[48]
How should we generate a place for it?

The Blessed One, the Tathagata, the All Good One, gave an oration:

O Vajrasattva and the rest of you Tathagatas who are in his company,
Listen!

The spontaneously formed abode of the great spirit is generated in a single instant, a single moment, within the magnificent palace of my consort's clear sky. Within it there is the spontaneously formed mandala of the great spirit, which as two aspects: The mandala that is spontaneously formed as a mandala, and the physical mandala of the great spirit.

This is the second chapter: Taking up the Topic.

THE SPONTANEOUSLY FORMED MANDALA OF THE GREAT SPIRIT

Then again, Vajrasattva and the rest of the Tathagatas addressed the Blessed One, the Tathagata, the All Good One, with these words:

Blessed One,
Tathagata,
All Good One,
How is it with the spontaneously formed mandala of the great spirit?

Tathagata,
All Good One,
How is it with the physical mandala of the great spirit?

The Blessed One, the Tathagata, the All Good One gave an oration:

Blessed One Vajrasattva
And the rest of you Tathagatas who are his entourage,
Listen!

At the precise moment that there is awareness
A pride is created
In a luminescence of the five families,
The consorts of the five families,
The eight Bodhisattvas,
The eight female Bodhisattvas,
The eight wrathful ones,
And the eight wrathful women.

The physical mandala of the great spirit is created
In a luminescence where the deities are our nerves.[49]
This is the spontaneously formed mandala of the great spirit.

This is the third chapter: The Spontaneously Formed Mandala of the Great Spirit.

THE NERVES

Then again the Tathagatas in the Blessed One's entourage addressed the Blessed One, the Tathagata, the All Good One with these words:

Blessed One,
Tathagata,
All Good One,
How is it with the nerves of the body?

The Blessed One, the Tathagata, the All Good One gave an oration:

O Tathagatas who are the Blessed One's entourage,
Listen!

The nerves of the body are these four: the open, the knotted, the sharp, and the severed. There are the ones that are transparent and that wrap around. With the nerves of great bliss and the nerves for the life-force, there are six kinds.

The nerves for the life force are wrapped up. There is one mind-nerve for the All Good One. There are two eye nerves, and two ear nerves. There are two nose nerves, and two tongue nerves. There are four nerves for the four kinds of consciousness, and there are four nerves for the four senses. There are the nerves for the objects of the four kinds of consciousness. All these nerves have a solid form.

Then there are the nerves for the goddesses of the four times:
In the beginning, the nerves attach themselves to a life-force,
They abide in life, and are attached to it,

But when we pass on from life,
The nerves are destroyed.
When they are destroyed,
The nerves become empty.
You must know that these are the nerves
Of the goddesses of the four times.

When we are joined to a life-force,
We are conscious of touch.
There are nerves that arouse our senses,
So that we may comprehend the characteristics
Of the things we touch.
These are the nerves of our physical senses.
You must understand that the true self-nature of the things we touch
Is our physical nerves.

The characteristics of our experience are three:
The object, the sense, and the consciousness.
When these come together,
There is a sensation that something is happening.

The nerves are not to be designated as being a self,
Which is what the Tirthakaras do.
They are not to be designated as being permanent.
They are not to be designated through a process of negation.
They are not to be designated through defining characteristics.

These are the nerves of our bodies.

This is chapter four: The Nerves.

THE NERVES ABIDE IN THE WAY OF THE LETTERS

Then again the Blessed Ones, the Tathagatas, addressed him:

Blessed One,
Tathagata,
All Good One,
In what way do these nerves abide?

The Blessed One said:

The transparent nerve is wrapped up, while the A and the Kṣa abide in the way of the nerves of great bliss. The nerve for the life-force is wrapped up, while the nerve of the Unmoving and the nerve of the All Good One must be understood to be Tha and Kṣa. The true nature of these two nerves is the lord-mother of the vajra dominion. You must know that this is the nerve for the All Good One.

Then again, we attach a different A to it. You must know that the open, the knotted and the rest of the four are Ṭa ta, and Ḍa da, and Ḍha dha, and also Ṇa na.

These eight: Ka kha, Ga gha, Pa pha, and Ba bha, are the two nerves for the eyes, the two nerves for the nose, the two nerves for the tongue, and the two nerves for the ears.

The four consciousnesses and the material sensory organs,
The nerves of the four sense organs: The eye, ear, nose, and tongue are these four: Tsa, Tsha, Dza, and Dzha.

The nerves of the *lingga*, the secret organ, are these four: Ya, Ra, Wa, and La.

With these four: Nga, Nya, Ma, and O, and these four: Ṣa, Śa, Sa, and Ha, using colors and shapes for them, the nerves abide in the way of the letters.

This is the fifth chapter: The Nerves Abide in the Way of the Letters.

BEING NATURAL

Then again that entourage of Blessed Ones, those Tathagatas, addressed the Blessed One, the Tathagata, the All Good One:

Blessed One,
Tathagata,
All Good One,
What is the true nature of all sentient beings?

The Blessed One, the Tathagata, the All Good One, gave an oration:

O Tathagatas,
Entourage of Blessed Ones,
Listen!

The great originator,[50]
The Blessed One,
Abides in fullness.
The Blessed One dwells naturally
In all living things.

From the beginning,
This is the mandala of the Victorious Ones.
We may make attributions about it,
Based on our reversions,
But there is no self-originating liberation
Other than this.

This is chapter six: Being Natural.

TRUE ENLIGHTENMENT

Then again the entourage of Tathagatas addressed the Blessed One, the Tathagata, the All Good One:

Using which methods are we to understand the meaning of the great perfection?

The Tathagata, the All Good One gave an oration:

O Tathagatas,
Entourage of Blessed Ones,
Listen!

Equanimity without conceptualizations
Is the embodiment of the Dharma.
The embodiment of the Dharma is like the sky.
I arise from it in a body that is like a rainbow.
I do not hold what I take in,
Like the moon on water.

In the two nerves of method and wisdom
The letters of the vowels and consonants are clear.
They are illuminated in four wheels,
Until they become non-dual,
And, through this, the playfulness of the All Good One
Is taught to be the profundity of the vowels and consonants.

In this, the A and the beautiful Ta
Expand into branches with the Pa,

And the general objectives of the entire world
Become evident as the profundities spoken of by the Buddhas.

E Ma Ho!
This is the practice field of the Buddha!
It is not a place that you will find
By seeking for it.
It is not to be realized
By conforming to the six Dharmas.
That would be like blind men scrutinizing the sky.

The path of purity,
Which goes higher and higher,
Is not in agreement
With the effortless Dharma.

To move through such paths
Is like going to the end of the sky.
You will not get there.

This is the seventh chapter: True Enlightenment.

Complete Perfection

Then again the Tathagatas, that entourage of Blessed Ones, addressed him:

Blessed One,
Tathagata,
All Good One,
How does the great perfection
Arise from out of the playfulness of the All Good?

The Blessed One, the All Good One, gave an oration:

That which abides nowhere,
And is not to be conceptualized,
Comes from the vowels and consonants.
So it is that likewise and for this reason
This is taught to this,
And this also attains this.
This is the heart-essence,
And because of this
It is a great wonder
That this comes from this.

The this of the past,
And the this of the present,
And likewise the greatness there is
In the presence of this,
Are, in this way, like pathways made of this.
This is the true nature of this.

The comprehensive pathway is like this:
It comes from the moon,

Along with its structure.

It is a total equanimity.
You will not see it by looking in any direction.
The true nature of this has been primordially pure,
Since the primordial.

This is the eight chapter: Complete Perfection.

NATURAL GREATNESS

Then again the entourage of Tathagatas addressed him:

Blessed One,
Tathagata,
All Good One,
As this has been naturally pure from the primordial,
How are we to rely on methods and wisdom?

The Blessed One, the Tathagata, the All Good One, gave an oration:

O Entourage of Tathagatas,
Listen!

The wisdom of greatness is difficult to find.
You will succeed by depending on wisdom and methods.
Just by the name,
It would seem I am teaching something else,
But directly experienced happiness
Comes from ourselves.

This is the ninth chapter: Natural Greatness.

FREEDOM FROM EFFORT AND SEEKING

Then again the entourage of Tathagatas addressed him:

Blessed One,
Tathagata,
All Good One,
What is the meaning of perfection without search or effort?

The Blessed One, the Tathagata, the All Good One, gave an oration:

Entourage of Tathagatas,
Listen!

O Tathagatas,
Entourage of Blessed Ones,
The meaning of the great perfection's being without search or effort
Is that the magnificent self-originating wisdom of the mind
Arises by itself, from the very beginning,
Without any search for it.
From out of this dominion,
Which has no depth or limit.
This is what it means
To be primordially free from an attitude of seeking.

Again that entourage of Blessed Ones, those Tathagatas, addressed him:

If it is so,
That the great perfection is primordially free from an attitude of seeking,
Then, O Blessed One, Tathagata, All Good One,

From what causes do there occur the magnificent virtues of the Buddha:
His powers, fearlessness, markings, and exemplary features?

The Blessed One, the Tathagata, the All Good One, gave an oration:

Entourage of Blessed Ones,
Tathagatas,
The magnificent virtues of the Buddha:
His power, fearlessness, and the rest,
Are for circumstances involving those of the lower vehicles,
But the great perfection's being without effort or search
Is itself lacking in any difficulty that would come from an effort or search.
As soon as we understand the meaning of the great perfection,
The great perfection that is free from effort or search
Will emerge from out of itself.

Again the entourage of Tathagatas addressed him:

Blessed One,
If yogins of the future would meditate on the meaning of the great perfection, how are they to meditate?

The Blessed One gave an oration:

Entourage of Tathagatas,
If yogins of the future
Would meditate on the meaning of the great perfection,
They must settle themselves in this reality that is primordially unborn,
Where their own minds are unborn,
Then meditate.

Again the entourage of Tathagatas addressed him:

Blessed One,
Through settling into reality,
How will we get miraculous powers, fearlessness, and the rest?

The Blessed One gave an oration:

Great miracles are not difficult.
All the wonders and the powers
Come from themselves,
Right when we reflect on them in our thoughts.

We settle ourselves,
Without searching for some invisible reality,
And meditate on that.

If we hunt for this and this,
This will also not emerge from this.

This is the tenth chapter: Freedom from Effort and Seeking.

THE REALITY OF LIVING NATURALLY

That entourage of Tathagatas addressed the Blessed One:

Blessed One,
Tathagata,
All Good One,
What is the meaning of the reality of living naturally?

The Blessed One gave an oration:

Entourage of Tathagatas,
The reality of living naturally
Is that Vajrasattva is the magnificent sky,
The openness of the All Good,
The dominion of the Dharma.
It is the great path of purity
That liberates everyone.
It is not born.
It does not stop.
It does not contemplate anything.

We study our objective with friendship,
So we do not do anything with great compassion.
This is the greatest of the great profundities.
We do not praise its virtues in any way.
We do not develop on these objectives.
We are liberated into liberation
Without any effort.

Self-originating wisdom is not to be sought.
We teach the path of liberation
After we are liberated.

This is the eleventh chapter: The Reality of Living Naturally.

OUR OWN BODHICITTA IS UNSPEAKABLE

Again that entourage of Tathagatas addressed him:

Blessed One,
Tathagata,
All Good One,
What does it mean to say our own Bodhicitta is unspeakable?

He have an oration to that entourage of Tathagatas:

The unspeakability of our own Bodhicitta
Is that the reality that is the basis for all things
Is primordially unborn.
The reality of this supreme secret
Will not be heard elsewhere
Through the organ of our ears.
In the same way,
The organ of our tongue
Does not have even an atom to say about this.

This is the twelfth chapter: Our Own Bodhicitta is Unspeakable.

THE BODHICITTA IS NOT ENSNARED BY THE KARMA OF LIVING BEINGS

Again that entourage of Tathagatas addressed him:

Blessed One,
Tathagata,
All Good One,
Is our own Bodhicitta entrapped in our karma,
Or is it not?

The Blessed One gave an oration:

The sorrows of living beings
Are entirely pervaded by the Bodhicitta,
So there is a playfulness.
We do not generate this.
It is equal to the end of the sky.

In particular,
It may resemble anything at all.
To say: "It is karma"
Is merely an attribution.
Something that is under the control of karma
Is not self-originating wisdom.
The same is true when a cause itself
Is a vajra condition.

That which is unborn
Has no ending.

From the primordial,
Our heart-essence is already enlightened.
This dominion is not shaken
By thoughts about a search.

This is the eleventh chapter: The Bodhicitta is not Entrapped by the Karma of Living Beings.

THE BODHICITTA IS NOT A SEEKING ATTITUDE

Again that entourage of Tathagatas addressed him:

Blessed One,
Tathagata,
All Good One,
Is the Bodhicitta that is free from an attitude of seeking
Something to put our hopes in or to pray for?

The Blessed One gave an oration:

The dhyāna of greatest virtue
Is dhyāna itself.
It is not something to think about.
It is a Dharma that is not to be contemplated,
And not to be studied.

Wisdom is born from ideas themselves.
We may give it a name,
Calling it a door of refinement,
And we may use a seclusion of the mind
To seek our path.
We may hold onto our seclusion,
As described in the Āraṇyaka Tantra,[51]
But our attributions will become our ideas,
And we will meditate on them,
Giving names to causes and results,

And removing both virtue and evil.

To say: "These things happen in this world,"
Is to gleefully take things up or cast them off,
Envisioning this to be supreme.

This is the fourteenth chapter: The Bodhicitta is Not a Seeking Attitude.

THE BODHICITTA DOES NOT HAVE THE FAULTS THAT THE NON-DUALISTS HAVE

Again that entourage of Tathagatas addressed him:

Blessed One,
Tathagata,
All Good One,
As the Bodhicitta is not a seeking attitude
Is this absence of a contemplation free from the faults
In the position of the Non-dualists,[52]
Or is it not?

The Blessed One gave an oration:

Attachment and non-attachment
Are paths of words.
According to the middle way,
They are like echoes from rocks.

The Blessed Ones give orations that say:
"Happiness and sorrow have a common cause."

This is the fifteenth chapter: The Bodhicitta Does Not Have the Faults of the Non-dualists.

GREAT WISDOM COMES FROM ITSELF

Again the entourage of Tathagatas addressed him:

Blessed One,
Tathagata,
All Good One,
This great spirit that is the Bodhicitta,
Is it a wisdom that comes from itself, or not?

The Blessed One gave an oration:

Even lust, hatred, and ignorance
Come from the pathway of the Bodhicitta.
Even the five kinds of wonder there are in doing everything
Are an unborn reality.
They are my ornaments.

This is the sixteenth chapter: Great Wisdom Comes from Itself.

THE WAY TO UNITE WITH TOTAL PERFECTION

Again that entourage of Tathagatas addressed him:

Blessed One,
Tathagata,
All Good One,
What is the meaning of the view
In which methods and wisdom are non-dual,
And the contemplation in which we are entirely perfected?

The Blessed One gave an oration:

Our ideas about the sky are unborn,
And these ideas are themselves like the sky.
The unattached sky is blue.
Our own great objectives appear to us
In the sky.

This is the seventeenth chapter: The Way to Unite With complete Perfection.

FREEDOM FROM ATTACHMENT

Again that entourage of Tathagatas addressed him:

Blessed One,
Tathagata,
All Good One,
Is this method,
Which unites methods with wisdom,
Free from attachments, or not?

The Blessed One gave an oration:

The happiness of the present,
And the happiness that comes later on,
Occur to us directly or from behind,
But they are problem areas.
You must not rely on them.

This is the eighteenth chapter: Freedom from Attachment.

NATURALLY BEING
A PRIMORDIAL HEART OF GREATNESS

Again that entourage of Tathagatas addressed him:

Blessed One,
Tathagata,
All Good One,
Has this Bodhicitta that is free from attachment
Existed naturally in a heart of greatness since the primordial, or not?

The Blessed One gave an oration:

The three times are one.
There is no difference.
With nothing before it,
And nothing following it,
It has arisen from the primordial.
It is encompassed by the embodiment of the Dharma,
For it is one.
The greatest of the great
Is to live naturally.

This is the nineteenth chapter: Naturally Being a Primordial Heart of Greatness.

TOTAL FREEDOM FROM PRAYER

Again the entourage of Tathagatas addressed him:

Blessed One,
Tathagata,
All Good One,
Is the Bodhicitta,
Which by nature is primordially unborn,
Free from prayer, or not?

The Blessed One gave an oration:

Joining with the three kinds of existence
Is just a name,
For they appear as an illusion.
Those who look for a time to do their practices
Will not succeed this time.
To practice praying that we may be free from tasks
Is like talking about the definition of emptiness.

This is the twentieth chapter: Total Freedom from Prayer.

THERE ARE NO SCRIPTURAL REFERENCES ON THE BODHICITTA

Again that entourage of Tathagatas addressed him:

Blessed One,
Tathagata,
All Good One,
Is this Bodhicitta that is free from prayer evident in the scriptures, or not?

The Blessed One gave an oration:

It is one.
It is entirely without form.
The yogin abides
In the bird-paths of the sky.

How would he maintain Dharmas
That exaggerate this unoriginated, unborn heart-essence,
Whether it is external or internal?
The external is, in fact, the internal.
There is no object
For our knowledge of profound things to understand.
Name in the world
Is also a force of reversion.
For this reason,
We are free from the equanimity of samadhi.
Our vows regarding this,
Whether former or latter,

And our natural composition,
Exist as if they were domains,
But we do not part from this
In any of the three times.

There is nothing that we attribute as a name for this vow.
It is a circle of great wisdom.

This is chapter twenty-one: There are no Scriptural References on the Bodhicitta.

THERE IS NO EMPOWERMENT INTO EQUANIMITY

Again that entourage of Tathagatas addressed him:

Blessed One,
Tathagata,
All Good One,
Is the empowerment for the Bodhicitta
Transmitted in this equanimity, or not?

The Blessed One gave an oration:

Immovability is the seal for our embodiment.
Unshakability is wisdom.
It is because we do not take
That we are selfless.
When there are no words of unhappiness,
There is equanimity.

Everything that entraps us,
And everything we do,
Whatever it may be,
And whatever its object is,
Comes from ourselves.
In this,
We are either men or women.

This is chapter twenty-two: There is No Empowerment into Equanimity.

THE EQUANIMITY OF ENLIGHTENMENT HAS NOTHING TO CAST OFF OR TAKE ON

Again that entourage of Tathagatas addressed him:

Blessed One,
Tathagata,
All Good One,
Is there an empowerment into the equanimity of the Bodhicitta, or not?
Are there things to cast off and take up, or not?

The Blessed One gave an oration:

This is not a basis on which
We must live with horrendous sorrow.
Those who keep to the A and the Par
Desire to tremble in the bliss of illusion.
This is also a problem,
As it is a holding onto something.

When we are not sure that there is one true nature,
However we look at things
Will be the way that we see them.

The desire for appearances,
And a seeking attitude,
Are pleasant,
But they have the major problem
That they are impediments.

To meditate on apparel,
As the door to all the branches of enlightenment
Is like the moon on water.
It happens without attachment and without stain,
But to meditate on this
Would seem to be a practice field for children.

We take on the form of the great wrathful lord,
Whose angry frown and costume are a mandala.
The letters are actually there,
But we do not find real peace.

We may cut off the head of a banana tree,
And we may burn its seeds in a fire,
But it will not be controlled.
It will somehow generate
Into a bounteousness of hundreds and thousands of emanations,
And flowers will be born.

Using the power of the un-signified
Will not free us from this central point.

This is chapter twenty-three: The Equanimity of Enlightenment has Nothing to Cast Off or Take On.

TEACHING THE METHOD BY WHICH WE ARE TO ATTAIN GREAT BLISS IN WHAT IS MERELY AN ILLUSION FROM BODHICITTA THAT DOES NOT CAST OFF OR TAKE ON ANYTHING

Again that entourage of Tathagatas addressed him:

Blessed One,
Tathagata,
All Good One,
Are there methods by which we are to attain great bliss through this Bodhicitta that does not cast off or take on, or not?

The Blessed One gave an oration:

The yogin who dwells in this without talking
Is fortunate.
He will not divide himself from others,
And will play in the land of spontaneously formed illusion.

This is chapter twenty-four: Teaching the Method by which We are to Attain Great Bliss in What is Merely an Illusion from Bodhicitta that Does Not Cast Off or Take On Anything.

ALL LIVING BEINGS ARE BUDDHAS BY THEIR VERY NATURE

Again that entourage of Tathagatas addressed him:

Blessed One,
Tathagata,
All Good One,
If there is a method by which we are to attain great bliss in what is merely an illusion, will it not then be the case that all living beings are Buddhas by their very nature?

The Bhagawan[53] gave an oration:

There is a great bliss in the objects that we comprehend.
This is, in fact, the purity of the world.
The lights from all the directions are gathered into it,
To form the directions, the boarders, the above, and the below.

The colors of a rainbow may not be definite,
But instantiations of their classes of color actually do appear.
In this same way,
The lack of motion in moving atoms
Is the most important from among the five elements.

This is chapter twenty-five: All Living Beings are Buddhas by their Very Nature.

TEACHING THAT THE ACCUMULATIONS ARE SPONTANEOUSLY FORMED AND ARE FULLY COMPLETE BY THEIR VERY NATURE

Again that entourage of Tathagatas addressed him:

Blessed One,
Tathagata,
All Good One,
As all living beings are Buddhas by their very nature,
Are there those who are poor in their savings,
And those who are totally perfect by their very nature,
Or not?

The Blessed One gave an oration:

This does not abide in a conventional name
For the past, the future, or the present.
It has no birth or ending.
On carefully investigation,
This is the unified greatness of the three times.
The awareness of equanimity does not structure it.
In is not a dedication toward some single direction.
We may display it as an ornament in our collection,
But it is naturally present,
So it will not be disclosed.
There is no dedication in this,
For it is present spontaneously.

It is pure from the primordial.
It is ambrosia.

According to the scriptures on the twelve impulses,[54]
The wisdom that has three embodiments
Appears where it is spontaneously formed by its very nature.
This is not something to be apprehended
By higher contemplations.

So he spoke.

This is chapter twenty-six: Teaching that the Accumulations are Spontaneously Formed and Are Fully Complete by Their Very Nature.

TEACHING THAT THE MASTER OF THE ASSEMBLY AND HIS JEWELRY ARE SPONTANEOUSLY MADE BY THEIR VERY NATURE

Again that entourage of Tathagatas addressed him:

Blessed One,
Tathagata,
All Good One,
Are the master of the assembly and his jewelry made by their own natures, or not?

The Blessed One gave an oration:

The thought in our minds is the master of ceremonies.
Due to his power to enfold them,
He is the organizer.
When we come to see this,
And make it real,
We will have a perfect settling into equanimity.
When we apprehend this for a mere instant,
We are united.

We will like it,
So there are samaya.
We move with the dance steps of methods,
For non-dual union is deluxe.

So did he give his oration.

This is chapter twenty-seven: Teaching that the Master of the Assembly and his Jewelry are Spontaneously Made by their Very Nature.

TEACHING THAT IT IS NOT NECESSARY TO DO AN OCEAN OF RITES, BEGINNING WITH THE TORMAS, AND THAT WE WILL SUCCEED BY SETTLING INTO EQUANIMITY

Again that entourage of Tathagatas addressed him:

Blessed One,
Tathagata,
All Good One,
Are the oceans of rites,
Beginning with the Tormas,
Carried out by settling into equanimity, or not?

The Blessed One gave an oration:

When we throw something away without holding onto it,
It is a Torma.
There is nothing else to do,
So the rites are over.
We clear away these obstructions to non-conceptual wisdom,
Then we understand the mantra words of unspoken equanimity.

This is chapter twenty-eight: Teaching that it is Not Necessary to Do an Ocean of Rites, Beginning with the Tormas and that We Will Succeed by Settling into Equanimity.

TEACHING THAT THERE ARE MAJOR EMOTIONAL FETTERS IN DOING RITES, SUCH AS THE TORMAS

Again that entourage of Tathagatas addressed him:

Blessed One,
Tathagata,
All Good One,
Will the performance of rites, beginning with the Tormas,
Bring about emotional problems, or not?

The Blessed One gave an oration:

When we make offerings to our gurus,
Distributions,
And all things that are meritorious,
While our minds are lacking in non-attachment,
And are not unshakable,
These things become great shackles.

This is chapter twenty-nine: Teaching that there are Major Emotional Fetters in Doing Rites, Such as the Tormas.

THE TRUE NATURE OF THIS EXISTS SPONTANEOUSLY

Again that entourage of Tathagatas addressed him:

Blessed One,
Tathagata,
All Good One,
Is there a true nature that is spontaneously made?

The Blessed One gave an oration:

Doing this about this,
Becomes an obstruction.
When we understand this about this,
We will not make up a thisness in this.

This is chapter thirty: The True Nature of This Exists Spontaneously.

TEACHING THAT REALITY IS TOTALLY UNCHANGING

Again that entourage of Tathagatas addressed him:

Blessed One,
Tathagata,
All Good One,
What does it mean when you say that this is spontaneously made and exists without changing?

The Blessed One gave an oration:

There is nothing that is left out,
For this is completely perfect.
It does not change.
It abides in honesty.
It is as smooth as the sky.
It is not a Dharma that becomes powerful due to something else.

The great bliss there is
In remaining spontaneous
Is an unparalleled wisdom.
It is something we are aware of
Through our own powers.
The Dharma does not come from anywhere else.
This is both easy and difficult.
It is difficult because it is easy.
It is not evident to direct perception.

It is totally pervasive.
To depend on saying:
"This is to be perceived directly,"
So not something that Vajrasattva would do.

This is chapter thirty-one: Teaching that Reality is Totally Unchanging.

TEACHING THAT IF WE ARE ATTACHED TO THE JOYS OF CONCEPTUALIZATION THERE WILL BE PROBLEMS

Again that entourage of Tathagatas addressed him:

Blessed One,
Tathagata,
All Good One,
If we are attached to the joy there is in conceptualizations,
Will that be a problem?

The Blessed One gave an oration:

This amazing and miraculous playfulness is effortless.
It is like the sky.
When we do not visualize anything at all,
Ignorance happens by itself, right away.

This is a path on which all sentient beings are equal.
It dwells naturally within all living things.
The childish have delusions that it has been polluted,
As if the medicine were seeking out the doctor.

So he spoke.

This is chapter thirty-two: Teaching that If We Are Attached to the Joys of Conceptualization There Will be Problems.

TEACHING HOW YOGINS OF THE FUTURE MUST TAKE THE MEANING OF THE GREAT PERFECTION INTO THEIR EXPERIENCE

Again that entourage of Tathagatas addressed him:

Blessed One,
Tathagata,
All Good One,
How are yogins of the future to bring the meaning of the great perfection
Into their experience?

The meaning of the great perfection
Does not refer to a cause,
A condition,
Or a result.

We must dwell on it without being disturbed or searching.
This is a reality that has been spontaneously realized
From the very beginning.
The actualization of this is Buddhahood.

The true nature of the great perfection
Is to dwell in great equanimity,
Without being distracted into great stupidity,
And without visualizing anything at all.

At the moment we do this,
Our Buddhahood is evident
From within ourselves.

In this reality,
Which is not visible as an object,
There is nothing for our intellects to seek,
So we have no seeking attitude about it.

We ponder this state without distraction
For a long while.
An embodiment of the Dharma is the result.

When we settle into equanimity in this pervasive state,
Without thinking about it,
The result will come spontaneously,
Without any study.

This is chapter thirty-three: Teaching How Yogins of the Future Must Take the Meaning of the Great Perfection into Their Experience.

The Tantra of Vajrasattva's Magnificent Sky is complete.

THE TIBETAN TEXTS

THE EFFULGENT VAJRA LIGHT OF THE BODHICITTA

From the mTshams brag Edition of the rNying ma rGyud 'bum

Volume One, pages 571-586.

ཀ

༄༅། །གནས་ཐམས་ཅད་དུ་ཡང་སྐད་ཅིག་ཏུ། །མི་མཐུན་ཕྱོགས་ཀྱིས་མི་ཉམས་རྒྱལ་བ་ཀུན་གྱི་ཐུགས་ཀས་འདི་རིམ་བརྒྱུད་ཤོག །སེམས་བསྒོམ་རྡོ་ལ་གསེར་ཞུན
རྫོགས་སོ།། ༄། །རྒྱ་གར་སྐད་དུ། བོ་དྷི་ཙིཏྟ་བཛྲ་སཏྭ་ཧཱ་ན་ཏ་ནཱ་མ། བོད་སྐད་དུ། བྱང་ཆུབ་སེམས་རྡོ་རྗེ་འོད་འཕྲོ་བའི
རྒྱུད་ཀྱི་རིམ་པ་ཞེས་བྱ་བ། བཅོམ་ལྡན་འདས་དཔལ་གྱི་དཔལ་སྐུ་བསམ་མ་བརྗོད་པ་ལས་འདས་པ་ལ་ཕྱག་འཚལ་ལོ། །འདི་སྐད་བདག་གིས་ཐོས་པའི་དུས་ཀྱི་ཚེ། བཅོམ
ལྡན་འདས་དཔལ་རྡོ་རྗེ་སེམས་དཔའ་ཉིད། ཀུན་ཏུ་བཟང་པོ་འོག་མིན་གྱི་གནས། རིག་པའི་ཕོ་བྲང་། བསམ་གྱིས་མི་ཁྱབ་པའི་དབྱིངས། བྱིན་རླབས་ཆེ་འཕྲུལ་རྣམ་པར
འཕྲུལ་པ་ཞེས་བྱ་བ་ན། བྱང་ཆུབ་སེམས་དཔའ་རྡོ་རྗེ་སེམས་དཔའ་ལ་སོགས་པ་རིགས་དང་ཐབས་གཅིག་གོ། །དེའི་ཚེ་རྡོ་རྗེ་སེམས་དཔས། བཅོམ་ལྡན་འདས
དཔལ་ཀུན་ཏུ་བཟང་པོ་ལ་འདི་སྐད་ཅེས་གསོལ་ཏོ། །དམ་ཚིག་ཉམས་པར་གྱུར་པ་ལ། །གསོ་བའི་ཐབས་ཤིག་སྟོན་དུ་གསོལ། །ཞེས་ཞུས་པས། བཅོམ་ལྡན་འདས་ཆོས
ཀྱི་རྒྱལ་པོ་ཀ་འཁྱིལ་པ། སེམས་དཔའ་ཆེན་པོ་དེ་ཉིད་ཅིག །ཤིན་ཏུ་རྣལ་འབྱོར་ལྡན་ཡིད་ལ། །རྣལ་འབྱོར་ལས་ཀྱང་རྣལ་འབྱོར་མཆོག །འཕགས་པ་ལས་ཀྱང་འཕགས

571

པས་ན། །རྡོ་རྗེ་རྒྱལ་བ་ཀུན་གྱི་མེས། །རྗེ་བཙུན་དམ་པ་ཀུན་ཏུ་བཟང་། །རྡོ་རྗེ་འཆང་རྒྱལ་འཛེགས་པའི་སྐྱབས། །ཉམས་པའི་ཆད་པ་བྱུང་བ་ལ། །མགོན་བཙུན་དེ
ལས་གཞན་མེད་དོ། །དམ་ཚིག་སེམས་ཉིད་ཡིན་པར་རྟུ། །འགྲོ་བའི་མགོན་པོས་ཡང་དག་གསུངས། །སེམས་ཉིད་དངོས་པོ་མེད་པ་ལ། །མཉམ་པའི་ཆད་པས་ཅི་ཞིག
གཅད། །གང་ལས་ཉམས་ཏེ་ཅི་ཞིག་ཉམས། །གང་ལས་ཉམས་ཏེ་ཇི་ལྟར་ཉམས། །ཉམས་པར་སེམས་པ་དེ་ཉིད་ཡིན། །ལྷུང་བར་འཛིན་པ་དེ་ཉིད་ཡིན། །སེམས་ཉིད
དག་པའི་ཆུས་བཀྲུས་ན། །དག་པར་མ་འགྱུར་གང་ཡང་མེད། །སྟོང་ཉིད་དོན་པའི་དོན་རྟོགས་ན། །བདེ་དང་སྡུག་བསྔལ་མིང་ཡང་མེད། །བདེ་དང་སྡུག་བསྔལ་སྡུག་མི
སྡུག །བདག་དང་བདག་མེད་སྟོང་མི་སྟོང་། །དེ་བཞིན་ཉིད་དུ་འཛིན་པ་ཡང་། །དེ་ཉིད་ཡིན་པས་དངོས་པོ་མེད། །དེ་ལ་ཐ་སྙད་ཅི་བཏགས་ཀྱང་། །ཐིག་ཏུ་ཕབས་པར
གཞལ་འགྱུར། །མ་བཅོས་རང་བཞག་རིག་པས་མཚོན། །ཇི་ལྟར་ནམ་མཁའ་བཞིན་གྱུར་ན། །དེ་ཚེ་ཆད་པ་འབྱུང་བར་འགྱུར། །ཆོས་ཉིད་མཐོང་བར་གྱུར་པ་ཡང་། །ཇི
ལྟར་རང་གི་མཛུབ་རྩེ་ལ། །རང་གིས་རེག་པའི་རྟུས་བྱུང་ན། །དེ་ཚེ་ཆོས་ཉིད་མཐོང་བར་འགྱུར། །ཞེས་གསུངས་སོ། །བྱང་ཆུབ་སེམས་རྗེ་བཙུན་དམ་པ་རྡོ་རྗེ་འོད་འཕྲོ

572

ཀ [illegible]

༄༅། །བའི་རྒྱུད་ལས། ཉམས་པ་ཆད་པ་མི་འབྱུང་བའི་ལེའུ་སྟེ་དང་པོའོ༎ ༎ཀྱེ་སེམས་དཔའ་ཆེན་པོ། ཉམས་པ་བཞིས་ནི
གང་ལ་བྱ། །ཆད་པ་ཞེས་ནི་ཅི་ལ་བྱ། །ཉམས་དང་ཆད་པར་འཛིན་པ་ཡང་། །དེ་ཉིད་ཡིན་ཏེ་དེ་མི་འབྱུང་། །འབྲས་བུ་སྒྲུབ་དང་བསྒྲུབ་པ་རུ། །འདོད་པ་དེས་ཀྱང་མི་ཉེ་དེ།
ལོང་བས་ནམ་མཁའ་འཚོལ་བ་བཞིན། །བྱང་ཆུབ་སེམས་ཀྱི་རང་བཞིན་འདི། །རྟག་དཀར་བརྗོད་དུ་རྩོལ་ཙམ་མེད། །རྟོགས་གི་ཡུལ་བཞིན་མེད་པས་ན། །སོ་སོ་སྐྱེ་བོའི
བློས་མ་རེག །བྱང་ཆུབ་གང་ཡིན་སེམས་ཉིད་གང་། །ཀུན་གཞི་རང་བྱུང་ཡེ་ཤེས་ལ། །ངང་གིས་སྤྲོས་མེད་ཆེན་པོ་ལ། །ཆེ་བའི་ཡོན་ཏན་བཅལ་དུ་མེད། །དེ་ཉིད་སེམས
ཡིན་བྱང་ཆུབ་སེམས། །ཧེ་རུ་ཀ་ཡི་རྩེ་མོ་ཡིས། །རྫས་ཀྱི་དངོས་པོ་ཀུན་སྤྲོག་ཀྱང་། །རང་གི་དངོས་པོ་སྤྲོག་མི་ནུས། །དེ་བཞིན་བྱང་ཆུབ་སེམས་ཀྱིས་ཀྱང་། །ཀུན
ཤེས་རང་རིག་མར་ཤེས་ཏེ། །ཤེས་པ་ཉིད་ནི་མ་ཤེས་པའོ། །འདི་ལ་ཚུལ་སྒྲུབ་བྱར་ཡང་མེད། །དག་དང་མ་དག་གཉིས་མེད་དེ། །རང་བྱུང་དག་པ་ཆེན་པོ་ལ། །མེད་ཅེས
བྱ་བ་བརྟགས་པ་ཉིད། །བརྟགས་པ་ཉིད་ལ་མ་གནས་ན། །བྱང་ཆུབ་སེམས་ལ་གནས་པ་ཡིན། །གནས་པ་ཉིད་ན་གནས་མེད་པས། །གནས་ཞེས་ཐ་སྙད་མི་གདགས་

573

སོ། །དུས་གསུམ་སངས་རྒྱས་སེམས་ལས་བྱུང་། །སེམས་ལ་ཐ་སྙད་ཡོད་ཅེའམ། །སེམས་ལས་ཀུན་འབྱུང་ཐམས་ཅད་སེམས། །སེམས་ནི་སྐྱེ་མེད་དེ་བཞིན་ཉིད།
རང་གསལ་ཐམས་ཅད་ས་ལ་ལེ་མཁྱེན། །མཁྱེན་པ་ཉིད་ཀྱང་སེམས་ཡིན་པར། །སེམས་དཔའ་ཆེན་པོས་རིག་པར་གྱིས། །བྱང་ཆུབ་སེམས་རྗེ་བཙན་དམ་པ་རྡོ་རྗེ་འོད་འཕྲོ
བའི་རྒྱུད་ལས། ཐམས་ཅད་སེམས་སུ་བསྟན་པའི་ལེའུ་སྟེ་གཉིས་པའོ༎ ༎ཀྱེ་སེམས་དཔའ་ཆེན་པོ། སེམས་ལ་འཁོར་བ་ཐམས་ཅད
བྱུང་། །སྣང་ནི་འདས་པ་དེ་བཞིན་ཏེ། །བྱུང་བ་ཡིན་ཏེ་དེ་ཉིད་ཡིན། །ཡིན་ཞེས་བྱ་བ་མཚོན་པ་ཙམ། །ཡང་དག་ཉིད་ལ་ཡིན་པ་མེད། །ཀུན་ཡིན་གང་ཡང་མིན་པའི
ཕྱིར། །ངས་ཀྱང་ཡང་དག་རིག་པ་བཞིན། །སྐལ་ལྡན་རྣམས་ཀྱིས་ཤར་ཤེས་པར་བྱའོ། །རྡོ་རྗེ་སེམས་དཔའ་གཞན་ཡང་ནི། །ཉོན་མོངས་པ་ཉིད་བྱང་ཆུབ་ལམ། །ཕྱིན
ཅི་ལོག་ཉིད་བྱང་ཆུབ་སྐྱེ། །ཡང་དག་པ་ཉིད་ཕྱིན་ཅི་ལོག །ཐམས་ཅད་སེམས་ཀྱིས་བྱས་པ་ཡིན། །སེམས་ཉིད་རང་ལ་ཡོད་པས་ན། །རང་བྱུང་ཡེ་ཤེས་རང་ལ་ཡོད། །
གལ་ཏེ་རང་ལ་མེད་ན་ནི། །དེ་ནི་རང་བྱུང་ཡེ་ཤེས་མིན། །གཞན་ནས་བཙལ་ཞིང་སྒྲུབ་དགོས་པས། །རྒྱུ་རྐྱེན་གཉིས་ལ་རག་ལུས་པས། །དེ་ལ་རང་བྱུང་ཡེ་ཤེས་མེད། །

574

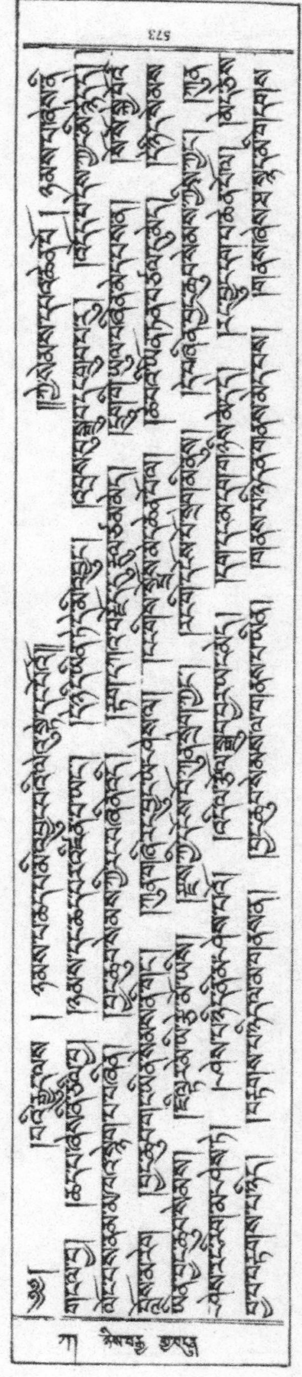

575

༄༅། །རྒྱུ་དང་རྐྱེན་ལ་རག་མ་ལུས། །ཡང་གསལ་ཕྲག་གཅིག་དྲི་མ་མེད། །རྒྱུ་རྐྱེན་མ་བསྐྱེད་རང་བྱུང་སྐུ། །མ་བསྒྲིབས་གསལ་བས་ཡེ་ཤེས་སོ། །གདོང
ནས་སྣ་ཚོགས་བྱང་ཆུབ་ལ། །བཅལ་བའི་བསམ་པ་བས་དབྱིངས་མི་བསྒྱུར། །འདི་བསྟན་དོན་ལ་བརྟེན་ནས་ནི། །སྒྱུ་མ་པའི་ཐབས་ཀྱིས་བསྒྱུར་བའི་ཕྱིར། །འཚམ་པར
མཛད་པའི་སྤྲུལ་སྐུ་ལ། །རིག་པའི་དོན་ནི་བསྟན་པར་བྱ། །གལ་ཏེ་དོན་འདི་མ་ཤེས་ཤིང་། །བྱང་ཆུབ་སེམས་ཀྱི་རྒྱུ་མེད་ན། །རྒྱལ་བ་རྣམས་ཀྱང་རྨོངས་པར་འགྱུར།།
གལ་ཏེ་གཞན་ལ་རྟོལ་བ་ནི། །ནོམ་པ་དོན་དཔའི་བཅུ་ན་མོ་ཞིག །རྟུལ་བརྩེ་བའི་བཅུ་ན་མོ་དེས། །རྟུལ་འཛོམ་རྙེད་མི་འགྱུར། །འདི་ལས་ཀུན་ཁྱུང་འདི་ལ་སོན། །འདི
ལས་མ་ཁྱུང་གཅིག་ཀྱང་མེད། །བྱང་ཆུབ་སེམས་རྡོ་རྗེ་བཅོམ་ལྡན་འདས་རྡོ་རྗེ་སེམས་དཔའ་དེ་ཡིས་ངོས་ཕྱེ་བའི་རྒྱུད་ལས། ཐམས་ཅད་སེམས་ལས་བྱུང་བར་བསྟན་པའི་ལེའུ་སྟེ་གསུམ་པའོ།།
།།དེ་ནས་རྡོ་རྗེ་སེམས་དཔས་གསོལ་པ། ཀྱེ་བཅོམ་ལྡན་འདས་སེམས་ཀྱི་ངོ་བོ་གང་ལགས། བཅོམ་ལྡན་འདས་ཀྱིས་བཀའ་སྩལ་པ། སེམས་དཔའ
ཆེན་པོ༔ སེམས་ཀྱི་རང་གི་ངོ་བོ་ནི། །ཅི་ཡང་མིན་ལ་ཅི་ཡང་སྣང་། །དཔག་མེད་བརྗོད་བྲལ་བསམ་མི་ཁྱབ། །འདི་ཞེས་མཚོན་དུ་མེད་པ་ནི། །སེམས་ཀྱི་ངོ་བོ་རང་དེ

576

གསུངས་སོ། །འཁོར་བའི་སྡུག་བསྔལ་སྣང་བ་ཡང་། །རང་ཡིན་གཞན་ལས་དེ་མི་འབྱུང་། །བདེ་དང་ཐར་པ་ཡོངས་སྤྱོད་ཀྱང་། །ཆོས་ཉིད་དབྱིངས་ལས་མ་གཏོགས་པ།
རྡུལ་ཕྲ་ཙམ་ཡང་མེད་པར་གསུངས། །སྐུ་དང་རྒྱན་གྱི་འཁོར་ལོ་ཡང་། །རང་གི་སེམས་ཡིན་གཞན་ན་མེད། །སངས་རྒྱས་ཆོས་དང་དགེ་འདུན་ཡང་། །རང་ཡིན་དེ་ལས
གཞན་ན་མེད། །དེ་ཕྱིར་བཀུར་བའི་ཡུལ་ཡང་མེད། །བསྒྲུང་མེད་སྒྲུབ་མེད་རྩོལ་བ་མེད། །ཁ་དོག་དབྱིབས་དང་གནས་རིགས་མེད། །བདེ་དང་སྡུག་བསྔལ་རྒྱུ་འབྲས་མེད།།
མེད་པ་མ་ཡིན་ཀུན་བདག་ཉིད། །ཡོད་པ་མ་ཡིན་བརྗོད་དུ་མེད། །བདག་མེད་གཞན་མེད་ཚེ་འཕོ་མེད། །མེད་པ་མ་ཡིན་ཐམས་ཅད་འབྱུང་། །འབྱུང་བ་མ་ཡིན་དེ་ཉིད
ཡིན༔ །ཀུན་གཅིག་ཡེ་ཤེས་ཁྱབ་པའི་ངང་། །ནམ་མཁའ་འདི་ནི་ཡེ་རྒྱུན་འབྱུང་བ་བཞིན། །སྤྲོ་གསལ་མེད་པའི་ངོ་བོ་གཅིག །འདི་ནི་རང་རིག་བྱང་ཆུབ་སེམས། །འདི་ཞེས
བསྟན་དུ་མེད་པའོ། །ཅི་ཡང་མེད་ལས་ཅིར་ཡང་སྣང་། །རང་བྱུང་སྙིང་པོ་མཆོག་གི་དོན། །སྣང་བ་ཉིད་ན་སྣང་མེད་པས། །སྣང་བ་མེད་པའི་ཚུལ་གྱིས་སྣང་། །མེད་ཅེས
བྱ་བའི་བརྗོད་པ་ཙམ། །དེ་ཉིད་ལ་ཡང་གནས་མི་བྱ། །གལ་ཏེ་གནས་ན་གོལ་ས་ཡིན། །གང་ཞིག་གོལ་ཏེ་ཅི་ཞིག་གོལ། །གང་དུ་གོལ་ཏེ་ཇི་ལྟར་གོལ། །གོལ་བར་སྣང་བ

577

༄༅། །དེ་ཉིད་ཡིན། །དེ་ཉིད་དངོས་པོ་མེད་པས་ན། །དེ་ཕྱིར་དེ་ལ་གནས་མི་བྱ། །གལ་ཏེ་གནས་ན་འཛིན་པ་ཡིན། །ཞེས་གསུངས་པས། །རྡོ་རྗེ་སེམས་
དཔའ་ཉིད་ལ་གནས་པར་གྱུར་ཏོ། །བྱང་ཆུབ་སེམས་རྗེ་བཙུན་དམ་པ་རྡོ་རྗེ་འོད་འཕྲོ་བའི་རྒྱུད་ལས། སེམས་ཀྱི་ངོ་བོ་བསྟན་པའི་ལེའུ་སྟེ་བཞི་པའོ།།
༈ ཀྱེ་སེམས་དཔའ་ཆེན་པོ། སེམས་ཀྱི་ཡོན་ཏན་ངས་བཤད་ཀྱིས། །སེམས་དཔའ་ཁྱེད་ཀྱིས་ཉན་པར་གྱིས། །སེམས་ཀྱི་ཡོན་ཏན་ཆེན་པོ་ནི། །སྟོང་གསུམ་རྡུལ་
སྙེད་སངས་རྒྱས་ཀྱིས། །བསྐལ་པ་བྱེ་བར་བརྗོད་བྱས་ཀྱང་། །དེ་ལ་བརྗོད་པར་མི་ནུས་ཏེ། །དེ་ནི་མ་བསྒྲིབས་ཀུན་ཏུ་གསལ། །དེ་ནི་ཀུན་གྱི་སྙིང་པོ་ཉིད། །སྡུག་བསྔལ་བྱེ་
བས་གདུངས་པ་ཡང་། །དེ་ལ་གཡོས་པ་རྡུལ་ཙམ་མེད། །བདེ་དང་སྡུག་བསྔལ་ཐམས་ཅད་ཀུན། །དེ་ཡི་ངང་ལས་སྐྱོང་ཆེན་པོ་སྐྱེ། །དེ་ཡི་དུས་ན་དེ་མི་འཛིན། །ཅི་ཡང་
མི་དམིགས་མཚོས་ཀྱི་སྐུ། །མི་འགྱུར་རང་བཞིན་དེ་ལ་འབྱེད། །འགྱུར་བ་མ་ཡིན་དེ་ཉིད་ཡིན། །སྐྱེ་མེད་བསྐྱེད་མེད་ཡི་གེ་མེད། །རྩིས་ལས་འདས་པས་ལྷུན་གྲུབ་སྐུ། །དེ་ར་
གཞན་ལ་དེ་རིམ་མཚོན་པའི་སྒྲོན། །ཀུན་ཏུ་ཞུགས་པས་བསྐལ་བ་ཐབས་སོ། །ངང་གིས་མི་འཕྲོག་དངོས་གྲུབ་པས། །དོན་དུ་ཕྱག་རྒྱ་རྫོགས་པ་ཡིན། །འདི་ཡི་དོན་རྟོགས་སྐྱེས་བུ་

578

ནི༔ ༔བཀུར་བ་མེད་ཅིང་བརླབས་བརྗོད་མེད། །མཚོན་པ་མེད་ཅིང་སྒོམ་པ་མེད། །བསྒྲུང་བ་མེད་ཅིང་རྟོག་པ་མེད། །སྤང་མེད་བླང་མེད་བྱང་ཆུབ་སེམས། །སྤྱོད་དུ་བྱ་མེད
ཐམས་ཅད་རྫོགས། །འདི་ནི་རང་བྱུང་རྒྱལ་པོ་ཡིན། །སངས་རྒྱས་ཀུན་གྱི་བདག་ཉིད་ཡིན། །འཕྲུལ་སྐུ་ཀུན་གྱི་ས་ཅུ་ང་རང་ཡིན། །རང་བཞིན་གསལ་བས་མཐུན་པ་མེད། །
དེ་ལྟར་སྣང་བ་མ་ལུས་ཀུན། །འདི་ལས་བྱུང་ཞིང་འདི་ལ་འདུས། །སྙིང་དང་ཡོན་ཏན་གཉིས་མེད་དོ། །སྣང་མེད་དེ་རང་མེད་འགོག་འགྱུར་མེད། །བྱས་པ་མེད་པར་ཐམས་ཅད
གྲུབ༔ ༔ཕྱིན་པ་མེད་པར་ཐམས་ཅད་སྟོན། །བསྟན་པ་མེད་པར་ཀུན་ལ་བ། །འདི་ནི་སེམས་ཀྱི་ཡོན་ཏན་ཞེས། །བཅོམ་ལྡན་ཀུན་ཏུ་བཟང་པོས་གསུངས། །བྱང་ཆུབ
སེམས་རྗེ་བཙུན་དམ་པ་འོད་འཕྲོ་བའི་རྒྱུད་ལས། སེམས་ཀྱི་ཡོན་ཏན་བསྟན་པའི་ལེའུ་སྟེ་ལྔ་པའོ།། ༈ དེ་ནས་རྡོ་རྗེ་སེམས་དཔས། ཀྱེ་
བཅོམ་ལྡན་འདས་འདི་ཉམས་སུ་བླང་བའི་ཐབས་བཤད་དུ་གསོལ། སྟོན་པས་བཀའ་སྩལ་པ། ཀྱེ་སེམས་དཔའ་ཆེན་པོ། ཉམས་སུ་བླང་དུ་མེད་པས་ན། །བླང་དུ་མེད
པའི་ཚུལ་གྱིས་བླང་། །བླང་བ་མི་སྤྱོད་རྟོག་པ་མེད། །རྟོག་པ་མེད་ལ་གནས་མི་བྱ། །རྣམ་པར་མི་རྟོགས་ལ་བ། །ག་ལེ་བ་རང་ཡང་རྟོག་པ་མེད། །མི་བརྟག་ས་དེ་བ་

ཀ། ཤེས་བྱ་ ཀུན་འདུས་རྨ་པ

༄༅། །ཉིད་ཀྱི་གཞི། །རིག་པ་རྗེ་བཞིན་ཀླུང་ས་སུ་བཞུགས། །འོད་གསལ་རྟོག་བྲལ་རིག་པའི་ཀློང་། །རྗེ་བཞིན་ཉིད་དུ་ཡེ་གསལ་ཁྱབ། །བསམ་མེད་དྲན་
མེད་མི་གཡོ་བ། །ཡོན་ཏན་ཆེན་པོ་བསམ་གཏན་ནི། །བསམ་གཏན་ཉིད་པས་བསམ་དུ་མེད། །མེད་པ་ཉིད་ལས་མི་གནས་ཤིང་། །རྟོག་པ་ཉིད་ལས་མི་གཡོ་བ། །
འདི་ནི་རྟོགས་པའི་རྒྱལ་པོ་ཞེས། །རྒྱལ་བ་ཀུན་གྱིས་ཡང་དག་པར་བཤད། །མི་བསམ་མི་དཔྱོད་དེ་བཞིན་ཉིད། །རྒྱལ་རྒྱུ་རྫས་ཞེས་པར་བྱ། །མི་གནས་པ་ལ་གནས་པ་
ནི༑ །འདི་ནི་གནས་པ་ཆེན་པོ་ཞེས། །ཀུན་བཟང་སེམས་དཔས་ཡང་དག་པར་བཤད། །བར་བཤད་དུ་མེད་པའི་དོན་འདི་ནི། །རྒྱལ་བ་རྣམས་ཀྱིས་མ་བཤད་དེ། །རྒྱལ་བ
ཁྱིམ་ཀུན་གསུང་མི་ཟབ་ཟླུམ། །དཔྱར་ཉིད་ཀུང་མ་བཤད་འདོད། །བྱང་ཆུབ་ཀྱི་སེམས་རྡོ་རྗེ་བཙུན་རྒྱལ་མ་པའི་འཁོར་འཁྲུལ་བའི་རྒྱུད་ལས། བསམ་མེད་ཉམས་སུ་བླང་དུ་མེད་པའི་ལེའུ་སྟེ་
ལྔ་པའོ༎ །དེ་ནས་ཡང་རྡོ་རྗེ་སེམས་དཔས་གསོལ་པ། ཀྱེ་བཅོམ་ལྡན་འདས་བྱང་ཆུབ་ཀྱི་སེམས་གང་ལགས། བཀའ་སྩལ་པ། སེམས
དཔའ་ཆེན་པོ་ཉོན་ཅིག །བྱང་ཆུབ་སེམས་ཀྱི་མཚན་ཉིད་ནི། །ཀུན་ཡིན་གང་ཡང་མ་ཡིན་ནོ། །འབྱུང་ཆེན་བཞི་དང་ལྷ་པོ་ཡང་། །བྱང་ཆུབ་སེམས་ཉིད་ཡིན་པར་

579

བཤད༑ །ཕྱི་དང་ནང་དང་ཕྱོགས་དང་རིས། །འཁོར་བ་མྱ་ངན་འདས་པ་དང་། །རྒྱུ་དང་འབྲས་བུ་སྣང་བ་དང་། །སངས་རྒྱས་སེམས་ཅན་ཕོ་མོ་དང་། །ཁ་དོག་དབྱིབས་
དང་གནས་དང་རིགས། །རྒྱུ་དང་རྐྱེན་མཚན་ཉིད་དང་། །མཚན་མ་རྩེ་སྣང་ཚིག་འདུག་པ། །དེ་ཉིད་བྱང་ཆུབ་སེམས་ཉིད་དེ། །གཞན་ནས་འོང་ས་དང་བཅལ་བ་མེད། །
དེ་རྣམས་ཡིན་པའི་དོན་ལ། །དེ་རྣམས་རིལ་དུ་མ་ངེས་པས། །དུ་མ་འང་ཡིན་པ་རམ་གསུངས་སོ། །ཐམས་ཅད་མ་འགགས་པར་སྣང་བས། །གཅིག་ཀྱང་ཡིན་པར་
མ་བཤད་དེ། །གཅིག་དང་དུ་མ་ལས་གྲོལ་བ། །མཚན་ཉིད་གང་དུ་མ་ངེས་པ། །དེ་ཉིད་བྱང་ཆུབ་ཆེས་ཀྱི་སྐུ། །ཐམས་ཅད་དེ་བོ་ལྷུན་གྱིས་གྲུབ། །བཙལ་བ་མེད་པར་
ཡས་ངས་རྒྱས། །ཕྱིན་པ་མེད་པར་ཀུན་ལ་སོན། །སྤྱོད་པ་མེད་པར་ཐམས་ཅད་བརྟུས། །མ་སྤངས་སྒྲིབ་པ་ཀུན་དང་བྲལ། །འཁོར་དང་མྱ་ངན་འདས་པ་དང་། །སངས
རྒྱས་སེམས་ཅན་འགྲོ་བ་རྣམས། །བྱང་ཆུབ་ལམ་དུ་སྣང་བ་ཡང་། །དེ་ལས་དེ་བྱུང་རྫུ་འཕྲུལ་ལས། །མཚོན་པའི་ངོ་བོར་ཀུན་དགུ་ཀྱང་། །མཚོན་དུ་མེད་དེ་དེ་ཉིད་ཡིན། །
ཡི་གེ་ཞེས་བྱ་བ་མཚོན་པ་ཙམ། །མཚོན་གཞི་མཚོན་གཉིས་བརྗོད་པ་ཡང་། །མཚོན་བྱ་མཚོན་བྱེད་མེད་པས་ན། །མཚོན་པ་མེད་པའི་རྒྱུ་ལ་གྱིས་མཚོན། །དེ་ཉིད་མཚོན་པ་ཆེན་པོ

580

581

༄༅། །ཡི༔ ༔དེ་ཡི་དོན་ཀུན་རིག་ཤེ་སྣན། །འཁོར་དང་སྤྲུག་པ་སྤྱོ་ལ་བཀྲུལ་འཁོར་ཀུན། །བྱང་ཆུབ་སེམས་ཉིད་ཡིན་ཞེས་བཤད། །བྱང་ཆུབ་སེམས
རྡོ་བཙན་དམ་པ་འོད་འཕྲོ་བའི་རྒྱུད་ལས། བྱང་ཆུབ་སེམས་ཀྱི་རང་བཞིན་གང་ཡིན་བསྟན་པའི་ལེའུ་སྟེ་བདུན་པའོ།། །།དེ་ནས་བཅོམ་ལྡན་སྒྲེས
པ་ཆེན་པོས། འཁོར་ལ་ཚིག་ཏུ་བཀའ་བསྩལ་པ། ཀྱེ་སེམས་དཔའ་ཆེན་པོ། གང་ཞིག་མཉམ་ཉིད་རྟོགས་པ་ལ། །སྒྲིབ་དང་ཡོན་ཏན་གཉིས་ཀ་སྒྲིབ། །བདེ་ཆགས་སྤྲུག
བསྒྱུལ་སྤྱོད་འདོད་པ། །དམུས་ལོང་མཐའ་ལ་མདུད་འདོར་བ་བདྲ། །དོན་ཉིད་མ་བཅོས་མཉམ་པའི་དོན། །མ་འདྲེས་གསལ་བར་མ་རྟོགས་ན། །སྟོང་གསུམ་རྒྱལ་བའི
སྐུས་པ་ཀ་ང་ཡང་། །ཕན་མེད་མ་བཀག་དགོས་ཉིད་མི་འགྱུར། །བྱང་ཆུབ་ཉིན་གང་ལས་གཉིས་མེད་དེ། །ཀུན་གཞི་ཡངས་པའི་དང་དུ་གཅིག །དེ་ཕྱིར་བླང་དང་དོར་མེད་དེ། །
དེ་ཉིད་མ་གྲུབ་རང་སྣང་ཕྱིར། །ཁྲིད་དང་རྫོད་དང་ནེ་རྟོགས་ས་དང་། །གསལ་དང་མི་གསལ་འཕྲུང་འཕྱོག་སྒྲོང་། །སྐྱོང་དང་རྟོག་དང་འགག་འཆོས་དང་། །མཚན་མ་སྤྱུང་ཚོར
མཐར་ལས་པ། །ཡིན་ནས་གསལ་མེད་ངང་གིས་ཞི། །བརྟགས་མེད་ཡེ་ནས་ཆོས་སྐུ་ཉིད། །མ་སྤྲུས་རོལ་པས་བདག་ཉིད་རྒྱན། །བདག་ཉིད་མ་མཐོང་དམུས་ལོང་

582

ཉིད༔ ༔མི་རྟོག་དོན་ལ་བླང་དོར་མེད། །སྒྲིབ་ཉིད་མཉམ་པར་དོན་རྟོགས་ན། །ཀུན་ཏུ་བཟང་ཞེས་དེ་ལ་བྱ། །ཧེ་རུ་ཀ་མ་ཐབ་གསལ་སྟོང་ཉིད་ལ། །སྒྲིན་དང་ཡུ་ལྷུང་ས་འཛིན
དང་སྒྲོག །སྐུ་རང་ངང་ཉི་ཟླ་མ་འདྲེས་གསལ། །མ་བཅའ་གསལ་ལ་ངོ་བོར་ཡིན་ནས་གཅིག །རྣལ་འབྱོར་སེམས་ཀྱི་མ་བཅའ་ཀློང་ལ། །སྒྲིབ་ཡོན་སྣང་ཡང་བླང་དོར་མེད། །ཐེག་པའི
རྒྱུ་བྲག་མ་ལུས་པ། །མ་འདྲེས་ཡོངས་རྫོགས་སྤྱོད་བླང་བྲལ། །གསལ་མེད་མི་རྟོག་ཀུན་མ་བྱེན་པ། །ངོ་བོ་ཉིད་དེ་ནི་དམིགས་སུ་མེད། །བྱང་ཆུབ་སེམས་རྡོ་བཙན་དམ་པ་འོད
འཕྲོ་བའི་རྒྱུད་ལས། གོལ་ས་སེལ་བ་ཞེས་བྱ་བའི་ལེའུ་སྟེ་བརྒྱད་པའོ།། །།དེ་ནས་དེ་བཞིན་གཤེགས་པ་ཉིད། །མི་གསུང་རྣམ་དག་ཆེན་པོ་ལ།།
ཏིང་ངེ་འཛིན་ལ་སྙོམས་པར་ཞུགས། །རྡོ་རྗེ་སེམས་དཔའ་བཅོམ་ལྡན་འདས། །མི་གསུང་གཞག་པ་དོན་གང་ཞིག །བདག་ལ་ཧེ་རུ་ཀ་ར་སྤྲུལ་མཛོད། །ཀྱེ་སེམས
དཔའ་ཆེན་པོ། ཀུན་སྣང་དབུས་གཅིག་དགོངས་པས་མ་བྱེན། །གང་ལ་ཅི་ཡང་མ་སྨྲས་ཏེ། །སྒྲིང་པོའི་དོན་ལས་གཡོ་བ་མེད། །གསུང་མེད་དོན་འདི་མི་ཤེས་པར། །གང
ཞིག་ཐམས་ཅད་མཉམ་མ་རྟོགས་པ། །དེ་ནི་ལོང་བའི་ཚོགས་སུ་ཡིན་ཞེས། །བཅོམ་ལྡན་དེ་བཞིན་གཤེགས་པས་གསུངས། །གང་ཡང་མ་འདྲེས་མ་བཀག་གསལ། །བསྒྱུས

༄༅། །པས་སྤྱི་དོར་བྱང་ཆུབ་སྙིང་། །དེ་ཉིད་རྟོག་མེད་བླང་དོར་ཐལ། །ཀུན་ཁྱབ་ཡེ་དལ་མ་ལུས་གཞིས། །མིང་ཚིག་བརྗོད་ཡིས་མཚོན་དུ་མེད། །མཚོན་མེད་ཡེ་
ཤེས་སྐུ་ཡི་མཆོག །ཡི་གེ་མེད་གསལ་ལ་གོ་བའི་གསུང་། །རྟོག་མེད་འོད་གསལ་ཐུགས་ཀྱི་མཆོག །མ་བཅོས་ལྷུན་གྲུབ་ཡེ་ནས་གནས། །འདི་ནི་ཚིགས་མེད་དོན་པོ་ཆེ། །
དོན་ཉིད་དེ་ཙམ་ཡང་མ་ཡིན་པས། །ཤེས་པ་གང་ལའང་བསམ་མ་མེད་བསམ་གྱིས་མི་ཁྱབ་པར། །དེ་ལྟར་བསམ་པ་བསམ་ཆེན་ཡིན། །ཀཱ་ཡ་བེདྐ་ཧེ་ཤྲུ་བུར། །བཅལ་མེ་རུས་མ
པ་ཀུན་གྲུབ་ཕྱིར། །མ་བཅོས་ལྷུན་གནས་དོན་གྱི་མཆོག །བྱང་ཆུབ་སེམས་རྗེ་བཙན་དམ་པ་འོད་འཕྲོ་བའི་རྒྱུད་ལས། ། མཉམ་པ་རབ་ཞུག་པའི་ལེའུ་སྟེ་དགུ་པའོ།།
||ཀྱེ་སེམས་དཔའ་ཆེན་པོ ། མེད་པ་དང་ནི་ཕྲུལ་པ་དང་། །གཅིག་པུ་དང་ནི་ལྷུན་གྱིས་རྫོགས། །བདག་ལ་འཁྲུལ་དང་རེས་མེད་དང་། །བདག་སྣང་
བདག་ཏུ་ལྷུན་གྲུབ་པས། །བཅལ་མེད་ལ་བསྒྱུར་དམ་ཚིག་མཆོག །ཡེ་ནས་བསྒྱུར་བས་བསྒྱུར་དུ་མེད། །མ་བསྒྱུར་ཐུབ་པས་དམ་ཚིག་མཆོག །ཐམས་ཅད་བདག
ཉིད་ཆེན་པོ་བས། །གཞན་ལ་བཅལ་བ་ཅི་ཡང་མེད། །རྟོག་མེད་བསམ་མེད་གང་ལ་མི་འགོག །དེ་ལྟར་སྤྱོད་ལམ་སྤྱོད་ལེན་བྲལ། །མཉམ་ཉིད་ངང་ལས་མི་འདའ་བ། །

583

རྫོགས་ཆེན་དམ་ཚིག་གཅིག་པུར་བཤད། །བྱ་བསམ་མེད་པས་དོན་གྲུབ་པ། །ལྷུན་གྱིས་གྲུབ་པའི་དམ་ཚིག་ཡིན། །ཡག་དང་མཉན་པས་མ་སྙོམ་པ་དང་། །མཆོད་དང་
དབྱངས་ལེན་སྦྱིན་གཏོང་བ། །མ་ཆགས་རྫོགས་ཆེན་སྤྲོས་མེད་ན། །བྱས་ན་ཐམས་ཅད་ཉེ་ཚེ་བའི་རྒྱུ། །གང་ཡང་དང་དུ་མ་བླངས་ན། །སྤྱོད་པ་སྤྱོད་མེད་ཆེན་པོ་ཡིན། །
ཉིད་པ་ཉིད་སྤྱོད་ཉིད་དབང་སྒྱུར། །རིག་པའི་རྒྱལ་པོ་སྙམས་པས་མ་འདས། །གང་གིས་སྐྱོང་བསྟན་དུ་མེད། །བྱང་ཆུབ་སེམས་རྗེ་བཙན་དམ་པ་འོད་འཕྲོ་བའི་རྒྱུད་ལས །
སྤྱོད་ལམ་བསྟན་པའི་ལེའུ་སྟེ་བཅུ་པའོ།། ||ཀྱེ་སེམས་དཔའ་ཆེན་པོ ། རང་བྱུང་ཡེ་ཤེས་བྱང་ཆུབ་སེམས། །བདག་ཉིད་ཆེན་པོ་ཆོས་སྐུ་མཆོག །
སྤྲོ་སྐུར་གཉིས་ཞི་མཉམ་ཉིད་དོན། །དུས་ཀུན་བརྟགས་ཆེན་རྡོ་རྗེའི་སྐུ། །རང་བཞིན་དེ་ཉིད་རྟག་མི་ནུས། །ཡེ་ཤེས་རྒྱུད་དུག་ལ་རུང་། །ཚིག་ཏུ་རྟག་རྒྱུན་གང་བརྗོད་ཀྱང་། །
རིག་པའི་རྒྱལ་པོ་ངང་ཉིད་ལ། །འཕོ་འགྱུར་རྟག་མི་རྟག་དང་བྲལ། །ཐུན་མོང་ཡེ་ཤེས་སྐྱེ་འགག་ཅན། །དོན་བྱེད་ནུས་པ་མ་ཡིན་ཕྱིར། །བླང་དོར་མེད་ན་དོན་གྱིས་བྲལ། །འདས
དང་མ་འོངས་ད་ལྟ་ཉིད། །རྟག་པར་མི་འགྱུར་དེ་ལྟའི་ཕྱིར། །ངོ་བོ་ཡི་རྟག་པ་བརྗོད་འདས་པས། །སྐུས་ཀྱང་རྟག་པར་རུང་མ་ཡིན། །འདས་དང་མ་འོངས་ད་ལྟར་དུ། །འབྱུང་

584

ཀ། [illegible]

༄༅། །བར་མ་ངེས་དུས་གཅིག་ལ། །སྐད་ཅིག་མ་ཕྲད་རྡེས་གསལ་ལ་མཁྱེན་པ། །རྣམ་ཅིག་མཁྱེན་པར་བརྗོད་པ་ཡིན། །དེ་ལྟ་མོད་ཀྱང་འཛིན་རྟོག་བྲལ། །
དེ་ཉིད་དུས་གསུམ་ཡེ་གནས་ལ། །ལུང་བང་སྐྱེལ་དང་འབྲེལ་མི་ཕྱུར། །ཐོག་མེད་དུས་ནས་གནས་འགྱུར་ཡང་། །མ་སྦྱངས་དག་པས་སང་སངས་རྒྱས་ས། །ཁྲུ་མེད་དོན་
མཛད་འབྲིན་ལས་མཆོག །བྱང་ཆུབ་སེམས་རྡོ་རྗེ་བཙན་དམ་པ་ཡོད་འཁྲུལ་བའི་རྒྱུད་ལས ། སྐུ་གསུང་ཐུགས་རྫོགས་པ་ཆེན་པོ་འདི་ཡི་ལེའུ་སྟེ་བཅུ་གཅིག་པའོ།།
།།དེ་ནས་སྟོང་པ་འདི་ངང་ལས་མ་བསྐྱུགས་པ་པ་མའི་དེ་སྐད་གྲགས་པར་འགྱུར་རོ། །ཨོཾ་མ་ཧཱ་ཡཱ་ཤེས་ཀུན་བཟང་པ་གྲིགས་པ་པོ། །ཀུན་འབྱུང་ངེ་ཐོང་ངེ་དངས་
པས་མཐོང་རྒྱུ་འི་སྐུ། །རྟོག་མེད་ཀུན་མཁྱེན་བྱ་མེད་འབྲིན་ལས་མཛད། །རྣམ་དག་བྱང་ཆུབ་སེམས་ལ་ཕྱག་འཚལ་ལོ། །ཡེ་མ་མ་བཙལ་ལྷུན་གྲིས་གྲུབ་པས་བདག
ལ་བྱུས། །ངོ་བོ་བསྟན་དུ་མེད་པས་འདུས་མ་བྱས། །ཚིག་ལས་འདས་པས་སྤྲོས་བོ་བྱང་ཆུབ་སེམས། །སྐྱབས་མཆོག་ལས་འདས་ལ་ཕྱག་འཚལ་ལོ། །ཨེ་མ་ཧོ་
རྟག་མེད་བདུད་བཅོམ་མཆོག་འཕྲུལ་བདག །སྐུ་གསུང་ཐུགས་ཀྱི་མཛད་པ་ཅིར་ཡང་སྟོན། །ཐམས་ཅད་ཉིད་ལ་འདུས་པས་བདག་ཉིད་ཆེ། །མཛད་པ་ཅིར་ཡང་སྣང་ལ་

585

ཕྱག་འཚལ་ལོ། །ཨ་ཧོ༔ དེ་ནས་དེ་བཞིན་གཤེགས་པ་ཡིས། །རྡོ་རྗེ་འཛིན་ལ་བཀའ་བསྩལ་པ། །ཀྱེ་སྙིང་སྐུ་ར་བྲལ་ལ་དོན་གྱི་བཅུད། །དོན་སྟོན་རྟོག་མེད་མི་ལོང་
བཞིན༔ ༔སྣང་གྲང་མེད་སྟོན་ཐེག་པའི་མཆོག །ཐམས་ཅད་མངའ་མཛད་རྒྱལ་པོ་ཉིད། །རྣམ་ཏུ་རྟོག་མེད་ཐུགས་ཀྱི་དགྱེས། །མི་ནུབ་མི་སྤྲོས་བརྟུབ། །དོན་ལྡན
སྤྲུག་མེད་མཆོག་སྒྲུངས་པ། །མཆོག་ལྡན་ཐེག་ཆེན་ཡང་རྩེ་འི་དོན། །དམ་པོ་དད་མ་དེར་བསྟན་མ་སྟ། །ལས་ཅན་ཡོ་རྒྱུན་དུ་བསྒྲུབ་པར་བྱ། །ཞེས་གསུངས་ནི །
རྡོ་རྗེ་འཛིན་པ་དང་ །འཁོར་བྱང་ཆུབ་སེམས་དཔའ་ཆེན་པོ་གྲངས་མེད་པ་དང་ །གཞན་ལས་ལ་སོགས་པ་སྐུལ་འདུས་ནི ། སྐུ་ཉིད་ཀྱང་སྤྲོད་པོ་བྱང་ཆུབ་ལ་ཡང་མི་སྣ
ཏེ་མི་སྣང་བར་འགྱུར་རོ། །བྱང་ཆུབ་སེམས་རྡོ་རྗེ་བཙན་དམ་པ་ཡོད་འཁྲུལ་བའི་རྒྱུད་ལས ། བསྟོད་ཅིང་གཏད་པའི་ལེའུ་སྟེ་བཅུ་གཉིས་པའོ།། །།རྒྱུད
ཀྱི་རྒྱལ་པོ་མི་ནུབ་རྒྱལ་མཚན་རྡོ་རྗེ་བཙན་དམ་པ་རྡོ་རྗེ་ཡོད་འཁྲུལ་བའི་རྒྱུད་རྫོགས་སོ།། ༄། །རྡོ་རྗེ་སེམས་དཔའ་ནམ་མཁའ་ཆེ
རྒྱས་པའི་ཡི་གེ་མེད་པའི་རྒྱུད ། རྒྱལ་པོའི་རྒྱུད་དུ་གསུངས་པ ། ཡི་གེ་མེད་པ་འདི་གསུངས་པའི་ཚོན ། ཉིད་དང་ཐམས་ཅད་བཅུམ་ས་སྟོན་མཐོས་པའི་དཔོན་པས་སྒྲ་

586

THE TANTRA OF VAJRASATTVA'S MAGNIFICENT SKY EMBELLISHED AS

THE UNWRITTEN

From the mTshams brag Edition of the rNying ma rGyud 'bum

Volume One, pages 586-592

ཕྱག་འཚལ་ལོ། །ཨ་ཧོ༔ དེ་ནས་དེ་བཞིན་གཤེགས་པ་ཡིས། །རྡོ་རྗེ་འཛིན་ལ་བཀའ་བསྩལ་པ། །ཀྱེ་སྒྲོ་སྐུར་བྲལ་ལ་དོན་གྱི་བརྡུད། །དོན་སྟོན་རྟོག་མེད་མེ་ལོང་
བཞིན༔ ༔སྣང་གྲུབ་མེད་སྟོན་འཕགས་པའི་མཆོག །ཐམས་ཅད་མངའ་མཛད་རྒྱལ་པོ་ཉིད། །རྟག་ཏུ་རྟོག་མེད་ཐུགས་ཀྱི་དཀྱིལ། །མི་ནུབ་མི་སྒྲིབ་བརྟུལ་པ། །དོན་ལྡན
སྒྲགས་མེད་མཆོག་སྦྱངས་པ། །མཆོག་ལྡན་ཐེག་ཆེན་ཡང་རྩེའི་དོན། །དབང་པོ་དྭངས་མ་དེར་བསྟིམ་མི་སྐྱེ། །འཁོར་བ་ལོ་རྒྱུན་དུ་བསྐྲིམ་པར་བྱ། །ཞེས་གསུངས་ཏེ །
རྡོ་རྗེ་འཛིན་པ་དང་ །འཁོར་བྱང་ཆུབ་སེམས་དཔའ་ཆེན་པོ་གྲངས་མེད་པ་དང་ །གཞན་ལས་ལ་སོགས་པ་བསྐལ་བ་འདུས་ཏེ །སྐུ་ཉིད་ཀྱང་སྣང་དེ་ལ་བྱང་ཆུབ་པ་ལ་ཡང་མི་སྣ
ཏེ་མི་སྣང་བར་གྱུར་ཏོ། །བྱང་ཆུབ་སེམས་རྗེ་བཙན་དམ་པ་འོད་འཕྲོ་བའི་རྒྱུད་ལས །བསྟོད་ཅིང་གཏད་པའི་ལེའུ་སྟེ་བཅུ་གཉིས་པའོ།། །།རྒྱུད་
ཀྱི་རྒྱལ་པོ་མི་ནུབ་རྒྱལ་མཚན་རྡོ་རྗེ་བཙན་དམ་པ་རྡོ་རྗེ་འོད་འཕྲོ་བའི་རྒྱུད་རྫོགས་སོ།། །།ༀ། །རྡོ་རྗེ་སེམས་དཔའ་ནམ་མཁའ་ཆེ
རྫོགས་པའི་ཡི་གེ་མེད་པའི་རྒྱུད ། རྒྱལ་པོའི་རྒྱུད་དུ་གསུངས་པ ། ཡི་གེ་མེད་པ་འདིས་གསུངས་པའི་ཚོན ། ཉེ་དང་ཐག་མི་རིང་བ་རྣམས་སྔོན་མ་ཐོས་པ་འདི་ཐོས་པས་གྲོལ་

596

ཀ [illegible]

༄༅། །པར་གྱུར་ཏོ། །དེ་ནས་རྡོ་རྗེ་འཛིན་པ་ལ་སོགས་པ་འདུ་བ་རྣམས་དང་ །སེམས་དཔའ་དང་ །སེམས་མ་དང་ །སྒོ་བ་དང་ །སྒོ་མ་དམ་པའི་སྒོ་
སྲུངས་གཤིན་རྗེ་གཤེད་པོ་ལ་སོགས་པ་དང་ །བཅོམ་ལྡན་འདས་དཔལ་ལ་མི་བསྐྱོད་པ་ལ་སོགས་པ་དང་ །བཙུན་མོ་རྣམས་དང་ །དཔེར་ན་ཏིལ་གྱི་གང་བུ་བཞིན་དུ་ཁྱབ་
པར་གནས་སོ། །དེ་ནས་འཁོར་རྣམས་ཀྱིས་ཞུ་བ་ཞུས་པ །དེ་བཞིན་གཤེགས་པ་ཉག་གཅིག་གི །ཐུགས་སུ་ཆུད་པའི་དོན་མཆོག་དེ། །གཟུ་བོ་ཆེན་པོས་བཤད་དུ་
གསོལ༔ ༔མཚན་མ་རྣམས་ནི་སྤངས་པ་ཡི། །ཐབས་མཆོག་དམ་པ་བཤད་དུ་གསོལ། །ཡི་གེ་མེད་པ་བཤད་དུ་གསོལ། །ཡི་གེ་མེད་པ་ལས་སྣང་གཞི་འདི་ལ་ཉུ་སྐྱེ་དང་
པོའི༔ ༔དེ་ནས་བདག་པོའི་མཆོག་རྣམ་པར་སྣང་མཛད་ཀྱི་སྐུ་ར་བྱུང་ནས ། བཀག་པར་མ་མཛད ། འཛུམ་པར་མཛད ། འཁོར་གྱི་དོན་དེ་ཐུགས
ཆུད་ནས ། རིགས་ཀྱི་བུ་ཁྱེད་ཅེས་གསུངས་ཏེ ། ཁྱེད་རྣམས་ལེགས་པར་ཉོན་ཅིག་དང་ན། །རྒྱུད་འདི་ཤིན་ཏུ་བརྟག་དཀའ་སྟེ། །མཚན་མ་ཀུན་དང་བྲལ་བས་སོ། །དཔའ
བོ་ཆེན་པོ་འཛེམས་པའི། །ཤིན་ཏུ་བཟློག་པར་དཀའ་བ་ཡང་། །རང་བའི་རྩལ་གྱིས་རྣམ་པར་སྦྱང་། །འདྲེན་པ་དང་པོ་སྐྱེས་པ་ཡང་། །ཤིན་ཏུ་བཟློག་པར་རབ་ཏུ་དཀའ།།

587

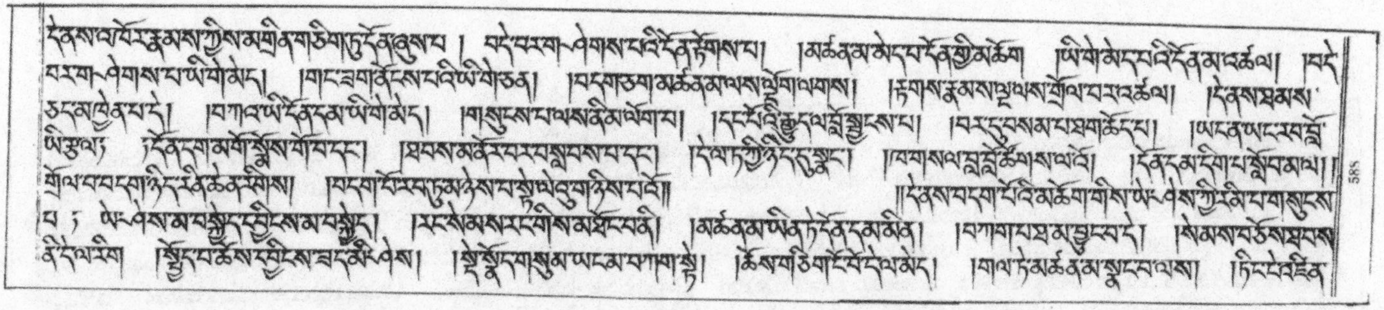

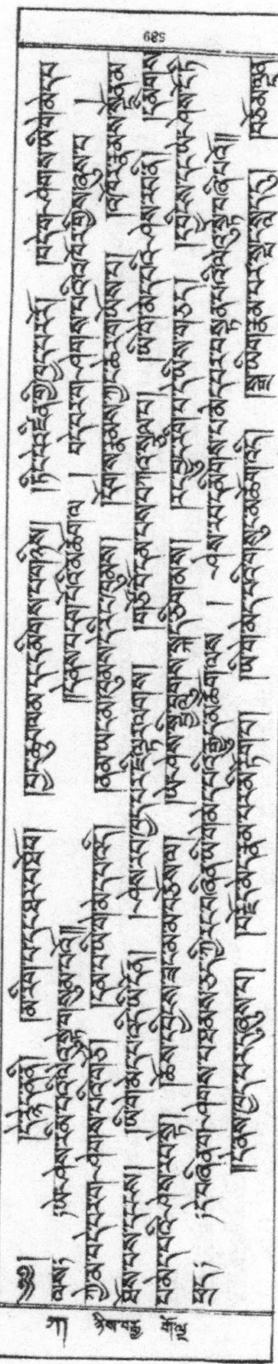

590

འདས་ཀྱིས་བཀའ་བསྩལ་པ་འཚལ། །ཡང་ཆེ་དང་དུ་བརྗོད་པ་བཀའ་བསྩལ་པ། རང་བཞིན་གནས་པའི་མཚན་ཉིད་དེ། །ཞི་བ་སྣང་དོར་གྲོལ་བ་གཞིར། །ཆོས་ཀྱི་རང་བཞིན་སྟོང་
པ་སྟེ; ;སངས་རྒྱས་ཀྱིས་ཀྱང་མ་གཟིགས་ཏེ། །མངོན་སུམ་མཐོང་བ་བཀག་པ་ཡིན། །གང་ཡང་མཐོང་བ་མེད་པ་ནི། །དེ་ནི་མཐོང་བ་ཆེན་པོའོ། །ཀུན་ཡང་དག་པ་ཆོས
དབྱིངས་སོ། །ཆོས་ཀྱི་འཁོར་ལོ་བསྐོར་བ་ཡང་། །སྐད་ཅིག་ཙམ་ཡང་བྱས་པ་མེད། །དོན་ནི་རྟོགས་པར་དམིགས་མེད་དོ། །ཡི་གེ་མེད་པའི་རྒྱུད་མཆོག་འདི། །དཔེར
ན་རྒྱལ་པོ་ཧྲ་སུ་ཏེ། །རྒྱུད་རྒྱལ་ཡི་གེ་མེད་པ་ལས། རང་བཞིན་གནས་པའི་ལེའུ་སྟེ་ལྔ་པའོ༎ ༎དེ་ནས་ཡི་གེ་མེད་པའི་གཙོ་མཆོག་དེས། །
འཁོར་གྱི་ཞུ་བ་ཐུགས་སུ་ཆུད་ནས། །ཐེག་ཆེན་འདི་ཡི་སྙིང་པོའི་གནས། །བྱང་ཆུབ་སྙིང་པོ་ཆེ་ཡིས་ཀྱང་། །རིན་ཆེན་རིགས་སུ་གཡུང་ལྷུན་པས། །ལྷ་མི་བཅས་ཤེས་པར
བྱའི; ;ལམ་གྱི་མར་ནས་ཉེ་ལམ་སྟེ། །ཐབས་ཀྱི་མཆོག་ཏུ་གྱུར་པས་ན། །ཡི་གེ་མེད་པར་གྲགས་པའོ། །ཀླུམ་པ་དང་ནི་རང་གྲགས་པ། །ཐེག་པ་ཀུན་ལས་འདས
པའི; ;ཡི་གེ་མེད་པར་གྲགས་པའོ། །འདི་ཡི་རྒྱུ་ལ་ཞིམ་ཞེས་ན། །ཡི་གེ་མེད་པར་དབྱེ་བ་མེད། །འདི་ཡི་དོན་ནི་རང་གསལ་ལྡན་པ། །དེ་ཡིས་ཐེག་ཆེན་འབྲས་སུ

591

༄། །ཐོབ; ;རྒྱས་པ་ཆེན་པོ་ཡི་གེ་མེད་པ་ལས། བདག་པོ་མཉེས་པའི་ལེའུ་སྟེ་དྲུག་པའོ༎ ༎དེ་ནས་བདག་པའི་མཆོག་ལ། །
བྱང་ཆུབ་སེམས་དཔའ་དགྱེས་པ་ལ་སོགས་པའི་འཁོར་རྣམས་ཀྱིས་མགྲིན་གཅིག་ཏུ་ཞུས་པ། དཔལ་ཆེན་འཁྲུལ་པའི་རྣམ་རྟོག་འཇོམས། །སྐྱོ་ངས་པའི་བདུད་ལས་ཐར་པའི
མཆོག །ཉག་གཅིག་ཐུགས་ཆུད་རྟོགས་ངས་དེ། །ཁྱེད་ཀྱིས་བླ་མེད་དབང་ཞ་དུ་གསོལ། །དེ་ནས་སེམས་དཔའ་དགེས་པ་ལ་སོགས་པའི་རྣམ་པར་རྟོག་པ་མཁྱེན་ནས་བཀའ་བསྩལ
པ; ཁྱེད་ཅག་ལེགས་པར་བཙུན་ནས་ཉོན། །ཉག་གཅིག་ཐུགས་ཀྱི་དགོངས་པ་དེ། །ཁ་ཤད་ཀྱིས་སེམས་ཉིད་ལྷུན་པར་གྱིས། །སྐྱེ་རྒྱེ་མེད་པ་ཡིན་ནམ་མཁའ་བཞད་དེ། །དང་པོའི
ཚིག་ནམ་མཁའ་བཞིན་ཀུན། །བསམ་པ་ཡིད་ཚོར་ནུབ་པའི། །ཐམ་པ་ཡི་མི་དམིགས་ལས། །ནམ་མཁའ་བཞིན་ནི་བཀག་པའོ། །དོན་དམ་དབྱེར་མེད་ནམ་མཁའ་བཞིན། །
གང་ལ་བཀག་པ་མེད་པ་སྟེ། །བཀག་པ་མེད་པའི་གཏན་ཚིགས་སོ། །དོན་ཡོད་ན་བཀག་པར་འགྲོ། །མེད་པས་ནམ་མཁའ་བའི་མི་རྟོགས་ཀུན། །དགོངས་པའི་མཐའ་ནི
བཀག་མེད་དོ། །ཡི་གེ་མེད་པའི་རྒྱུད་ལས། ནུལ་བསྒྱུར་མཐོང་དུ་མེད་པའི་ལེའུ་སྟེ་བདུན་པའོ༎ ༎དེ་ནས་བདག་པོའི་མཆོག་ལ་ཡང་ཞུས་པ། །

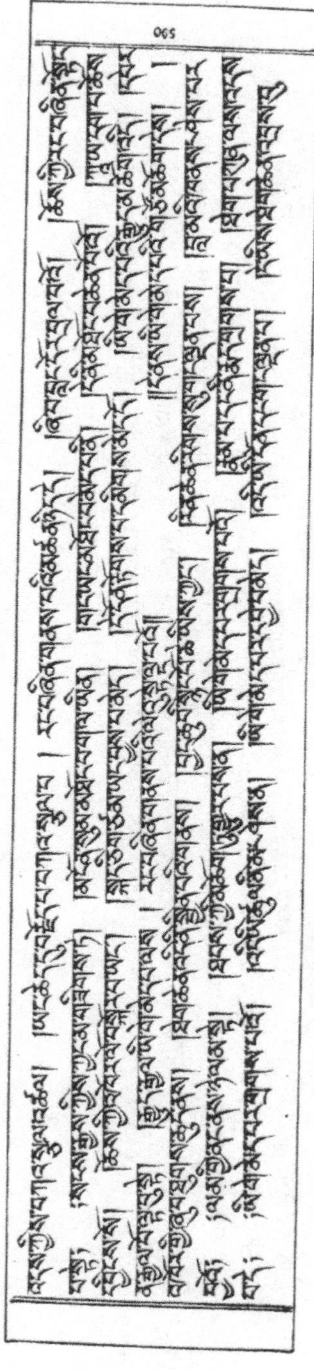

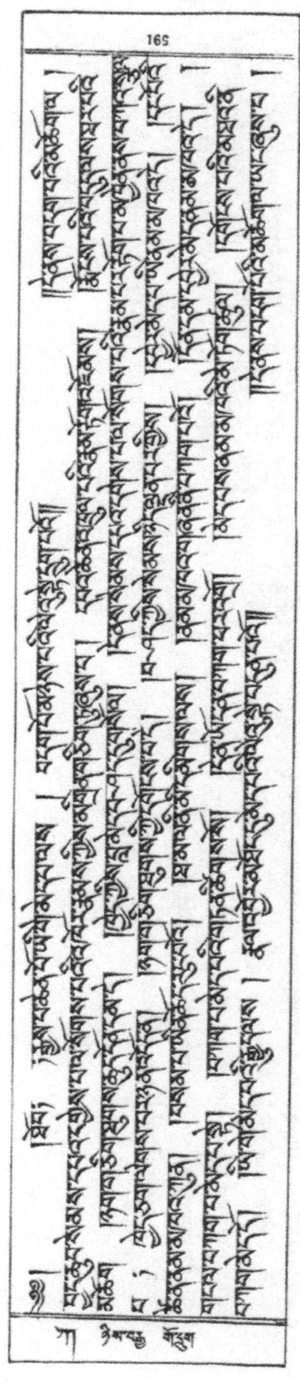

592

མཚན་མ་འདི་ནི་མིང་ཙམ་ཡང་། །སྨོན་པ་དེ་ཡང་དག་པ་ལ་ལགས་སམ། །མངའ་བདག་ཁྱེད་ཀྱིས་མཁྱེན་པར་ཞུ། །སློབ་རྣམས་སྐྱུངས་ཕྱིར་བཀའ་ན་སྐུལ་འཚལ། །ཁྱེད་ཅག
བསམ་པ་དམན་པ་ལ། །ཟབ་མོ་རྒྱུད་རྒྱལ་ཡི་གེ་མེད། །གསུས་དང་བཅས་པས་མཉན་པར་བྱེད། །ཕོ་རངས་ཆོན་གཅད་པར་བྱ། །དེ་ནས་རེད་ཙིང་གོམས་པ་ནི། |
ཡི་གེ་མེད་པའི་ཡན་ལག་ཡིན། །མཛད་སྤྱོད་གཏད་རྒྱུད་དང་བཅས་པ། །རིན་ཆེན་རིགས་ཞི་ཁར་དམ་ཏྲ་ལ། །བཀའ་ཡི་སྙིང་ནི་ཞེས་པ་ལ། །རྒྱུད་ནི་རིམ་པ་བཞིན་དུ
སྦྱིན། ༑ཡི་གེ་མེད་པ་རྒྱས་པ་ཆེན་པོ་ལས། །འབྲོ་ས་ལ་གཏད་པའི་ལེའུ་སྟེ་བརྒྱད་པའོ།། །།དེ་ནས་འཁོར་ལ་གདམས་ངག་ཏུ་གནང་བ། |
བསྒོམ་བསྒྲུབ་ཀུན་དང་བྲལ་བ་ཡི། །ཏིང་འཛིན་འདི་ནི་བཅལ་དང་བྲལ། །དང་པོ་ཞི་བ་དུ་བསྐུད་མི་ནུས། །བར་དུ་བསམ་པ་ཐུག་ཚོད་པ། །ཐམ་རས་མཐར་འཚེར་ཞེས
བརྗོད། ༑མི་དམིགས་པ་ལ་གང་གནས་པ། །དེ་ནི་རྩལ་དང་བྲལ་བའོ། །འདི་བ་རག་ཞིགས་པས་གཏད་རྒྱུ་དང་བཅས་པ་རྫོགས་སོ།། ||
འོད་ཀྱི་དགེ་སློང་བཻ་རོ་ཙ་ན་དང་། ། རྒྱ་གར་གྱི་མཁན་པོ་ཛྙཱ་ན་ག་ར་བྷུས་བསྒྱུར་ཅིང་ཞུས་ཏེ་གཏན་ལ་ཕབ་པའོ།། ||ཤྲཱི། །རྒྱ་གར

THE TANTRA OF VAJRASATTVA'S MAGNIFICENT SKY

EMBELLISHED FOR THE BRAHMINS

From the mTshams brag Edition of the rNying ma rGyud 'bum

Volume Two, pages 529-556.

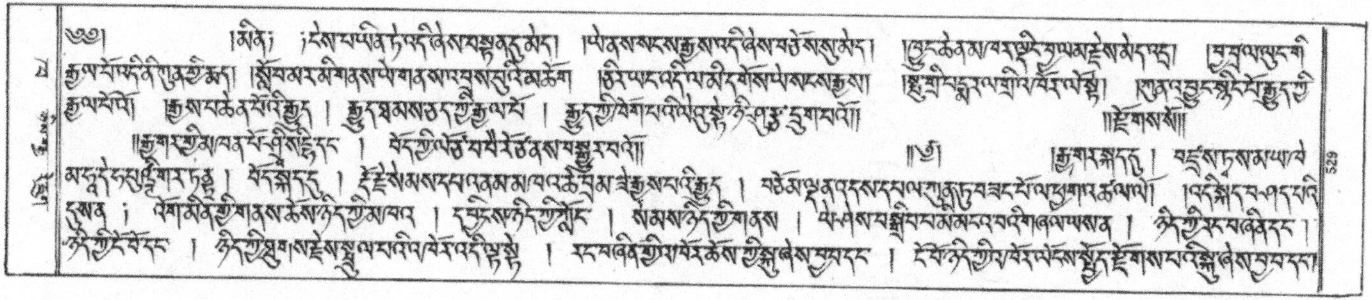

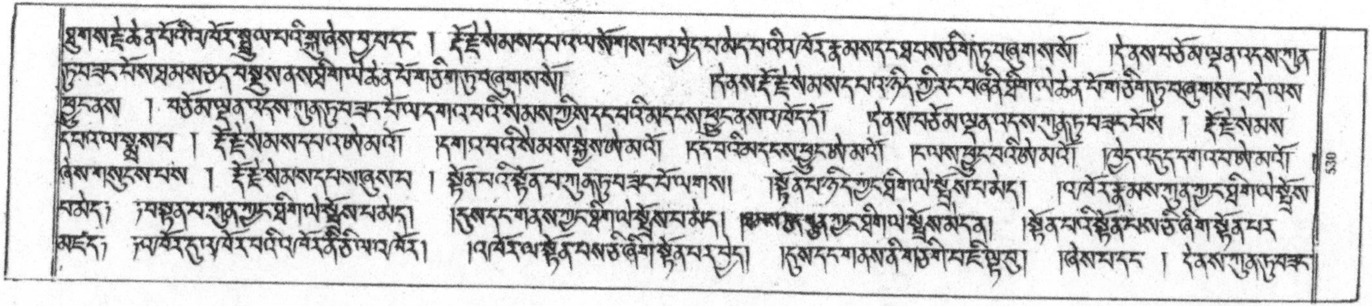

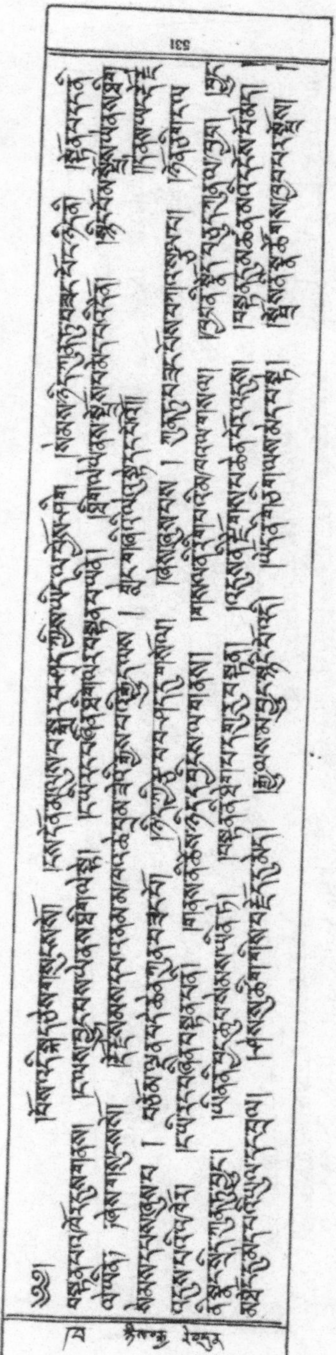

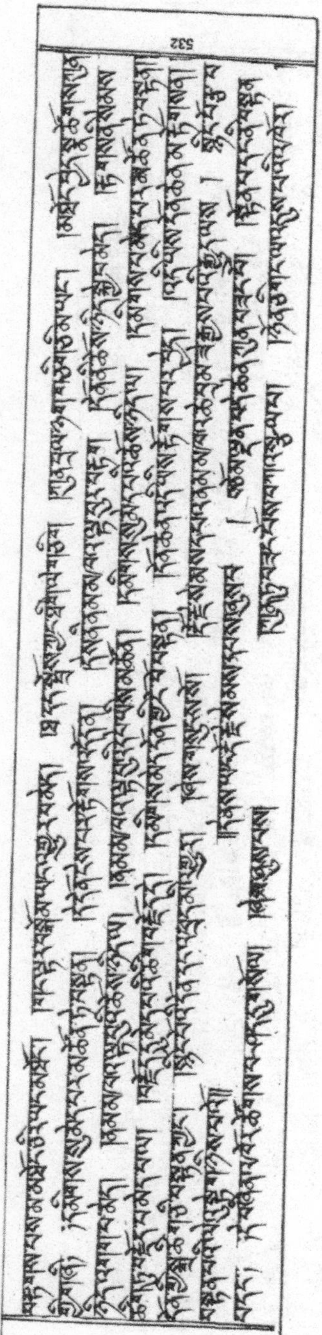

531

532

ཡ

༄༅། །སྟོན་པ་ཡང་འདི་རྣམ་གསུམ་སྟེ། །བསྟན་པ་ཡང་ནི་རྣམ་པ་གསུམ། །དེ་བརྗོད་པ་པོ་ཡང་གསུམ་དུ་བསྟན། །སྟོན་པ་གསུམ
ནི་པད་ཧྲ་ཧེ། །ཆོས་ཀྱི་རང་བཞིན་སྟོན་པ་དང་། །ཆོས་ཀྱི་ངོ་བོ་སྟོན་པ་དང་། །དོན་གྱི་སྤྲུལ་ཚིག་སྟོན་པའོ། །རང་བཞིན་སྟོན་པའི་སྟོན་པ་ནི། །སྐྱེ་བ་མེད་པའི
ཉིད་ཉུ་བས་ཡས། །ཇི་ལྟར་སྣང་བའི་ཆོས་རྣམས་ཀུན། །དེ་བཞིན་ཉིད་དུ་སྟོན་པར་བྱེད། །ངོ་བོ་སྟོན་པའི་སྟོན་པ་ནི། །ཇི་ལྟར་སྣང་བའི་ཆོས་རྣམས་ཀུན། །སྟོང་པ
ཉིད་ཀྱི་སྐུ་རུ་བྱུང་ནས། །ངོ་བོ་དཔག་མེད་པར་སྟོན། །སྤྲུལ་ཚིག་སྟོན་པའི་སྟོན་པ་ནི། །ཆོས་རྣམས་དོན་གྱི་སྒྲིར་བསྡུས་ནས། །མ་རིག་མི་ཤེས་སེམས་ཅན་ལ། །དེ་དོན་སྒྲ
ཚིག་སྤེལ་བས་ནས་སྟོན། །བསྟན་པ་རྣམ་པ་གསུམ་ནི་འདི་ལྟ་སྟེ། །ཆོས་སྐུའི་བསྟན་པ་དེ་བཞིན་ཉིད་དུ་བསྟན། །དེ་བཞིན་ཉིད་ལ་རྣམ་པར་རྟོག་པ་མེད། །ཧྲི
ཧྲ་ར་སྣང་བའི་ཚོགས་རྣམས་ཐམས་ཅད་ཀུན། །སེམས་ཀྱི་ངོ་བོ་ཡིན་པས་དེ་བཞིན་ཉིད། །དེ་ལ་གང་ཞིག་འཆེལ་ཤིང་སྒོམ་བྱེད་པ། །དེ་ཡིས་ཆོས་སྐུའི་བསྟན་པ་རྟོགས་པ་མེད།
སྣང་བ་མེད་པའི་ཆོས་ཉིད་བྱང་ཆུབ་སེམས། །མཐོར་དེ་བཞིན་ཉིད་དུ་མ་རྟོགས་ཏེ། །དེ་ལ་གཉུ་འཆེལ་ཤིང་སྒོམ་བྱེད་པ། །དེ་ཡིས་རང་སེམས་བཅོས་མེད་དམ་རིག །སྣང

533

སྲིད་ཆོས་དང་སྣང་སྲིད་བྱང་ཆུབ་སེམས། །སེམས་ཀྱི་དེ་བཞིན་ཉིད་ཀྱང་དེ་བཞིན་ཉིད། །དེ་བཞིན་ཉིད་དུ་མ་བརྟགས་སོ་སོར་མཐོང་། །དེ་བཞིན་ཉིད་དེ་ནི་དབྱིངས་ནས་ཆོས་ལ
ལོངས་སྤྱོད། །དུས་གསུམ་རྒྱལ་བས་བཙལ་ཡང་མི་རྙེད་དོ། །ལོངས་སྤྱོད་རྫོགས་པའི་བསྟན་པ་ལོངས་སྤྱོད་དོ། །ལོངས་སྤྱོད་ལྔ་ནི་ཆོས་ཉིད་ལོངས་སྤྱོད
ཅིག །སངས་རྒྱས་སེམས་ཅན་ཀུན་གྱི་ལོངས་སྤྱོད་དུ། །ལོངས་སྤྱོད་རྫོགས་པའི་ས་ལ་ལས་སྤྲུལ་དུ་མེད། །གཟུགས་ལ་སོགས་པའི་ལོངས་སྤྱོད་ལྔ་ལ་ནི། །གཅིག་ལ
ལྔ་ལྔ་ཉི་ཤུ་རྩ་ལྔར་སྤྱོད། །ཅུ་ལྔའི་ལོངས་སྤྱོད་དེ་ནི་སྐུ་ལྔར་རྫུ་ལ། །ཆོས་ཉིད་དོན་གྱི་ངོ་བོ་ཉིད་དུ་བཞག །སྤྲུལ་པ་སྐུའི་བསྟན་པ་ཐུགས་རྗེས་དོན
མཛད་དོ། །ཁམས་གསུམ་སེམས་ཅན་བསམ་པ་ཐ་དད་ལ། །སྐུ་དང་གསུང་དང་ཐུགས་ཀྱི་རྣམ་གསུམ་གྱིས། །ཁམས་པ་ཐམས་ཅད་སྐུ་གསུང་ཐུགས་རྗེས་བཏུལ། །དེ་བརྗོད
པ་པོར་ནི་རྣམ་པ་གསུམ་བསྟན་ཏེ། །ཤེ་ཀུ་ཏུ་ན་ལ་འབྱོར་རྩེ་ལ་བསྐུལ་བ་དང་སེམས་དཔའི་འཁོར། །སྟོར་ཞུགས་ཡིད་ཚེ་ས་སངས་རྒྱས་ས་ལ་གནས། །རིག་འཛིན་དང་དང
པོ་སྐུ་པ་སེམས་དཔའི་འཁོར། །མཐོང་བ་ཉི་རེས་སྒོམ་པའི་ས་ལ་གནས། །སེམས་པ་བསྐྱེད་མོས་པ་སྤྱོད་པའི་འཁོར་རྣམས་ནི། །རྒྱུ་དགེ་འབྲས་བུ་དགའ་འཛེམས་པ་ལ་གནས། །དེ

534

535

༄༅། །ཞི་སྐྱོན་པ་གསུམ་གྱི་ལེའུ་ཞེར་དུ་བསྟན། །རྡོ་རྗེ་སེམས་དཔའ་ནམ་མཁའ་ཆེ་བྲམ་ཟེའི་རྒྱས་པའི་རྒྱུད་ལས། ། སྟོན་པ་དང་ནི་བསྟན་པ་དང་དང་ལ་འཁོར་བསྡུ
བཞི་པའི་ལེའུ་སྟེ་གསུམ་པའོ།། །རྡོ་རྗེ་སེམས་དཔས་ཡང་ཞུས་པ། །བཅོམ་ལྡན་བདེ་ཆེན་ཀུན་བཟང་པོ། །ཉིད་ཀྱི་བྱ་མེད་པ་ཤད་དུ་གསོལ། །
ཞེས་ཞུས་པས། ཀུན་ཏུ་བཟང་པོས་བཀའ་སྩལ་པ། །ཉོན་ཅིག་དཔལ་འདུས་པའི་འཁོར། །བྱ་བ་མེད་པའི་དོན་འདི་ནི། །ཀུན་བཟང་དང་པོ་རང་བཞིན་ཏེ། །དང་པོ་རང་བཞིན
འགྱུར་མེད་ལ། །བསྒོམས་ཤིང་འཆེ་སན་བསྒྱུར་བ་ཡིན། །ཡེ་ནས་ལྷུན་གྱིས་གྲུབ་པ་ལ། །སྒྲུབ་ནས་ཡང་འཆིང་བ་ཡི། །དེ་ཡི་ནས་ཉམས་ཟིན་པས། །བྱ་བ་མེད་པའི་ཚིག་ཉིད
ཡིན། ། ཚིག་ཉིད་དང་པོ་རང་བཞིན་པས། །རང་བཞིན་དེ་ལ་བྱ་རྩོལ་མེད། །བཙོལ་སྒྲུབ་མེད་པའི་རང་བཞིན་ལ། །རྡོ་རྗེ་སེམས་དཔའ་འཁྲུལ་པ་འཆོས། །རྡོ་རྗེ་སེམས་དཔའ་འཁྲུལ
འཆོས་ན། །ཀུན་ཏུ་བཟང་པོ་འཆིང་བ་ཡིན། །དེ་ལྟར་སྣང་བའི་ཚིག་རྣམས་ཀུན། །ཀུན་ཀྱང་དང་པོ་རང་བཞིན་ཡིན། །མི་གནས་དམིགས་པའི་ཡུལ་དང་བྲལ། །སྤྲོས་མེད
བསམ་མེད་ཡུལ་ལས་འདས། །དེ་ལ་སྒོམ་གཞག་སུ་ཅི་རྟེན་པ། །བསྒྲལ་བ་ར་བཙལ་ལ་ཡང་རྟེན་པ་ར་དགའ། །ང་ལ་བཙལ་བས་གྲུབ་པ་མེད། །ང་ལ་བསྒྲུབས་པས་གྲུབ་པ་མེད། །ང

536

ལས་ལྷ་ཡུལ་མེད་ཀྱིས། །ང་ལམ་བགྲོད་ལམ་མེད་ཀྱིས། །ང་ལམ་སྒྲོང་སྒྲིབ་མེད་ཀྱི། །ང་ལ་བགྲོད་པས་ཐོབ་པ་མེད། །བདེ་ཆེན་ཆོས་སྐུ་སེམས་སུ་གཅིག་པའི་ཕྱིར། །སྐུ
གདུང་གསུམ་མེད་འཁྲེད་པར་མེད། །རང་བྱུང་ཡེ་ཤེས་ཡུལ་ལ་མི་རྟོག་པས། །རིག་པའི་ཡེ་ཤེས་ཡུལ་གྱིས་བཙལ་མི་དགོས། །མ་བཙལ་ཡེ་ནས་ལྷུན་གྱིས་གྲུབ་པའི་ཕྱིར། །
རྩོལ་བའི་ཕྲིན་ལས་ཡེ་ནས་བྱ་མི་དགོས། །ཡེ་ནས་སངས་རྒྱས་ལ་ཀུན་གནས་པས། །རིག་འཛིན་ས་ལམ་བགྲུ་སྦྱང་མི་དགོས། །ཡེ་ནས་ཀུན་བཟང་ལྷ་བསྒོམ་མི་དགོས། །
ཡེ་ནས་རྣམ་དག་དམ་ཚིག་བསྲུང་མི་དགོས། །མི་གནས་མི་རྟོག་ཅིར་ཡང་དགོངས་མེད་པས། །མི་རྟོག་མཉམ་པའི་ཡུལ་ལ་རང་བཞིན་གནས། །རྡོ་རྗེ་སེམས་དཔའ་ནམ་མཁའ
ཆེ་བྲམ་ཟེའི་རྒྱས་པའི་རྒྱུད་ལས། ། བྱ་བ་མེད་པའི་ལེའུ་སྟེ་བཞི་པའོ།། །རྡོ་རྗེ་སེམས་དཔས་ཡང་ཞུས་པ། ། །བཅོམ་ལྡན་བདེ་ཆེན་ཀུན་བཟང་
པོ། །ཐམས་ཅད་བྱང་ཆུབ་སེམས་སུ་ཇི་ལྟར། །སངས་རྒྱས་པའི་དོན་བཤད་དུ་གསོལ། །ཀུན་ཏུ་བཟང་པོས་བཀའ་སྩལ་པ། །ཉོན་ཅིག་དཔལ་འདུས་པའི་འཁོར། །ཆོས
ཀྱི་སྐུ་ནི་བྱང་ཆུབ་སེམས། །བྱང་ཆུབ་སེམས་ལ་མཚན་ཀྱི་སྐུ། །རྫུ་ལ་ཅ་མ་སྐུ་ཀུན་བཅོས་པ་མེད། །དེ་ན་སེམས་ལ་སངས་རྒྱས་མེད། །ཡོངས་སྤྲོས་རྡོ་རྗེ་གསུམ་རྣམ་དག་བ

ཡ

༄༅། །སེམས། །བྱང་ཆུབ་སེམས་ཀྱི་ལོངས་སྤྱོད་སྐུ། །སེམས་ལས་བྱུང་བའི་གཟུགས་རྣམས་ལ། །ལོངས་སྤྱོད་རྫོགས་པས་སྐུ་གཞན་མེད། །སྤྲུལ་
པའི་སྐུ་ནི་བྱང་ཆུབ་སེམས། །བྱང་ཆུབ་སེམས་ནི་སྤྲུལ་པ་ཡི་ལས། །འགྲོ་བའི་དོན་མཛད་གཞན་ན་མེད། །དུས་གསུམ་སངས་རྒྱས་ཐམས་ཅད་ཀྱི། །བྱང་ཆུབ་སེམས་ལས
གཞན་མེད་དོ། །སྒྲ་རབ་དག་པའི་སངས་རྒྱས་རྣམས། །རང་སེམས་མ་བཅོས་སྒྲ་རམ་སྒྲོར་རྟོགས། །དཀྱིར་བཞུགས་པའི་སངས་རྒྱས་རྣམས། །མ་བཅོས་པ་ཡི་རང་བཞིན
དེ། །མ་བཅོས་མདེ་བཞིན་རྟོགས་སུ་རུང་། །དཀྱུར་འགྲོ་བའི་དོན་ཡང་མཛད། །སྤྱད་ནས་འབྱུང་བའི་སངས་རྒྱས་རྣམས། །རང་བྱུང་སེམས་ཉིད་འདི་ཡི། །སྤྱི་ཆས་ཚོལ་བས
ལྡང་མ་བསྟན། །དཀྱིར་ཏེ་འཛིན་སེམས་མེད་ཚོས། །མ་བཅོས་ལ་མཐུ་ཞུགས་ནས་སྒྲོན། །ཧེ་ཡཱ་ཤུ་ར་ཆེས་རྣམས་ལ། །བྱང་ཆུབ་སེམས་སུ་མ་རྟོགས་ཏེ། །བཅོས
པ་ཅི་སྒྲུབ་ཀྱང་འགྲུབ་མི་འགྱུར། །མཉེ་གསུམ་བཅོས་པས་འགྲུབ་པ་མེད། །བསྐལ་པ་བརྒྱ་མིར་ཕྲགས་པ་གྲུང་ཀུན། །མི་བཙུའ་ལ་བདེ་བ་ཐ་མི་ཐུབ། །སྐུ་གསུམ་སེམས་ལས
མ་བཅོས་བྱུང་། །སྐུ་གསུམ་སྐྱོན་པའི་སྒྲ་བརྗོད་ལས། །དེ་བཞིན་འཆོས་པར་བྱེད་པ་ཡི། །རྟོན་པས་བདེན་ཀྱང་ཡ་ཙི་སྤྱན་ཡང་། །ཉིད་ཀྱི་རང་བཞིན་སྟོན་པ་ཡིན། །རྡོ་རྗེ་སེམས

537

དཔལ་ནམ་མཁའ་ཆེ་ཁྲམ་ནི་རྒྱས་པའི་རྒྱུད་ལས། ། བྱང་སེམས་བཅོས་མེད་ཀྱི་ལེའུ་སྟེ་ལྔ་པའོ།། །རྡོ་རྗེ་སེམས་དཔས་ཡང་ཞུས་པ། །བཅོམ་ལྡན
བདེ་ཆེན་ཀུན་བཟང་པོས། །ཉིད་ཀྱི་ལྷ་སྒོམ་པ་ལ་དག་ཏུ་གསོལ། །ཀུན་ཏུ་བཟང་པོས་བཀའ་སྩལ་པ། །ཉོན་ཅིག་དང་ལ་འདུས་པའི་འཁོར། །རྟོགས་ཆེན་ཡ་སྒོམ་མདུ་མེད་པ
ནི། །ཀུན་ཏུ་བཟང་པོའི་སེམས་ཀྱི་ཡོན་ཏན་ཏེ། །བྱང་ཆུབ་སེམས་ཀྱི་ཆེ་བའི་ཡོན་ཏན་གྱིས། །བཙལ་ཞིང་སྒྲུབ་པའི་དཀའ་བ་སྤྱོད་མེད་གོས། །རྒྱུ་རྐྱེན་མེད་པས་བཙལ་བའི
ལས་མེད་གོས། །ཁྲུས་བུའི་རང་བཞིན་ཤ་ཞིག་ནས་སྒྲུབ་མེད་གོས། །ཆོས་ཉིད་རང་བཞིན་སྒོམས་པས་སྤུ་མེད་གོས། །མཐུས་པས་ནི་འཛིན་པའི་ཤ་ཉེན་པོ་མེད། །གཞན
ལ་མི་ལྟོས་སྒོམས་ནས་འཚོལ་མེད་གོས། །དམ་ཚིག་སྲུང་བའི་སྒོམ་པ་སུ་མེད་གོས། །འབྲིན་ལས་བཙལ་བའི་སྒོམ་པ་སུ་མེད་གོས། །ལམ་ལ་མི་སྤྲོད་ས་ལ་མི་སྤྱོད་སྟེ།
རང་ལས་ཆོས་ནི་གཞན་ཏུ་ཚོལ་མི་བྱེད། །ངན་སྤྱོད་ཡུལ་ལ་ཀུན་ཡལ་བར་སྤྱིན་གྱིད། །ཚིག་གིས་མི་ཐེབས་དབང་པོའི་སྤྱོད་ཡུལ་འདས། །རང་གི་རང་བཞིན་ངོ་སྤྲུལ་ཏེ་ཐིག་ལེར་གནས།།
མ་སྤྲོས་གཉིས་མེད་ཡོན་ལས་གཅིག་ཏུ་བསྡུན། །རང་བྱུང་ཡེ་ཤེས་མི་རྟོགས་གཡོས་པ་མེད། །རྒྱུ་འབྲས་དང་ལས་ནས་རྩོལ་དང་སྒྲུབ་པ་མི་བྱེད། །མ་བྱུང་བ་ལ་ནི་ངོས་པ་སྒོམ་མི་བྱེད།།

538

ཡ

༄༅། །མཉམ་པས་ན་འཛིན་པའི་དོགས་པ་མེད། །བདེ་ཆེན་བརྡལ་བ་ཆེན་པོའི་ཀློང་དཀྱི་ཡིན། །མི་སྣང་བས་ན་དམིགས་པའི་ཡུལ་དང་བྲལ། །ཆོས་ཉིད་
སྣང་བ་མེད་པའི་རང་བཞིན་ལ། །མི་རྟོག་མཁའ་མཉམ་ཆེན་པོ་རང་ངང་གིས་གནས། །ཆོས་ཉིད་སྤྲོས་པ་མེད་པའི་རང་བཞིན་ལ། །རིག་པས་མི་རྟོགས་ཏེ་དེ་འཛིན་མཐུད
ཚན། །གང་ཞིག་ངང་ལ་སྒོམ་པ་བྱེད་པ་དེས། །སྒོམ་པ་ཉིད་ཀྱིས་ངང་དང་ཕྲད་མི་འགྱུར། །ཆོས་ཉིད་མངོན་དུ་གྱུར་བ་ངང་ཡིན་པས། །ཐུག་པ་བསྒྲུབ་ལ་མི་སྐྱེ་རྒྱ་མ་བར
སྣང་མི་དགོས། །རང་བྱུང་ཡེ་ཤེས་སྐྱེ་འཛིན་མེད་པའི་ཕྱིར། །མ་རིག་ཏེ་ནི་འབྲལ་དང་བར་པོ་དགག་མི་དགོས། །རང་རྒྱུད་དུ་མ་དག་ཆོས་ཉིད་སྦྱོང་མི་དགོས། །ཡེ
ནས་དག་པས་གཅོད་སྤྱོ་བ་མི་དགོས། །ཡེ་ནས་ལྷུན་གྲུབ་རྩོལ་བསྒྲུབ་བྱ་མི་དགོས། །ངང་ཡེ་ངོ་བོ་ཀུན་གྱིས་མཐོང་དུ་རུང་ཕྱིར། །ངང་ཡེ་ཤེས་མངོན་དུ་གྱུར་པའི་ཆོས་རྣམས་ནི།
སྣ་ཚོགས་དབང་པོའི་ངོ་ལ་བསྟན་པ་ཡིན། །དེ་ལ་ངང་པོ་རང་བཞིན་ཀུན་རྟོགས་ཤེས། །དེ་ལ་ངང་པོ་རང་བཞིན་མ་མཐོང་ན། །ཀུན་བཟང་ངང་པོ་རང་བཞིན་བསྟན་མི་ནུས། །
རྟོགས་པ་ཆེན་པོའི་དོན་དང་སྒོམ་ལ་མེད་པས། །རྒྱུ་འབྲས་སྤང་བླང་བྱེད་པའི་ལུང་ལ་བཟུང་། །རྡོ་རྗེ་སེམས་དཔའ་ནམ་མཁའ་ཆེ་ཁྲོམ་རྣམ་རྒྱ་སྤྱོད་པའི་རྒྱུད་ལས ། ལྟ་བ་སྒོམ

539

མེད་ཀྱི་ལེའུ་སྟེ་དགུ་པའོ།། །།རྡོ་རྗེ་སེམས་དཔས་ཡང་ཞུས་པ། །བཅོམ་ལྡན་བདག་ཆེན་ཀུན་བཟང་པོ། །ཉིད་ཀྱི་དམ་ཚིག་བ་ལད་དུ་གསོལ།
ཀུན་ཏུ་བཟང་པོས་བཀའ་བསྩལ་པ། །ཉོན་ཅིག་ད་ལ་བརྟུལ་པ་ཤིག་པ་པོར། །མཉམ་སྦྱོར་དང་བྲལ་བའི་རང་བཞིན་གྱིས། །སྐྱེ་བའི་ཚེ་འཁྲུལ་སྣ་ཚོགས་ཡུལ་བྱུང་ནས། །
ཡུལ་མེད་རང་གི་རང་བཞིན་ཡེ་ཤེས་ཀྱི། །དེ་ལ་མི་རྟོག་རྟོགས་པའི་ཡུལ་ལས་འདས། །ཡུལ་ལ་མི་འཛིན་སྤྲོས་དང་ལྡན་མེད་པས། །མེད་པ་བྲལ་བ་གཅིག་ཏུ་ལྷུན་གྲུབ
སྟེ། །མཉམ་སྦྱོར་བར་སྤྱ་བའི་རྒྱལ་ཡེ་སེམས་ཀུན་དང་བྲལ། །ཀུན་བཟང་ང་ལ་བསྒྲུབ་པའི་དམ་ཚིག་མེད། །རྒྱུ་ཀྱེ་ན་མེད་པས་བསྲུང་ལ་ཞིང་བསྲུང་བ་མི་དགོས། །ལྷུན་གྲུབ་ཀྱིས་གྲུབ
པས་སྲུང་བའི་ཉམས་མེད་གོས། །ཡིན་ལ་ཡེ་བས་ལེགས་པར་བྱ་མི་དགོས། །རང་བྱུང་ཡེ་ཤེས་རྒྱུད་དང་ཀྱེ་ན་མེད་གོས། །བཟང་ངན་མེད་པས་བླང་དོར་བྱ་མི་དགོས། །དངོས
པོ་མེད་པས་མེད་པ་ཞེས་བྱ་བ་ཡང་། །ངོས་གཟུང་མི་ཐོད་པ་ཤེས་མ་འགགས་པས། །དེ་ལ་ཆུལ་པ་ཞེས་བྱ་བ་དགོས་པ་ཡིན། །སེམས་ཀྱི་ཀུན་གཅིག་གཅིག་ཏུ་རབ་ཏུ་གསལ་
ཡིན། །རྣམ་པར་སྣང་བའི་ཚོགས་རྣམས་ཐམས་ཅད་ཀུན། །ཡིད་ཆེས་སྐྱེད་དུ་བ་ལས་ཡས་རྫོགས་པའི་ཕྱིར། །ཀུན་གྱིས་རྟོགས་པ་ཞེས་སུ་ངེས་པ་ཡང་། །ཆོས་ཉིད་རང་བཞིན

540

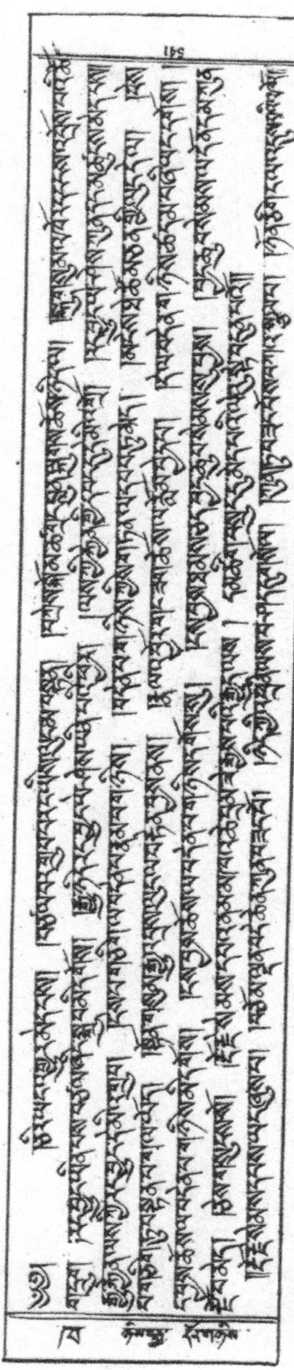

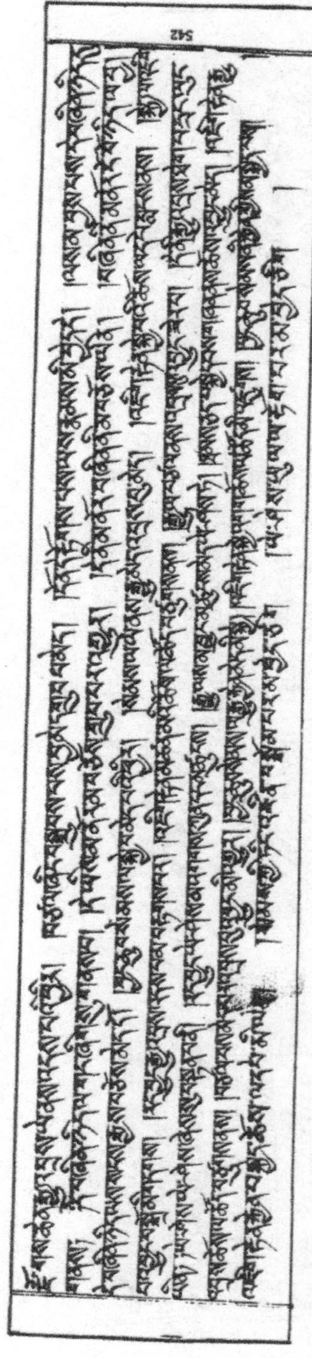

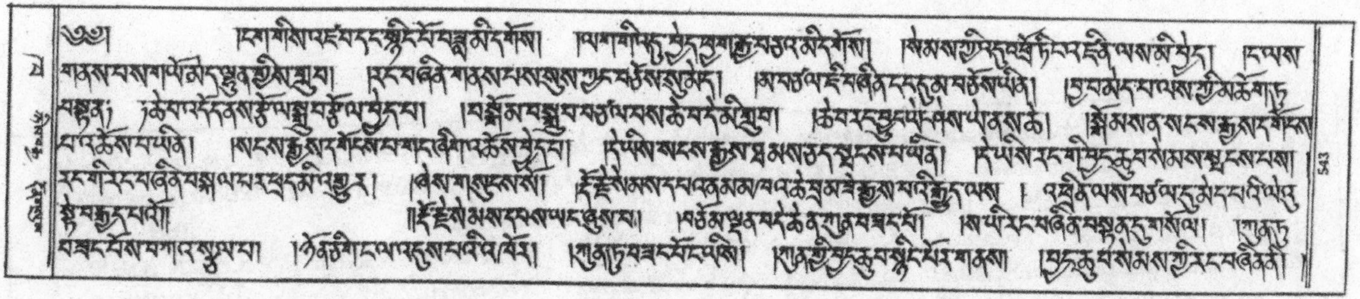

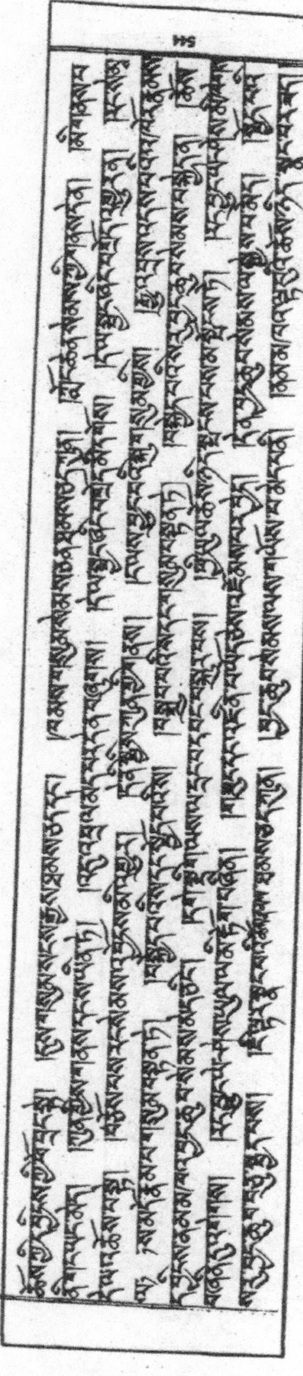

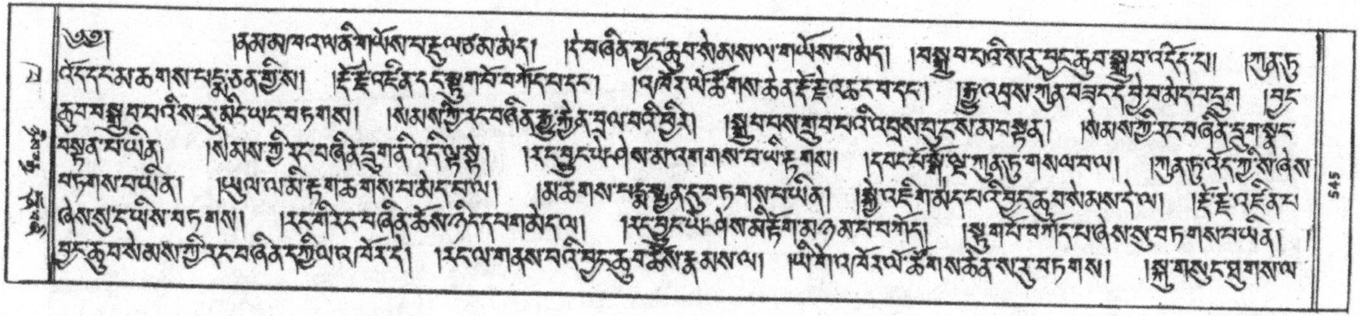

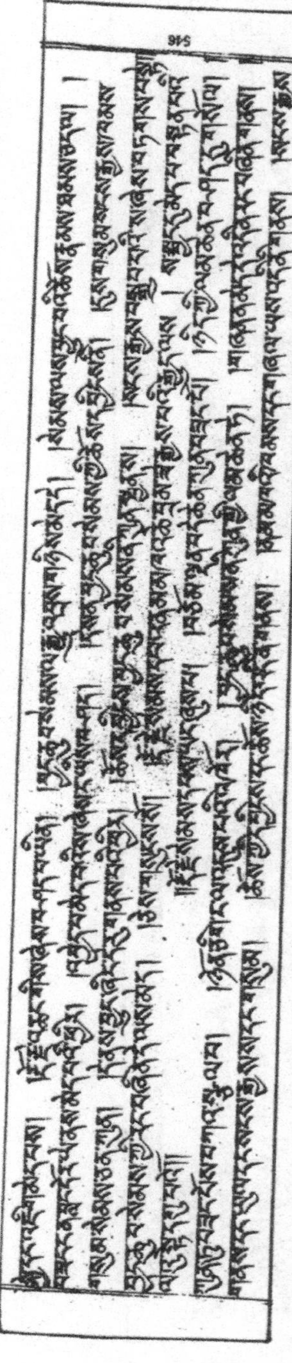

ཁ

༄༅། །ངོ་བོ་རང་ཡུལ་ལ་ནི་བྱང་ཆུབ་སེམས། །གཞན་དུ་བསྒྲོད་པའི་ལམ་རང་གནས་མེད་དེར། །བསྒྲོད་པས་ནམ་མཁའི་ལམ་ལ་ཕྱིན་པ་མེད། །རང་
སེམས་སྒྲིབ་བྲལ་ཆོས་ཀྱི་དབྱིངས་ཡིན་པས། །སྒྲིབ་བྲལ་དེ་ན་སངས་རྒྱས་ཐམས་ཅད་བཞུགས། །དེ་བས་ལམ་ལ་བསྒྲོད་པར་མ་བྱེད་ཅིག །རང་སེམས་མ་བསྒྲིབ་ནམ་མཁའི
རང་བཞིན་གསལ། །དེ་ན་དུས་གསུམ་སངས་རྒྱས་ཐམས་ཅད་བཞུགས། །དེ་བས་ལམ་ལ་བསྒྲོད་པར་མ་བྱེད་ཅིག །རང་སེམས་མ་བཅོས་ཆོས་ཉིད་དེ་རྗེ་བཞིན་ནས། །དེ་ལ
དུས་གསུམ་སངས་རྒྱས་ལྷུན་གྱིས་གྲུབ། །དེ་བས་ལམ་ལ་བསྒྲོད་པར་མ་བྱེད་ཅིག །སངས་རྒྱས་རང་སེམས་རྟོག་དང་བྲལ་བ་ཡིན། །བསྒྲོད་པས་རང་སེམས་རྟོག་བྲལ་དེར
མི་ཕྱིན། །ཀ་ལུ་ཏ་མ་རིག་ལམ་ལ་བསྒྲོད་ཀྱུ་རུ། །ཕྱིན་པའི་དུས་མེད་རྟོགས་པའི་ས་མེད་པས། །བསྒྲོད་པས་སངས་རྒྱས་ས་རུ་ཕྱིན་པ་མེད། །སངས་རྒྱས་རང་སེམས
རྟོག་དང་བྲལ་བ་ཡིན། །ལྟ་བ་སྒོམ་པས་ཏིང་འཛིན་ཡུལ་དང་བྲལ། །ཏིང་འཛིན་དེ་ཡིས་རྟོག་སྤྲོས་མཉམ་དང་བྲལ། །དམ་ཚིག་བསྲུང་བས་མཉམ་ཉམས་འཛིན
དང་གནས། །མཉམ་ཉམས་འཛིན་པས་རྟོག་མེད་མཉམ་དང་བྲལ། །འཕྲིན་ལས་བཅོལ་བས་སྒྲུབ་པའི་ཏིང་འཛིན་བྱེད། །སྒྲུབ་པའི་ཏིང་འཛིན་མི་རྟོག་མཉམ་དང་བྲལ། །

547

ལ་ལ་སྲུངས་པས་གནས་པའི་ཏིང་འཛིན་བྱེད། །བསྒོམས་པའི་ཏིང་འཛིན་རྟོག་མེད་མཉམ་དང་བྲལ། །ཆོས་ཉིད་བརྟགས་པས་གསལ་བའི་ཏིང་འཛིན་བྱེད། །ཏིང་འཛིན
གསལ་བས་རྟོག་མེད་མཉམ་དང་བྲལ། །ཡེ་ཤེས་གསལ་བས་རྟོགས་པའི་ཏིང་འཛིན་བྱེད། །གསལ་བ་རྟོགས་པའི་ཏིང་འཛིན་མཉམ་དང་བྲལ། །འདོད་པའི་ཏིང་
འཛིན་ཉིད་རྟོགས་པར་གསལ་བ་བདེས། །འདོད་པ་མེད་པའི་བདེ་བ་སྒྲུབ་པ་མེད། །ཏིང་འཛིན་མི་བྱེད་བས་ཀ་ཅག་ལམ་མི་སོག་ལས་པས། །རང་བྱུང་ཡེ་ཤེས་ལས་ཀྱི་དབང་མི་འགྱུར། །
རང་བྱུང་ཡེ་ཤེས་ཆེས་སྤྲོ་སྐྱེད་པོ་ད། །བཙལ་བས་མི་འགྲུབ་རང་བཞིན་གནས་པས་འགྲུབ། །སྒྲུབ་པས་བྱ་བའི་དོན་རྣམས་ཀུན་དང་བྲལ། །དོན་ཞེས་བྱ་བ་མེད་ཙམ་བཏགས
པ་ཡིན། །སངས་རྒྱས་མིང་དུ་འདོགས་པར་བྱེད་པ་ནི། །ངེས་པའི་ཡུལ་མེད་དྲང་བའི་ཡུལ་དུ་བསྟན། །ཞེས་གསུངས་སོ། །རྡོ་རྗེ་སེམས་དཔའ་ནམ་མཁའ་ཆེ་བྲམ་ཟེ
རྒྱས་པའི་རྒྱུད་ལས། ། ལམ་ལ་བསྒྲོད་དུ་མེད་པའི་ལེའུ་སྟེ་བཅུ་པའོ།། ||རྡོ་རྗེ་སེམས་དཔས་ཡང་ཞུས་པ། །བཅོམ་ལྡན་སྟོན་པ་ཆེན་ཀུན་ཏུ་བཟང
པོ། །རང་བྱུང་ཡེ་ཤེས་ཕ་དང་དུ་གསོལ། །ཀུ་རུ་བཟང་ཆེན་པ་ཀ་ཏུ་ལ་པ། །ཉིད་ཙམ་ཞིག་རང་ལ་བརྟེན་པའི་ངོ་བོར། །འཁོར་ཀྱི་སྒྲུབ་པའི་ཡེ་ཤེས་ནི། །ཡུལ་ལ་བརྟགས

548

549

༄༅། །ཡང་འདི་ཡེ་ཤེས་ཏེ། །གང་ཟླ་ལྷུན་ལ་ཡང་རྟོག་པ་སྤྱོད་པ། །དེ་ནི་རིག་སྤྱོད་ཡེ་ཤེས་ཡིན། །རིག་པར་གྲུབ་པའི་ཡུལ་འདི་ནི། །བྱང་ཆུབ་སེམས་ལ་བསྒྲུབ་པའི་ཕྱིར། །
དེ་ནི་ཡུལ་མེད་བྱང་ཆུབ་སེམས། །ཡུལ་ལ་རྟོག་པ་འདི་ཡེ་ཤེས་ཏེ། །ཡུལ་ལ་སྒྲུབ་པས་རང་གྲུབ་མིན། །ཡུལ་མེད་ཙམ་ན་གཞལ་ལ་མི་སྤྱོད། །རང་བྱུང་ཡེ་ཤེས་ཞེས་བྱ་བ། །ཡེ་
ཤེས་པ་ཕྱམས་ཤེས་པ་ཡིན། །རང་བྱུང་ཡེ་ཤེས་ཡོན་ཏན་ཤེས། །དེས་ན་རང་བྱུང་ཡེ་ཤེས་ཏེ། །ཡེ་ནས་ཤེས་པས་ཡེ་ཤེས་ཡིན། །ཡེ་ཤེས་ཞེས་བྱའི་འདི་ལ་བཏགས། །ཡེ་ཤེས་རང་
ལས་བྱུང་བའི་ཕྱིར། །དེ་ལ་དེ་ནི་བརྗོད་སྨྲ་མི་སྤྱོད། །དེ་ར་བརྗོད་སྨྲ་མ་མི་སྤྱོད་པས། །དེ་ར་བརྗོད་ཅིང་ཆགས་ཞེན་མི་འགྱུར། །ཟག་ཆགས་མེད་པའི་ཚེ་ན་དེ། །དུས་
གསུམ་སངས་རྒྱས་དགོངས་པར་ཡང་། །དུས་གསུམ་སངས་རྒྱས་ཐམས་ཅད་ཀྱི། །དགོངས་པའི་ཡུལ་ལ་མི་རྟོག་སྟེ། །མཉམ་པ་ཉིད་དུ་ཡེ་ནས་གནས། །དུས་གསུམ་
སངས་རྒྱས་ཐམས་ཅད་ཀྱི། །རང་བྱུང་ཡེ་ཤེས་ཐུགས་ལ་དགོངས། །ཡེ་ནས་རྟོག་པ་མེད་པའི་ཕྱིར། །སངས་རྒྱས་དགོངས་པ་མི་མཐོང་ངོ་། །རྟོག་པའི་ཡུལ་ནི་ཀུན་དང་བྲལ། །རང་
བྱུང་ཡེ་ཤེས་སངས་རྒྱས་དགོངས་པ་མཐོང་། །རང་བྱུང་ཡེ་ཤེས་ཡུལ་ལ་མི་རྟོག་པ། །རྣམ་རྟོག་རྟོག་པའི་བག་ཆགས་སོས་མི་འགྱུར། །ཡེ་ནས་ཉིད་ལ་བརྗོད་པ་བཏགས་པའི

550

བག་ཆགས་སུ་ཡིན། །མི་རྟོག་པ་ལ་བག་ཆགས་ཡོངས་ལས་མ་བསྒྱུངས། །མི་རྟོག་པ་ནི་རང་བྱུང་ཡེ་ཤེས་སྟེ། །སེམས་ཀྱི་རང་བཞིན་རང་སར་སོར་གྲོལ་ཕྱིར་བཤད། །རང་བྱུང་ཡེ་ཤེས
དེ་ལ་འགགས་པ་མེད། །བྱང་ཆུབ་སེམས་ཀྱི་རོ་ཀུན་སྣང་ལ། །རང་བྱུང་ཡེ་ཤེས་མི་ཕ་གག་གོ་སོར་གསལ། །རང་གི་ཉིད་ཀྱིས་སྣང་བ་དེ་ནི་སྤྲོ་དངས། །ཏིང་ངེ་འཛིན་མི
རྟོག་པ་བག་ཆགས་སོག་ས་མི་འགྱུར། །འདི་ནི་དུས་གསུམ་སངས་རྒྱས་དགོངས་པ་སྟེ། །གང་དུ་མི་རྟོག་རང་ལ་རྒྱུག་ནས་པ། །ས་ལ་མི་གནས་འགྲོ་བའི་དོན་མི་ཤེས་ནས།
ཆོས་སྐུ་བྱང་ཆུབ་སེམས་ལ་བརྟེན་གནས་ཏེ། །དུས་གསུམ་སངས་རྒྱས་ཀུན་གྱི་དགོངས་པ་འདུས། །རིག་པ་རྩེ་ཉམས་གསུམ་དོན་གསུམ་རྟོག་པར་གྲོལ། །རང་བྱུང་ཡེ་ཤེས་ཡུལ
ལ་མི་རང་གསལ་ལ་བ། །ཡེ་ཤེས་ལྷུ་ཡི་ཡུལ་ལ་ལྷ་ར་རྫོགས་པ་ཡིན། །ཡུལ་དང་དེ་ལྷུན་ཡེ་ཤེས་ལྷུ་ལ་སྣང་། །ཡུལ་དེ་ཡེ་ནས་ཡེ་ཤེས་ཡིན་པའི་ཕྱིར། །ཡུལ་དང་ཡེ་ཤེས
གཉིས་སུ་ངས་མ་བསྟན། །དེས་ན་ཡུལ་ཡང་རང་བྱུང་ཡེ་ཤེས་ཡིན་པར་བཤད། །རང་བྱུང་ཡེ་ཤེས་ཅི་ཡང་མེད་པ་ལ། །ང་ཡས་བྱུང་བའི་ཡི་གེ་རྗེས་སུ་གཞན་པ་ཡིས། །ཡུལ
ལ་བརྟེན་ནས་ཡེ་ཤེས་མི་བཏགས་པ། །རྣམ་པ་སྣང་བ་ཀྱི་ཡེ་ཤེས་བྱུང་བའི། །རྣམ་པར་བརྟགས་པའི་ཡེ་ཤེས་གཅིག་གི་ཞིང་ནི། །ཡུལ་གཅིག་རང་བཞིན་སོ་སོར་སྣང་བ་ལ།

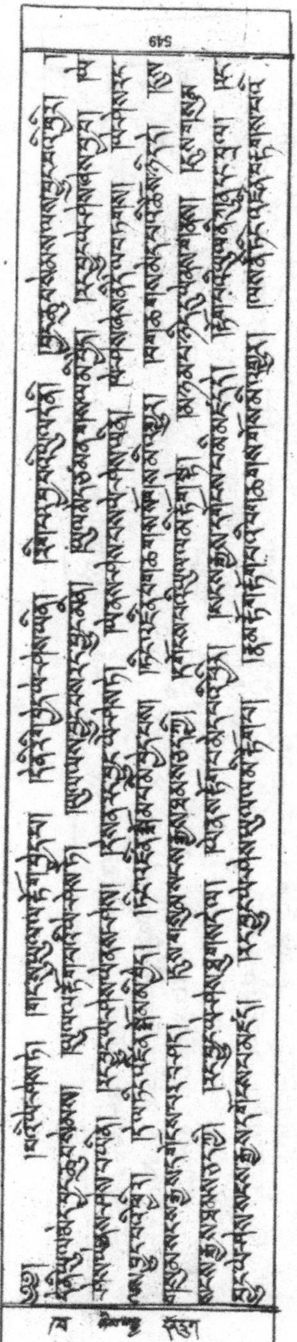

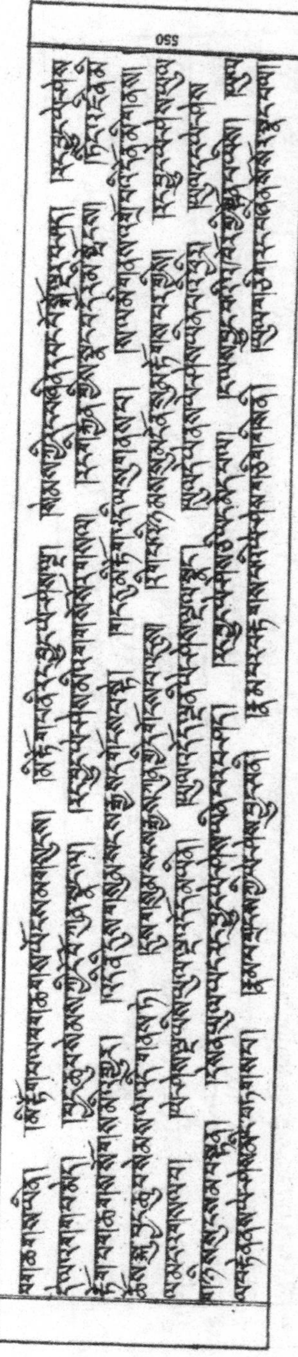

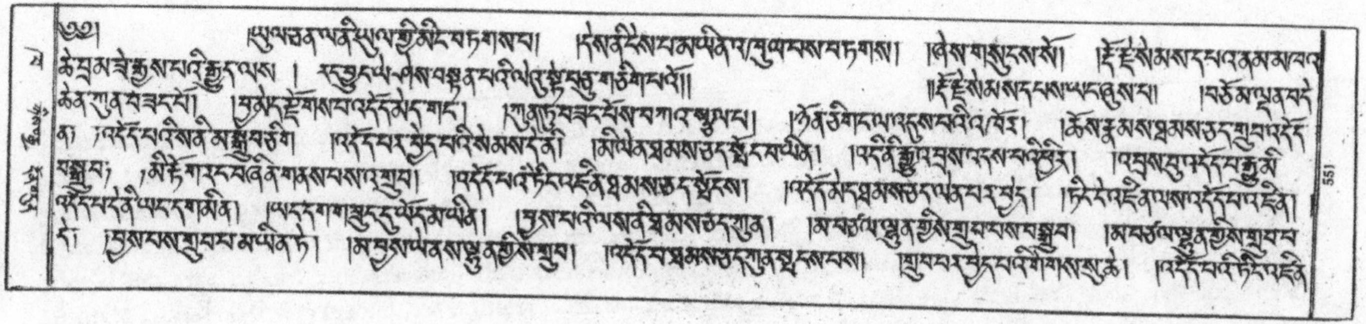

ཡེ

༄༅། ། ཡུལ་ཅན་ལྔའི་ཡུལ་ལ་ཀྱི་མིང་བཏགས་པ། །ངེས་དོན་རྟོགས་པ་མ་ཡིན་པར/ལུགས་མང་པས་བཏགས། །ཞེས་གསུངས་སོ། །རྡོ་རྗེ་སེམས་དཔའ་ནམ་མཁའ་
ཆེ་བྲམ་ཟེ་རྒྱས་པའི་རྒྱུད་ལས། ། རང་བྱུང་ཡེ་ཤེས་བསྟན་པའི་ལེའུ་སྟེ་བཅུ་གཅིག་པའོ།། །།རྡོ་རྗེ་སེམས་དཔས་ཡང་ཞུས་པ། །བཅོམ་ལྡན་བདེ་
ཆེན་ཀུན་ཏུ་བཟང་པོ། །སྤྲོས་མེད་རྟོགས་པ་འདོད་མེད་གང་། །ཀུན་ཏུ་བཟང་པོས་བཀའ་སྩལ་པ། །ཉོན་ཅིག་ང་ལ་འདྲིས་པའི་འ/ཚེར། །ཆོས་རྣམས་ཐམས་ཅད་གྲུབ་པ་འདོད་
ན། །འདོད་པ་འདི་ནི་མ་སྐྱེ་བཅིག །འདོད་པར་བྱེད་པའི་སེམས་དང་ནི། །མི་ལྡན་ཐམས་ཅད་རྫོགས་པ་ཡིན། །འདོད་ནི་རྒྱུ་རུ་བྲམས་འདས་པ་སྦྱོར། །འབྲས་བུ་འདོད་པ་བསྐྱེད་མི
བསྒྲུབ། །མི་རྟོག་ཀ་དག་རང་བཞིན་གནས་པས་འགྲུབ། །འདོད་པའི་ཏིང་འཛིན་ཐམས་ཅད་སྤོངས། །འདོད་མེད་ཐམས་ཅད་ལྡན་པར་སྤྱོད། །ཏིང་ངེ་འཛིན་ལས་འདོད་པ་འཛིན།
འདོད་པ་དེ་ནི་ཡང་དག་མིན། །ཡང་དག་གསུང་དུ་ཡོད་མ་ཡིན། །ཀུན་པ་འདི་ཡིས་ཐམས་ཅད་ཀུན། །མ་བཙལ་ལྷུན་གྱིས་གྲུབ་པས་བསྒྲུབ། །མ་བཙལ་ལྷུན་གྱིས་གྲུབ་པ་བ
ཏེ། །ཀུན་པས་གྲུབ་པ་མ་ཡིན་ཏེ། །མ་བཅོས་ལྡན་པ་ལྷུན་གྱིས་གྲུབ། །འདོད་པ་ཐམས་ཅད་ཀུན་ཏུ་སྤངས་པས། །སྒྲུབ་པར་བྱེད་པའི་གེགས་སུ་ཆེ། །འདོད་པའི་ཕྱི་དང་འཛིན

551

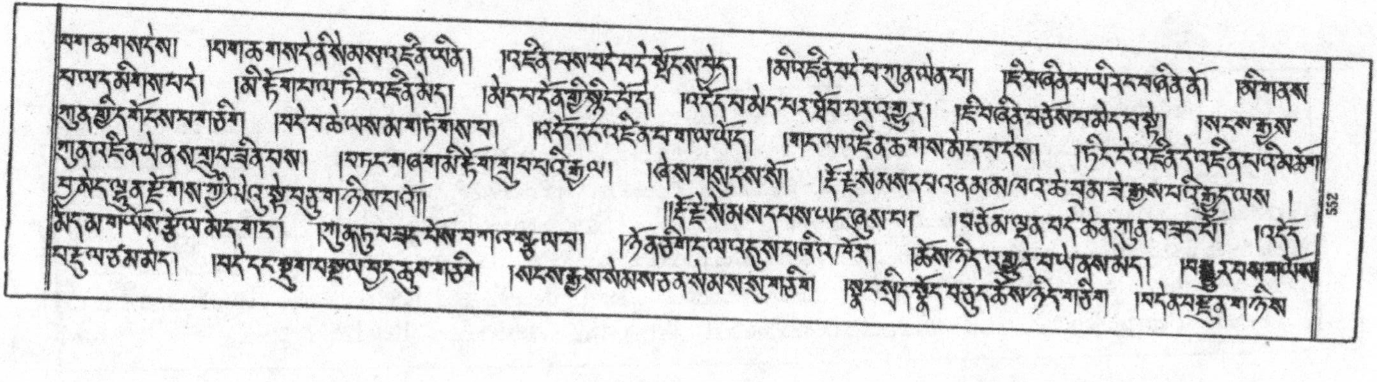

བག་ཆགས་སྡེས། །བག་ཆགས་དེ་ནི་སེམས་པར་འཛིན་པ་ཡིན། །འཛིན་ནི་མ་བདེ་བ་སྟོང་སྐྱེད། །མི་འཛིན་བདེ་བ་ཀུན་ལ་ཁྱབ། །ཇི་བཞིན་པ་ཡི་རང་བཞིན་ནོ། །ཤེ་གནས
པ་ཡང་མིགས་པ་དེ། །མི་རྟོག་པ་ལ་ཏིང་ངེ་འཛིན་མེད། །མེད་པ་དོན་གྱི་སྐྱེ་མེད་ཡོད། །འདོད་པ་མེད་པར་ཐོབ་པར་འགྱུར། །ཇི་བཞིན་བཅོས་པ་མེད་པར་སྤྱད། །སངས་རྒྱས
ཀུན་གྱི་དགོངས་པ་གཅིག །བདེ་བ་ཆེ་ལས་མ་གཏོགས་པ། །འདོད་དང་འཛིན་པ་ག་ལ་ཡོད། །གང་ལ་འཛིན་ཆགས་མེད་པ་དེས། །ཏིང་ངེ་འཛིན་དེ་འཛིན་པའི་སེམས
ཀུན་འདོད་པ་ཡོན་ཏན་ལྷུན་གྲུབ་ཟིན་པས། །ཐང་ཞིག་མི་རྟོག་གསལ་བ་འཁྲུལ། །ཞེས་གསུངས་སོ། །རྡོ་རྗེ་སེམས་དཔའ་ནམ་མཁའ་ཆེ་བྲམ་ཟེ་རྒྱས་པའི་རྒྱུད་ལས། །
སྤྲོས་མེད་ལྷུན་རྫོགས་ཀྱི་ལེའུ་སྟེ་བཅུ་གཉིས་པའོ།། །།རྡོ་རྗེ་སེམས་དཔས་ཡང་ཞུས་པ། །བཅོམ་ལྡན་བདེ་ཆེན་ཀུན་ཏུ་བཟང་པོ། །འདོད
མེད་མ་གཡོས་རྩོལ་མེད་གང་། །ཀུན་ཏུ་བཟང་པོས་བཀའ་སྩལ་པ། །ཉོན་ཅིག་ང་ལ་འདྲིས་པའི་འ/ཚེར། །ཆོས་ཉིད་འགྱུར་བ་ཡོང་ས་མེད། །བསྒྱུར་ལས་ཡོངས
བརྡུལ་ཙམ་མེད། །བདེ་དང་སྡུག་བསྔལ་བྱང་ཆུབ་གཅིག །སངས་རྒྱས་སེམས་ཅན་སེམས་སུ་གཅིག །སྣང་སྲིད་སྣོད་བཅུད་ཆོས་ཉིད་གཅིག །བདེན་པ་རྫུན་གཉིས

552

ཡ

༄༅། །ཀུན་ཏུ་ཆོས་ཉིད་མ་ཉམས། །བདེ་ལ་ཆགས་མེད་ཐུགས་བསྐྱེད་ལ་ཡིན། །རང་བཞིན་གནས་པས་ཀུན་ཀྱང་འགྲུབ། །ཀུན་གསལ་དེ་ལ་རྟོག་མེད་པས། །
དེ་ནི་རང་བྱུང་ཡེ་ཤེས་ཡིན། །ཡེ་ཤེས་བག་ཆགས་མི་སྒོམ་པས། །ལས་ཀྱིས་གོས་པར་ག་ལ་འགྱུར། །སྣ་ཚོགས་བསྒོམས་པས་གཅིག་མི་གསལ། །གསལ་བའི
ངང་འཛིན་གང་ཞེ་ན། །དེ་ལ་ངང་འཛིན་ཡོད་མ་ཡིན། །དེ་བཞིན་ཉིད་དང་གཅིག་པ་ལ། །སངས་རྒྱས་སེམས་ཅན་གཉིས་སུ་མེད། །བདེ་བ་ཕྱག་བརྒྱ་ལ་གཉིས
སུ་ནུས། །དགོ་བ་དང་ནི་སྡང་བར་བསྟན། །ཕྱོགས་བརྒྱ་བཅུ་པོ་རུ་བར་བསྟན། །དེ་ནི་ངེས་པའི་དོན་ལས་འགག་ལ། །རང་བཞིན་ཆེས་ལ་གཡོས་པ་མེད། །སངས་རྒྱས་རང
བཞིན་གཡོས་མེད་པར། །དུས་གསུམ་རྒྱལ་བའི་ཆོས་ཉིད་ཡིན། །དེ་ལ་སངས་རྒྱས་གུད་ན་མེད། །བྱང་ཆུབ་སེམས་ལས་མ་གཏོགས་པའི། །སངས་རྒྱས…
སེམས་ཅན་ཞེས་ག་མེད། །སེམས་ཉིད་མི་རྟོག་སངས་རྒྱས་ཡིན། །སངས་རྒྱས་ཀུན་ལ་སེམས་ཉིད་བསྟགས། །སེམས་ཉིད་མ་གཡོས་རྩོལ་དང་བྲལ། །
རྩོལ་བྲལ་དེ་ལ་བཅོས་སུ་མེད། །ཅེས་གསུངས་སོ། །རྡོ་རྗེ་སེམས་དཔའ་ནམ་མཁའ་ཆེ་བྲམ་ཟེ་རྒྱས་པའི་རྒྱུད་ལས། །མ་གཡོས་རྩོལ་བྲལ་གྱི་ལེའུ་སྟེ་བཅུ……

553

གསུམ་པའོ།། །རྡོ་རྗེ་སེམས་དཔས་ཡང་ཞུས་པ། །བཅོམ་ལྡན་བདེ་ཆེན་ཀུན་བཟང་པོ། །ཉིད་ཀྱི་རིག་པ་རྗེ་ཕྱིར་གསལ། །ཀུན་ཏུ
བཟང་པོས་བཀའ་སྩལ་པ། །ཉོན་ཅིག་ང་ལ་འདྲུས་པའི་ཞོར། །རིག་པ་སྐྱེ་བྲལ་ཆེན་པོར་གསལ། །རྟོག་པ་བསམ་སྤྱོད་མེད་པར་གསལ། །མི་རྟོག་བསམ་མེད
ངང་དུ་གསལ། །རིག་པ་རྟོག་འཛིན་མེད་པར་གསལ། །བསམ་མཐའ་ཞིག་སྣང་པོར་གསལ། །རིག་པ་དམིགས་གཏད་མེད་པར་གསལ། །མི་རྟོག་མ་ཉམས་པའི
ངང་དུ་གསལ། །རིག་པ་བྱ་བཙལ་མེད་པར་གསལ། །མཐའ་བར་དབྱིངས་པ་ཆེན་ཀློང་དུ་གསལ། །རིག་པ་དྲན་བསམ་མེད་པར་གསལ། །ཤེས་རིག་བསམ་མ་སྤྱོད
འདས་པར་གསལ། །རིག་པ་འཛིན་རྟོག་མེད་པར་གསལ། །མི་གཡོ་མ་ཉམས་པའི་ངང་དུ་གསལ། །རིག་པ་ག་ཏུ་དང་ཞེན་མེད་གསལ། །སྤྱོད་པའི་མཐའ
དང་བྲལ་བར་གསལ། །རིག་པ་རང་ལུགས་ཆེན་པོར་གསལ། །བྱ་བཙལ་ཉིད་ལས་འདས་པར་གསལ། །རིག་པ་མ་བཀག་གྲུང་པོར་གསལ། །མི་རྟོག་མ་ཉམ
པའི་ངང་ལ་གསལ། །རིག་པ་འཛིན་པ་མེད་པར་གསལ། །མི་རྟོག་སྒྲིབ་དང་བྲལ་བར་གསལ། །རིག་པ་བསམ་སྤྱོད་མེད་པར་གསལ། །ཤེས་པ་ཅིར་ཡང་མ་གཡོས་གསལ། །

554

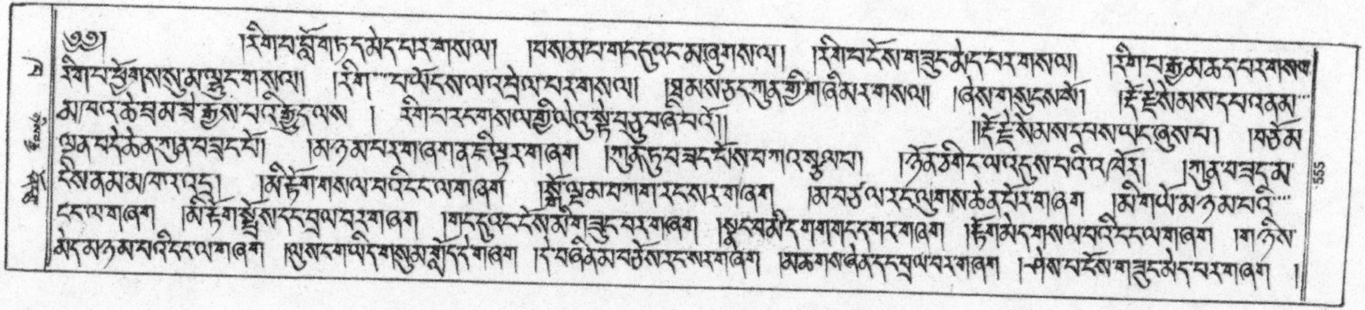

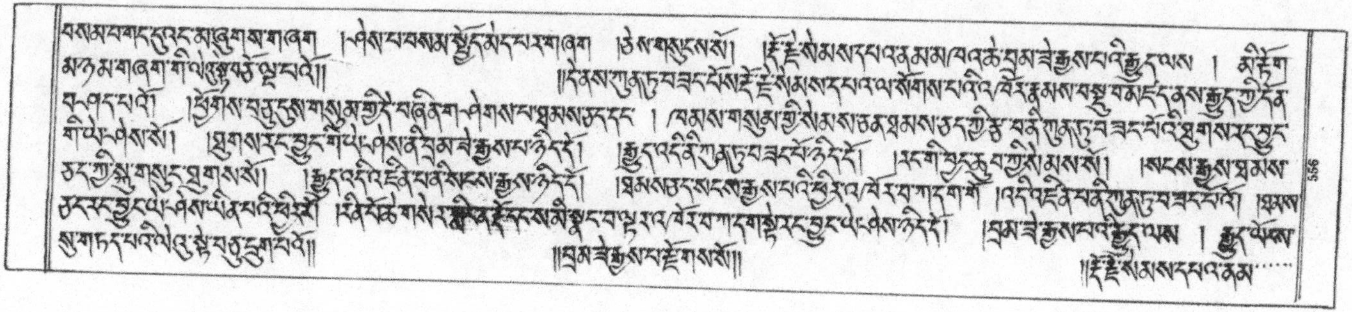

THE TANTRA OF VAJRASATTVA'S MAGNIFICENT SKY

EMBELLISHED FOR THE KING

From the mTshams brag Edition of the rNying ma rGyud 'bum

Volume Three, pages 119-165.

ཀ

༄༅། །ཨུ་ར་ཀྲི་ཀ་མི་ཏྲུ་ཨུ་ཏྲ། །།ཀྱཻ། །རྒྱ་གར་སྐད་དུ། བཛྲ་ས་ཏྭ། ཁ་སོ་མ་ཧཱ་རཱ་ཛ་ཏནྟྲ
ནཱ་མ། བོད་སྐད་དུ། རྡོ་རྗེ་སེམས་དཔའ་ནམ་མཁའ་ཆེ་རྒྱལ་པོ་རྒྱས་པའི་རྒྱུད། བཅོམ་ལྡན་འདས་དཔལ་ཀུན་ཏུ་བཟང་པོ་བདེ་བ་ཆེན་པོ་ལ་ཕྱག་འཚལ་ལོ། །
འདི་སྐད་བདག་གིས་ཐོས་པའི་དུས་གཅིག་ན། བཅོམ་ལྡན་འདས་དེ་བཞིན་ཉིད་ལེགས་པ་ཡང་དག་པར་རྫོགས་པའི་སངས་རྒྱས་ཀུན་ཏུ་བཟང་པོས་བསམ་གྱིས་མི
ཁྱབ་པའི་ངང་ངོ་བོ་བརྗོད་ལ་སྙོམས་པར་ཞུགས་སོ། །འོག་མིན་གནས་མཆོག་ཁྱད་པར་ཅན། །ཆོས་ཀྱི་དབྱིངས་ཀྱི་ཕོ་བྲང་ན། །ཡེ་ཤེས་སྒྲིབ་མེད་གཞལ་ཡས་ན། །
ཉིད་ཀྱི་རང་བཞིན་ཆོས་སྐུ་དང་། །ཉིད་ཀྱི་ངོ་བོ་ལོངས་སྐུ་དང་། །ཉིད་ཀྱི་ཐུགས་རྗེ་སྤྲུལ་སྐུ་དང་། །རྡོ་རྗེ་སེམས་དཔའ་ལ་སོགས་པ། །འབྱུང་བ་མེད་པའི་འཁོར
རྣམས་དང་། །ཐིག་ལེ་ཆེན་པོ་གཅིག་ཏུ་བཞུགས། །དེ་ནས་རྡོ་རྗེ་སེམས་དཔས་ཞུས་པ། །སྟོན་པའི་སྟོན་པ་ཀུན་ཏུ་བཟང་པོ་ལགས། །སྟོན་པ
ཉིད་ཀྱང་ཐིག་ལེ་སྤྲོས་པ་མེད། །བསྟན་པ་ཀུན་ཀྱང་ཐིག་ལེ་སྤྲོས་པ་མེད། །དུས་དང་གནས་ཀྱང་ཐིག་ལེ་སྤྲོས་པ་མེད། །ཐམས་ཅད་ཀུན་ཀྱང་ཐིག་ལེ་སྤྲོས

119

མེད་ན། །སྟོན་པའི་སྟོན་པས་ཅི་ཞིག་སྟོན་པར་མཛད། །འཁོར་དུ་འཁོད་པའི་འཁོར་ནི་ཅི་ལ་འཁོར། །འཁོར་ལ་སྟོན་པ་ཅི་ཞིག་སྟོན་པར་བྱེད། །དུས་དང་གནས་ནི་གཅིག་པ
ཇི་ལྟ་བུ། །ཞེས་ཞུས་པས། །རྡོ་རྗེ་སེམས་དཔའ་ལ་སོགས་ཀྱི། །འབྱུང་བ་རྣམས་བཞི་འཁོར་རྣམས་ལ། །བཅོམ་ལྡན་འདས་ཀྱི་ཐུགས་རྗེ་ཡིས། །
གསང་བ་འདི་ནི་རབ་ཏུ་བསྒྲགས། །འདི་ནི་གསང་བ་ཐམས་ཅད་ཀྱི། །གསང་ཆེན་རབ་ཏུ་ངེས་པ་ཡིན། །ཀུན་ཏུ་བཟང་པོ་ང་ཉིད་ནི། །སྟོན་པ་དང་ནི་བསྟན་པ་དང་། །
འཁོར་དང་དུས་དང་གནས་དང་ནི། །ང་ལས་བྱུང་བའི་ཐིག་ལེ་སྐུ། །ང་ཡི་རང་བཞིན་ཐིག་ལེ་ཡིན། །ཐིག་ལེ་ཡ་ནས་སྤྲོས་པ་མེད། །སྙིང་པོ་མ་སྤྲོས་ཐིག་ལེ་ཡིན། །ཀུན
ལས་བྱུང་བ་རྒྱུར་བ་ཡི། །ཚ་བའི་ཡོན་ཏན་རྫོགས་པའི་མཆོག །ཆོས་རྣམས་ཀུན་གྱི་དེ་བཞིན་ཉིད། །མཆོག་གི་སྙིང་པོས་ཐུགས་བརྒྱུད་པ། །འབྱུང་བ་ར་འཁོར་རྒྱས་ནང
བཞིན་འཛིན། །ཡང་དག་དོན་གྱི་སྙིང་པོ་ནི། །གང་ནས་བཙལ་ཡང་མི་རྙེད་དེ། །རང་རིག་སྒྲིབ་མེད་དག་པ་ཡིན། །དེ་ལ་རྟག་ཏུ་ཞུགས་གོམས་པ་ནི། །བསྐྱེད་པ་དམ་པ
དེ་ཡིན་ནོ། །དེ་ནི་མཐོང་ལམ་ཡིན་པར། །ཀུན་ཏུ་བཟང་པོས་རབ་ཏུ་བསྟན་ཏོ། །འགྲོ་བའི་སྡུག་བསྔལ་བྱང་ཆུབ་སེམས། །ཀུན་ཏུ་ཆུབ་པས་རྣམ་པར་རོལ། །དེ་ལ

120

ཀ

༄༅། །སྤྲོད་པ་མེད་བཞིན་དུ། །ནམ་མཁའ་འདི་མཐའ་ལྷུར་མཉམ་པར་གནས། །མཁའ་བ་འདྲ་ཀློང་ཞེན་མེད་རང་རིག་འདི། །མི་ཤིགས་རྡོ་རྗེའི་སྙིང་པོ་སྐུ། །
མི་འགྱུར་མཆོག་གི་སྙིང་པོ་ཡིན། །སྣང་བྲལ་འདྲ་ཤེས་གང་གནས་པ། །རྡོ་རྗེ་སྙིང་པོ་གྲུབ་པའི་མཆོག །རྡོ་རྗེ་ཡེ་ཤེས་རང་བྱུང་འཁོར་ལོ་ལྷུན། །ཞལ་འདུས་ཤེས་རྩེ་ཀྲོ་ལ་བ
བཟང་། །སངས་རྒྱས་ཀུན་དང་མཉམ་འགྱུར་བའི། །ཆོས་པ་ཀུན་སྐྱེད་མཆོག་གི་སྐུ། །གང་ཡང་འགྱུར་བ་མེད་པ་ཡི། །ཆོས་སྐུ་ས་གཞན་ཏུ་ཐེབ་པའི་ཕྱིར། །རང་བཞིན་ལྷུན
གྲུབ་ལྷུ་ལ་ལ་རོལ། །མཐོང་ཐོས་རེག་དང་དྲན་པ་ཡིས། །སྡིག་པ་ཀུན་ལས་རྣམ་པར་གྲོལ། །གདོད་ནས་རྣམ་དག་གྲོལ་བའི་ལམ། །འགྲོ་བ་ཀུན་ལ་རང་བཞིན་གནས། །
ཕྱིན་ཅི་ལོག་ཏུ་རྣམ་པ་རྟག་པ་ཏུ་ཤར། །གྲོལ་བ་རང་བྱུང་གཞན་ལས་མེད། །ཡང་དག་དོན་གྱི་སྙིང་པོ་འདི། །ཐམས་ཅད་མཁྱེན་པའི་ཡེ་ཤེས་ཀྱིས། །ཁྱད་པར་མེད་པར་ལྷུན་གྱིས
གྲུབ། །འབྲས་བུ་ཀུན་ཏུ་བཟང་པོའི་སྐུ། །ཞེས་གསུངས་སོ། །རྡོ་རྗེ་སེམས་དཔའ་ནམ་མཁའ་ཆེ་རྒྱལ་པོ་རྒྱས་པའི་རྒྱུད་ལས། སྙིང་གཞིའི་ལེའུ་སྟེ་དང་པོའོ།།
།།དེ་ནས་བཅོམ་ལྡན་འདས་ཀྱིས་རྡོ་རྗེ་སྙིང་པོའི་དོན་དེ་ཉིད་ལ་སྙོམས་པར་ཞུགས་ནས་ཚིག་ཏུ་བརྗོད་པ་འདི་ཉིད་བརྗོད་དོ། །ལྷུན་གྱིས་གནས་པའི

121

བདེ་ཆེན་ཏེ། །མངོན་སུམ་མི་གནས་ཀུན་ཏུ་ཁྱབ། །རང་བྱུང་ཡེ་ཤེས་རྩོལ་མེད་པས། །དབྱིངས་དང་ཡེ་ཤེས་དོན་ལ་ལས་འདས། །རྩོལ་སེམས་བདེ་བསྒོམ་མེད་ཀྱང་། །དེ་
ནི་རིག་པ་སྒྲོན་མ་ཆེན་ཡིན། །ཚིག་གི་ཐ་སྙད་མེད་པའི་ཕྱིར། །དགེ་དང་སྡིག་ལས་རྣམ་པར་གྲོལ། །ལྷུན་གྱིས་རྫོགས་པའི་ངོ་བོ་དེ། །སྤྲོད་དང་ལྟ་དང་འཛུགས་རྩོལ་མེད། །
གང་ལ་འང་འགྱུར་པ་མེད་པས་ན། །རང་བྱུང་ཡེ་ཤེས་རྩོལ་མེད་པས། །དབྱིངས་དང་ཡེ་ཤེས་དོན་ལ་ལས་འདས། །མི་རྟོག་ཡེ་ཤེས་ཆེན་པོ་ལ་ལས། །དགེ་བའི་འབྲས
བུ་བསྟན་མེད་པས། །བཟློག་ཅིང་སྤོང་བའི་ལམ་དང་བྲལ། །ཡིན་པའི་དོན་ཉིད་གཞིག་ཏུ་མེད། །སྣང་བ་ཞེས་མ་སྐྱེད་པོ་ང་མིན། །ནམ་མཁའི་མིང་ཡང་འཐོབ་པ
མེད། །སྒྲ་བྲལ་ལྷུན་གྲུབ་མཆོག་གི་སྐུ། །ཐ་སྙད་མི་འབྱུང་གཅིག་གི་ངང་། །གང་ཏུ་འང་མཐུན་མ་གསལ་བས། །ཚིག་ཡང་མཐུན་པ་དེ་བཞིན་ནོ། །དེ་བཞིན་སྙིང་
པོ་ཆེན་པོ་ཉིད། །དུས་གསུམ་རྒྱལ་བའི་གནས་སུ་ཆེ། །སངས་རྒྱས་དེ་ནི་ཡི་མ་འདྲ་བར། །མཆོག་གི་སྙིང་པོ་དེ་ཉིད་ནི། །འགྲོ་དྲུག་དེ་ཡི་རང་བཞིན་ནོ། །དེ་ལྟ་རེ་
བཞིན་དེ་ཡི་ཕྱིར། །དེ་ལ་དེ་བསྟན་དེ་ཡང་འཐོབ། །དེ་ནི་སྙིང་པོ་དེ་བཤད། །དེ་ལས་དེ་བྱུང་དོ་མཚར་ཆེ། །སྟོན་གྱི་དེ་དང་དཔྱད་ནི་སྟེ། །དེ་བཞིན་དེ་ཡི་གནས་སུ

122

ཀ

༄༅། །ཀྱེ༔ ཇི་ལྟར་རང་དེ་ཡི་ལ་མ་འདྲ་བས། །དེ་ནི་དེ་ཡི་རང་བཞིན་ནོ། །དེ་དང་འདྲ་བ་ཡོངས་ཀྱིས་ལམ། །ལྟ་བ་ལས་བྱུང་ཧེ་ན་བཅས་པའི། །
སྤྲུ་ཡི་ཕྱག་རྒྱ་རབ་སྤྲང་བདེས། །ཅིར་ཡང་མ་ཤུགས་བ་དེ་བཞིན་ནོ། །ཞེས་གསུངས་སོ། །རྡོ་རྗེ་སེམས་དཔའ་ནམ་མཁའ་ཆེ་རྒྱལ་པོ་རྒྱས་པའི་རྒྱུད་ལས། ། ལུང་གསུམ་བཅུ་ལ
སྤྲུལ་གྱི་ལེའུ་སྟེ་གཉིས་པའོ།། །དེ་ནས་བཅོམ་ལྡན་འདས་ཤེ་ཀུ་ཐབ་པའི་ཏིང་ངེ་འཛིན་ལ་སྙོམས་པར་ཞུགས་ནས་ཚིག་དུ་བརྗོད་པ་
འདི་ཉིད་རབ་བརྗོད་དོ། །འདི་ནི་གསང་ཆེན་རབ་ངེས་པའི། །རྒྱུ་བ་པ་རབ་གྲུབ་པས་བཅོམ་ལྡན་འདས། །འགྲོ་བ་ཀུན་ལ་རང་བཞིན་གནས། །ཕྱིན་ཅི་ལོག་ཏུ་ནམ་
བརྟགས་ཀྱང་། །སྒྲོ་ལ་བ་རང་བྱུང་གཞན་ལས་མིན། །བཙལ་དུ་མེད་པའི་སྙིང་པོ་འདི། །འགྲོ་བའི་ཕུག་བསྡལ་བྱུང་རྒྱུ་བསམས། །ཀུན་ཏུ་ཁྱབ་པས་རྣམ་པར་རོལ།།
དེ་ལ་བསྒྱུར་བ་མེད་པ་བཞིན་དུ། །ནམ་མཁའི་མཐའ་ལྟར་མཉམ་པར་གནས། །ཆོས་སྐུ་ཅིར་ཡང་མི་དམིགས་ཏེ། །འཁོར་བ་མྱང་འདས་པའི་ཆོས། །དེ་ལ་
གདོད་ནས་བགག་མེད་པའི་ཀློང་། །ཅིས་ཀྱང་གཞིག་ཏུ་མེད་པ་སྟེ། །དེ་ལ་སེམས་ཅན་རྣམ་པར་རྟོག །རྡོ་རྗེ་ལྟར་འཕྲད་པ་ཀུན་བྱུང་བས། །ཀུན་གྱི་ཡིད་བཞིན་ནོར་བུ་

123

སྟེ༔ །ཐམས་ཅད་མཉམ་པ་གཉིས་སུ་མེད། །མཉམ་དབྱིངས་དབྱེར་མེད་ཆེན་པོའི་དབྱིངས། །བསྐྱུས་ནས་འདུས་པར་གྲུབ་པ་མེད། །ཆོས་ཀྱི་སྐུ་ཉིད་ཅི་རུ་མི་
དམིགས། །མ་སྐྱེས་མི་འགག་ཅི་རུ་མི་དགོངས། །གང་ཡང་མི་འགྱུར་མཉམ་ཆེན་པོ། །རྩལ་བཞིན་འབྱུང་བ་ཡིད་བཞིན་ནོར། །འབྱུང་འཇུག་མི་འགག་ཅིར་ཡང་
སྣང་། །མཆོག་གི་སྙིང་པོ་མཐའ་རྡོན། །དམ་པ་ཡིན་ཏེ་སྤྲོས་དང་བྲལ། །དེ་ཡང་འགག་པ་མེད་བཞིན་དུ། །ཀུན་འབྱུང་རིན་ཆེན་འབྱུང་པོ་འབར། །ཀུན་གློང་ཀུན་
འདུས་ཀུན་གྱི་ཀློང་། །རྡོ་རྗེ་འདུས་པ་བདེ་ཆེན་སྐུ། །མཉམ་སྙོམས་འདུས་པ་ཕུས་པའི་ངང་། །མཉམ་དབྱིངས་ཡེ་ཤེས་ཆེན་པོའི་མཆོག །མི་དམིགས་མི་
སྤྲོ་སྣང་བ་མེད། །མཆོག་གི་སྙིང་པོ་དམ་པ་ཡིན། །དེ་བཞིན་ཉིད་ཀྱང་དབུ་མར་མིན། །མི་དམིགས་བདེན་པ་གཉིས་མི་མངའ། །བདེན་གཉིས་ལྡན་པས་བརྒྱུར་
པའི༔ །བྱང་ཆུབ་སེམས་དཔའ་ཡང་མེད། །ཞེས་གསུངས་སོ། །རྡོ་རྗེ་སེམས་དཔའ་ནམ་མཁའ་ཆེ་རྒྱལ་པོ་རྒྱས་པའི་རྒྱུད་ལས། ། གསང་བ་མཛོད་དུ་
བསྟན་པའི་ལེའུ་སྟེ་གསུམ་པའོ།། ༎དེ་ནས་བཅོམ་ལྡན་འདས་ཀྱིས་དོན་གྱི་སྙིང་པོའི་ཏིང་ངེ་འཛིན་ལ་སྙོམས་པར་ཞུགས་ནས་ཚིག་དུ་བརྗོད་

124

ཀ རྩེ་བསྡུས 125

༄༅། །པའི་དོ་བ་རྫོང་དེ། །བསྒོམ་དུ་དངོས་པོ་མེད་པ་སྟེ། །ཚིག་གིས་དེ་ལ་མཚོན་དུ་མེད། །དེ་ལ་རྒོད་བྱིང་མེད་ཡེ་ཤེས་གསལ། །དེ་ཡི་སྣང་བ་ཐམས་
ཅད་གྲོལ། །ཡི་ལྡ་མི་སྐྱེད་མི་སྐྱུང་ཞིང་། །མི་སྒོམ་པ་ཉིད་སྒོམ་པ་ཡིན། །ཅི་ཡང་སྒྲུབ་ཏུ་མེད་པ་ལ། །དམིགས་པ་བསྒྲུབ་ཡོད་པ་མིན། །སྤང་ཞིང་བཙལ་བའི་གནས་
མེད་དེ། ;ཡ་སྤྲུངས་བམ་ས་གསུམ་ཡེ་ནས་རང་སར་རྒྱས། །དབང་པོ་ནི་སྤྱོད་ཡུལ་མ་ཡིན་ཏེ། །ཚིག་གིས་མཚོན་པ་རང་ལ་འགྱུར། །སྒོམ་ཞེས་གདགས་སུ་མེད་པ་ཡིན།
ཚིག་གིས་མཚོན་དུ་མེད་པའི་ཕྱིར། །ངག་ཏུ་ཅི་སྨྲ་ཐམས་ཅད་དང་། །དབྱིངས་དང་ཡེ་ཤེས་ཉིད་ཀྱི་རང་བ་སྟོབ། །འདི་ནི་སྒྲིབ་པའི་སྒྲོན་མ་ཆེན་ཡིན། །ཆོས་རྣམས་ཀུན་རང་བཞིན་
ཉིད་ཀྱིས་སྟོང་། །ངོ་བོ་ཉིད་ཀྱིས་མ་སྤྲུལ་ལྷུན་པའི། །རྣམ་པར་དག་པའི་བདག་ཉིད་དེ། །ལམ་གྱིས་བཅོས་སུ་མེད་པ་ལ། །ཐེག་དམན་རྟོག་པ་ཞེན་པ་ཡིས། །རང་རྒྱུད་
འདོད་གཞུང་སྒྲིབ་ཅི་ལོག །སོ་སོ་རང་སྤྱོད་ནས་རྣམ་བརྟགས་ཀྱང་། །ལོ་ནི་བརྒྱ་བ་མང་རང་བསྐལ་པའི། །ཡེ་ཤེས་མཆོག་གི་དམ་པ་འདིར། །མ་བསྒྲུབ་ལྷུན་
གྱིས་རྫོགས་པ་ལས། །གྲོལ་བ་རྒྱུ་ཐབས་གཞན་ལས་མིན། །དམ་ཚིག་ནོར་བུ་རིན་པོ་ཆེ། །ས་གཞི་རྒྱ་མཚོ་རྡོ་རྗེ་གླུ། །ཐུལ་པ་གཅིག་པུ་སྟོང་པ་རྫོགས་སོ། །

126

།ཐམས་ཅད་ནམ་མཁའི་མཚན་ཉིད་དེ། །སྣ་ཚོགས་འཇིག་རྟེན་བམ་ས་གཡོ་དང་། །རྒྱལ་བ་མངོན་བྱུང་ཐམས་ཅད་ཀུན། །ནམ་མཁའི་དབྱིངས་སུ་མཉམ་པ། །
དུས་བཞི་ཕྱོགས་བཅུ་གང་ནའང་མེད། །རྒྱལ་སྲས་ཡབ་ཡུམ་ལ་སོགས་པ། །ཐམས་ཅད་ནམ་མཁའི་ངང་དུ་ཐིམ། །དེ་ཤེས་དེ་ལས་མི་འདའ་བ། །ཡེ་ཤེས་སླ་མེད་
སྨད་པོ་ཆེ། །འབྱུང་བ་ཆེན་པོ་བཅོམ་ལྡན་འདས། །ཆུ་བ་བར་གནས་པས་བཅོམ་ལྡན་འདས། །འགྲོ་བ་ཀུན་ལ་རང་བཞིན་གནས། །ཕྱིན་ཅི་ལོག་ཏུ་རྣམ་བརྟགས་ཀྱང་། །
མདོར་བསྡུས་དམ་པ་མ་ལུས་ལས། །གྲོལ་བ་རང་བྱུང་གཞན་ལས་མེད། །གཉིས་མེད་བྱང་ཆུབ་མཆོག་འབྱུང་བ། །ཡེ་ཤེས་མི་འགྱུར་ཐིག་ལེ་འདི། །ཐུབ་གནས་གཅིག་
པུ་སྟོང་པ་རྫོགས། །ཟད་མེད་རིན་ཆེན་གཏེར་ཡིན་ཏེ། །ཀུན་ལ་ཁྱབ་ཅིང་སྣ་ཚོགས་སྐྱེན། །འདི་ནི་བཅོམ་ལྡན་འདས་ཉིད་དོ། །སེམས་ཅན་སྙིང་པོ་ཡིན་པའི་ཕྱིར། །འགྲོ་བ་
ཀུན་ལ་རང་བཞིན་གནས། །ཞེས་གསུངས་སོ། །རྡོ་རྗེ་སེམས་དཔའ་ནམ་མཁའ་ཆེ་རྒྱལ་པོ་རྒྱས་པའི་རྒྱུད་ལས། །གབ་པ་གསང་བ་མངོན་དུ་བྱུང་བའི་ལེའུ་སྟེ་བཞི་པའོ།།
།དེ་ནས་བཅོམ་ལྡན་འདས་ཀྱིས་སྤྱན་ཅིག་ཤེས་མ་གོས་པའི་ཏིང་ངེ་འཛིན་ལ་སྙོམས་པར་ཞུགས་ནས་ཆེད་དུ་བརྗོད་པ་འདི་བརྗོད་དོ། །བླ་མེད་དཔེ་བ

ཤ ཉེ

༄༅། །པའི་མཆོག་ཉིད་ལས། །ཉོན་མོངས་ལྔ་དང་ལྡན་པ་ཡིས། །ལས་སུ་གཉེར་བྱས་ཆོ་ག་དེ་ལ། །བསྒྲུབ་པར་བྱ་བཅུད་པར་དེ། །དེ་ཉིད་མཆོག་ཏུ་
གྲུབ་པ་ལ། །བསྒྲུབ་པ་པར་བྱེད་པ་བཟླན་མེད། །གཙང་དང་སྣ་བའི་སྒྲོ་མེད་ན། །དེ་ནི་ཐེག་མཆོག་ལྷ་ལ་མཁས། །དེ་ལ་སྐྱོན་ཀྱིས་བསྒོམ་མེད་པས། །ཇི་ལྟར་ལས་ངན་སྤྱོད་
པ་རྣམས། །བླ་མེད་ཐེག་པའི་སྤྱོད་དུ་བསྒྲགས། །རང་གི་བྱང་ཆུབ་སེམས་སུ་རྟོགས་ནས། །གཞན་ལ་སྤྱུ་རྣམ་པར་དག་འགྱུར་ན། །མཐོང་ལུ་མི་སྒྱུར་བས་ན། །ཟླན་མེད་པའི་
གནས་སུ་འགྲོ། །གཙང་སྣ་མེད་པའི་ཐབས་ཟབ་ཞིང་། །དགེ་སློང་འབྱུག་ཅིང་སྐུར་བྱེད་པ། །སངས་རྒྱས་མེད་པ་བཞིན་ང་ལ་སྦྱོར། །ཀླབ་ང་མདེ་སྤྲེ་སྤྲེ་ག་ཏུ་ཚིང་། །སྒྲིག་པ་
འབར་བ་སུ་སྤྱོད་པ། །ཐེག་པའི་དོན་ལ་མཁས་པ་སྟེ། །རང་སེམས་བརྟན་པོ་རྣམ་དག་ན། །སྤྱོད་པའི་སྐྱོན་ཀྱིས་མི་གོས་ཏེ། །སངས་རྒྱས་མཉེས་ཏེ་ཆེས་ཁྱུང་འཛིན། །
བླ་མེད་ལམ་ལ་ཡི་ནས་གནས། །བདེ་གཤེགས་རྒྱལ་བའི་སྐུ་ཉིད་ལས། །དཔག་ཚིང་སྤྲིན་ཏུ་དུ་མིན་སྤྱོར། །སྤྲིན་ཅིས་བསྒོ་རུ་མེད་པ་སྟེ། །ཡང་སང་སངས་རྒྱས་དང་ལེགས་ངས
རྒྱས། ༔ །འདུས་མ་བྱས་པའི་སྙིང་པོ་ཡང་དེ། །བསྒྲུབ་ཏུ་མེད་དེ་བསྒྲུབ་པར་གསུངས། །དེ་རྟོགས་སྒྲུབ་པས་མཐག་ཏུ་ནི། །རྒྱལ་བ་རྣམས་དང་དབྱེར་མེད་དེ། །མཚམས་མེད་ 127

ལྷ་ཡིས་སྒྲིབ་མི་ནུས། །ཆོས་རྣམས་ཀུན་གྱི་དོན་སྟོན་པ། །དེ་ནི་ཤིན་ཏུ་བདེ་བའི་དོན། །ཡང་དག་ཆོས་མཆོག་དེ་བཞིན་ཉིད། །གཙང་སྣ་མེད་པ་ཀུན་སྤྱད་ཅིང་། །སྙིང་རྗེ་མེད་
པར་ཀུན་བསད་པ། །མཆོག་གི་མཆོག་ལྷ་མཆོག་གི་སྐུ། །དེ་བཞིན་གཤེགས་པ་ཀུན་གྱི་སྐུའོ། །ཞེས་གསུངས་སོ། །རྡོ་རྗེ་སེམས་དཔའ་ནམ་མཁའ་ཆེ་རྒྱལ་པོ་རྒྱས་པའི་རྒྱུད་
ལས ༔ ཐེག་པའི་འཁོར་ལོ་བསྐོར་བ་བླ་ན་མེད་པའི་ཐེག་པ་སྟེ་ལེའུ་ལྔ་པའོ།། །།དེ་ནས་ཡང་བཅོམ་ལྡན་འདས་ཀྱིས་རང་གི་ཀྱིལ་འཁོར་ཐམས་ཅད་ལ་བུ
བ་དང་བ་ཤང་གཅིས་མཆོད་ནས་རྒྱལ་པོ་ཡིན་པའི་ཏིང་ངེ་འཛིན་ལ་སྙོམས་པར་ཞུགས་ནས་ཆ་དང་དུ་བརྗོད་པ་འདི་བརྗོད་དོ། །རང་གི་བྱང་ཆུབ་སེམས་རྟོགས་ནས། །རང་བྱུང་ཡེ་ཤེས་
རང་ཤར་ན། །བདག་ལས་དཀྱིལ་འཁོར་མེད་ཤེས་ཏེ། །དཀྱིལ་འཁོར་བདག་པོ་བདག་ཉིད་ལ། །ཚོས་རྣ་བྲི་རྣམས་དབུལ་མི་འབྲུ། །འདོད་ཡོན་ལྔ་པོས་མཆོད་བྱ་ཞིང་། །
མཉམ་པའི་སྒྲུབ་རྫས་བ་ཤང་གཅིག་ཡིས། །ལུས་སྐུ་ཟླ་ཞིང་མཆོད་བྱེད་པ། །དེས་ནི་རིགས་རྣམས་ཀུན་མཉེས་ཏེ། །ངེས་མེད་སྟོང་དང་སྟོང་ཉིད་དུ། །བ་ཤང་གཅིག་མི་
གཙང་ཞུ་ཁྲག་རྣམས། །བློ་ལྡན་མཁས་པས་རབ་བཀང་སྟེ། །བདག་ཉིད་དཀྱིལ་འཁོར་ཆེན་པོ་ལ། །ཉི་མ་རེ་རུ་བ་རེ་དབུལ་བར་བྱ། །མི་དམིགས་མཁའ་དབྱིངས་རྣམ་པར 128

129

༄༅། །དེ་ནས། །རང་བྱུང་ཡེ་ཤེས་ཀློང་ནས་འཕྲོས། །ངང་གིས་ཤར་ཅིང་རང་བཞིན་འབྱུང་། །མཁས་པས་མི་གཙང་སྣ་ཚོགས་པ། །སྤྱོད་པས་རྣམ་དག་
ནང་སྦྱུགས་ནས། །བདག་ལ་བདག་གིས་མཆོད་བྱས་ན། །[illegible]ལ་བའི་དཀྱིལ་འཁོར་མ་ལུས་མཉེས། །ཐབས་ལ་མཁས་པ་ཆེན་པོ་ཡིས། །རང་རིག་དཀྱིལ་འཁོར་རང་གི་
སེམས། ༈ གདོད་ནས་ལྷུན་གྱིས་གྲུབ་པ་དེ། །བདག་ཉིད་དཀྱིལ་འཁོར་ཡིན་པ་ལ། །མི་གཙང་བས་ན་མཆོད་བྱས་པས། །འབྱུང་བ་རྒྱུའི་དཀྱིལ་འཁོར་མཆོད་པ་དང་། །
ཀུན་སྤྱོད་དངོས་གྲུབ་རང་གིས་སེམས་བས། །ཆུར་བྱུང་དང་དངོས་གྲུབ་ཆེན་པོ་འདིས། །བདག་མཆོད་དཀྱིལ་འཁོར་འབྱུང་བ་ར་ལས། །དཀྱིལ་འཁོར་རབ་ཏུ་འབར་བ་ཡི། །ཁྲོ་
བདག་ཆེན་པོས་ཡུལ་བསྒྲུབ་ནས། །ཡི་གེ་སྔོན་དུ་བྲིས་པ་བཞིན། །དཔའ་བོའི་སྙིང་དུ་འབྱུང་འགྱུར་ཡང་། །ཞི་བ་མ་བཅོས་ཆོས་ཀྱི་སྐུ། །འཁོར་འཁྱུར་མེད་པ་མཐོང་
ཡིན་པས། །འདུས་མ་བྱས་པའི་ཆོས་ཉིད་ནི། །འདོད་ཞེས་མི་མཆེད་ཚིག་ལས་འདས། །སྐུ་ཡི་ཕྱག་རྒྱ་རྫོགས་པར་གསལ། །ཉོན་མོངས་ལ་ལྷ་ནི་རྒྱལ་བའི་ཞིང་། །
ཉོན་མོངས་ལ་བསོགས་པ་སྤྱོད་ནས་འདས། །བྱ་རྒྱུ་བསང་དག་རྒྱས་གཞན་ནས་མིན། །འདོད་ཆགས་ལ་སོགས་དཀྱིལ་འཁོར་ཉིད། །དཀྱིལ་འཁོར་ཆེན་པོ་མཆོག་གི་མཆོག །

130

གང་ཞིག་དེ་ལ་འཇུག་བྱེད་པ། །སྙིང་པོའི་དཀྱིལ་འཁོར་བུ་ལྟར། །ཡིད་ལ་འཕྲད་པ་སྣ་ཚོགས་འགྲུབ། །གསང་སྔགས་བདག་བློ་མི་འགྱུར་བ། །ཀུན་གཞི་རིག་པའི་རྩེ་མོ་
ཤར། ༈ དཀྱིལ་འཁོར་བདག་པོར་ཅིར་ཡང་སྣང་། །སྣང་མེད་མ་སྐྱེས་དབྱིངས་སུ་རྫོགས། །ཞེས་གསུངས་སོ། །རྡོ་རྗེ་སེམས་དཔའ་ནམ་མཁའ་ཆེ་རྒྱལ་པོ་རྒྱས་པའི་
རྒྱུད་ལས། མཆོད་པ་མི་དམིགས་པར་བསྟན་པའི་ལེའུ་སྟེ་དྲུག་པའོ།། ||དེ་ནས་བཅོམ་ལྡན་འདས་ཀྱིས་བསྒོམ་དུ་མེད་པའི་ཏིང་ངེ་འཛིན་
ལ་སྙོམས་པར་ཞུགས་ནས་ཚིག་ཏུ་བརྗོད་པའི་བརྗོད་དོ། །སངས་རྒྱས་བྱང་ཆུབ་གང་བསྒྲུབ་པ། །ཡི་གེ་མེད་པའི་དོན་ལ་བལྟ། །སྙིང་པོ་མེད་པའི་གསུང་ལ་བརྟག །སྒྲ་
བ་མེད་པའི་ཚིག་ཉིད་ལ། །མཐའ་ཙམ་ལ་བཞག་ན་སྒོམ་པ་ཡིན། །དེ་དང་དེ་རུ་ཉི་ཚེ་མ་བཙལ་ན། །དེ་ལས་དེ་བཞིན་དེ་མི་འགྱུར། །ཡང་དག་སངས་རྒྱས་ལམ་དུ་འབྱུང་། །
ཅིར་ཡང་མི་སྣང་ནམ་མཁའི་དབྱིངས། །དེ་བཞིན་བདེ་ཆེན་སྒྲུབ་དང་བྲལ། །མིང་མིག་སྣང་མེད་ཆོས་ཉིད་ལ། །སྒོམ་པ་ཡིད་ལ་མི་འབྱུང་བ། །མཐའ་ཙམ་ལ་བཞག་འགོམ་
པའོ། ༈ ནང་དང་ཕྱི་རོལ་དོན་ཉིད་ལ། །ཆགས་མེད་གནས་པ་བདེ་བའི་ཡུལ། །དེ་ལ་གང་འགོག་གཟུང་ལ་མ་མཆོག །སངས་རྒྱས་ཀུན་དང་དེ་ཞི་དང་། །སྟོན་པ་རྡོ་རྗེ་ཀུན་གྱི

ཀ

131

༄༅། ཐུགས་ཀྱང་ །ཡེ་ཤེས་ལྷ་ལྔ་ནམ་སྙིང་པོའི་སྙིང་། །གསུང་བའི་སྙིང་པོ་ངེས་པ་ཡིན། །འབྲས་བུ་ཀུན་གྱི་ཡི་མ་ཆུར་པ། །ཡེ་ཤེས་རྡོ་རྗེ་མཁའ་
འདྲ་སྟེ། །ཅི་ཡང་མི་དམིགས་གསལ་དེ་སྤྲུལ་ལས། །དུས་བཞི་སངས་རྒྱས་མ་ལུས་ཀྱིས། །བསྐལ་པ་གྲངས་མ་དུ་བཅུ་ལ་སྦྱར་ཀྱང་། །སངས་རྒྱས་ཀྱིས་ཀྱང་
མི་གྲགས་ཏེ། །དམིགས་མེད་ནམ་མཁའ་འདྲ་བུ་ཡི་དབུས། །དམིགས་སུ་མེད་པ་རྟོགས་ནས་སྒོམ། །སངས་རྒྱས་བྱང་ཆུབ་སེམས་ཀྱང་དཔའ་ཉིད། །དགོངས་
སུ་མེད་པའི་དོན་ལ་དགོངས། །དཔྱད་དུ་མེད་པའི་དོན་ལ་སྤྱོད། །གཞིག་ཏུ་མེད་པའི་སྙིང་པོས་བཞིག །བསམ་དུ་མེད་པའི་དོན་ལ་བསམ། །གང་ཡང་བསྒོམ
དུ་མེད་པའི་ངང་། །དེ་བཞིན་བཞག་ན་བསྒོམ་ཞེས་བྱ། །མི་སྐྱེ་མི་འགག་རྣམ་པར་དག །གདོད་ནས་བརྗོད་དུ་མེད་པ་ལ། །སྤྲོས་མེད་ཚོགས་ལ་ལས་འདས་པའི
སྤྱོད། །རང་གི་ངོ་བོ་རབ་སྟན་དུ་མེད། །ཡེ་ནས་རྟོགས་པ་མེད་ཕྱོགས་རྒྱ་ལ་བས། །རང་ཤར་བ་སྐྱེ་ཤེས་བུ་གྲུབ་མེད་རས། །དེ་ལ་སྤྱོད་ས་པ་མི་དགོས་ཏེ། །ངང་ངོས་མེད
ངོ་བོ་ཉིད་ཀྱིས་པ་དག །མི་འགྱུར་རྡོ་རྗེ་ཐེག་པ་འདི། །ཐེག་པའི་མཆོག་སྟེ་ལྷུན་མེད། །གདོད་ནས་སྟོང་པའི་ཚིག་ཉིད་ལ། །དངོས་པོ་རབ་སྟོན་པར་མ་གསུངས

132

ཏེ། །དེ་ལྟ་མ་ཡིན་ཕྱོགས་རྒྱུ་ལ་འབྱུང་། །མི་ཆགས་མི་རྟོགས་མི་གནས་པས། །ཏིང་ངེ་འཛིན་ནི་ཡོ་ཆགས་མི་གནས། །བདུད་རྩི་བྱང་ཆུབ་སེམས་ཉིད་དེ་ནི། །
བསམ་མེད་ནི་བ་སམ་བསྒོམ་དུ་མེད། །ཤེས་རབ་ཐབས་ཀྱི་ཚོགས་གཉིས་ནས། །དེ་ཕྱིར་སེམས་ལས་སངས་རྒྱས་མེད། །ཡིད་མའི་ཐ་སྙད་དུ་བཙམ་ཡང་། །འདི་ལ
མེད་པས་སྒོ་སྐུར་མེད། །ཉེ་བ་ཙམ་དམིགས་བྱའི་ཡུལ་མེད་པས། །བསྐལ་པར་བྲུ་བ་ཡོད་པ་མིན། །བྱང་ཆུབ་སེམས་ལ་གཏིང་དཔག་མེད། །ཧེ་སྐྱུར་བརྗོད་པའི་ཡུལ
ལས་འདས། །མི་ཏུ་གདགས་པའི་ཧེ་ཆ་མེད་པས། །སྒྲ་ཐུགས་མ་འདྲེས་དམ་པའི་མཆོག །འདི་ནི་བརྟན་གཉིས་བསྐུལ་བ་མི་དགོས། །ཡི་གེས་མཚོན་དུ་རྡུལ་ཙམ
མེད། །བརྟགས་པ་རང་ཀ་ལ་ཡོད་པ་མིན། །རྣར་སྒྲོ་ཉམས་ཀྱིས་བསམ་དུ་ཡང་། །མ་བུས་མ་ས་གྲིག་ལོ་སྐྲ་མེད་པས། །བྱང་ཆུབ་ཡིན་ཞེས་བསམ་མི་རུང་།།
ཞེས་གསུངས་སོ། །རྡོ་རྗེ་སེམས་དཔའ་ནམ་མཁའ་ཆེ་རྒྱལ་པོ་རྒྱས་པའི་རྒྱུད་ལས། བསམ་བཞིན་བསྒོམ་དུ་མེད་པའི་ལེའུ་སྟེ་བདུན་པའོ།།
།།དེ་ནས་བཅོམ་ལྡན་འདས་ཀྱིས་བསམ་ཞིང་བསྒོམ་དུ་ཡོད་པའི་ཏིང་ངེ་འཛིན་ལ་སྙོམས་པར་ཞུགས་ནས་ཆེད་དུ་བརྗོད་པ་འདི་བརྗོད་དོ། །སྒྱུ་མེད་བྱང་ཆུབ་སེམས

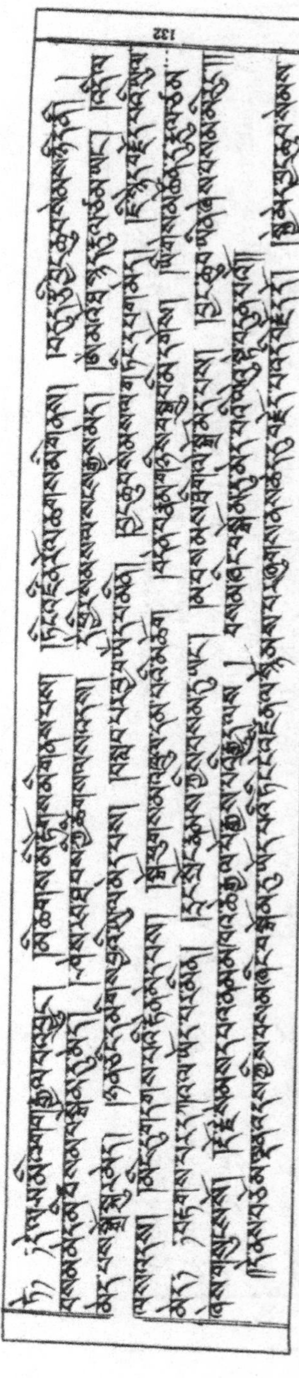

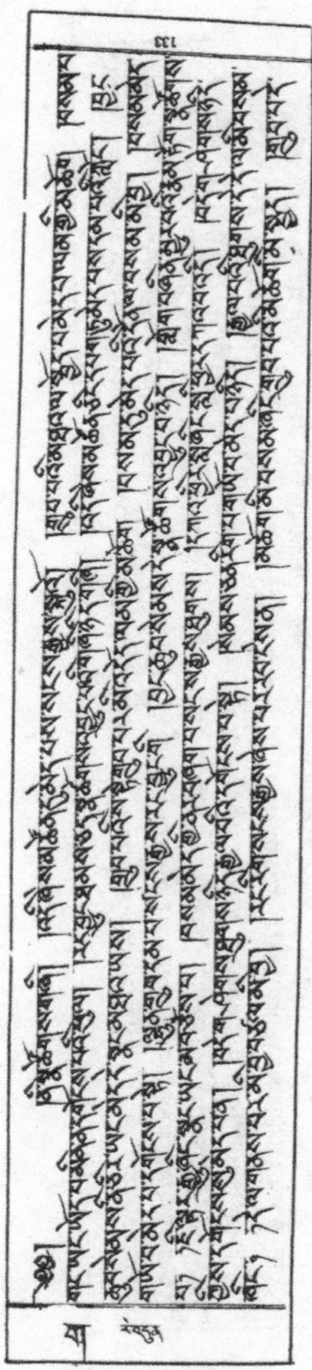

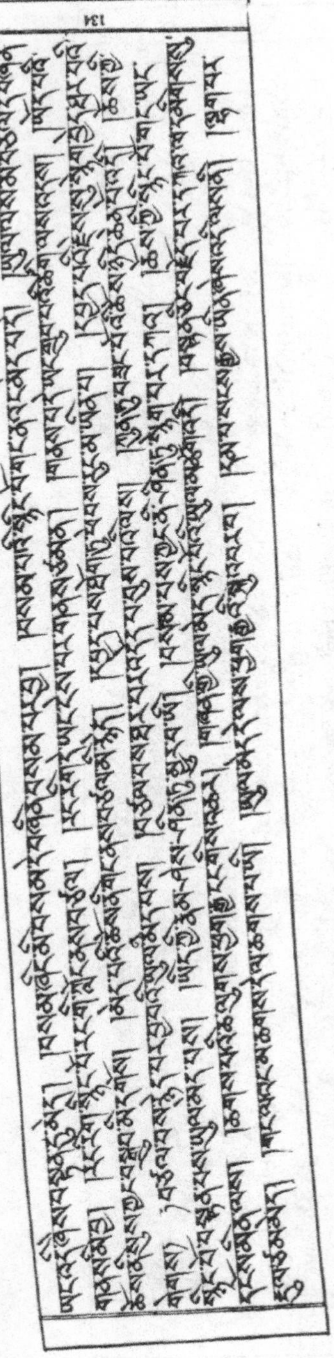

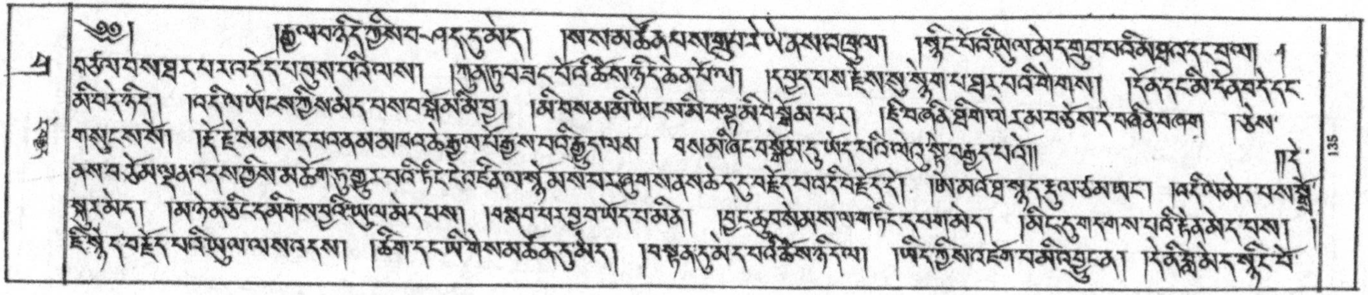

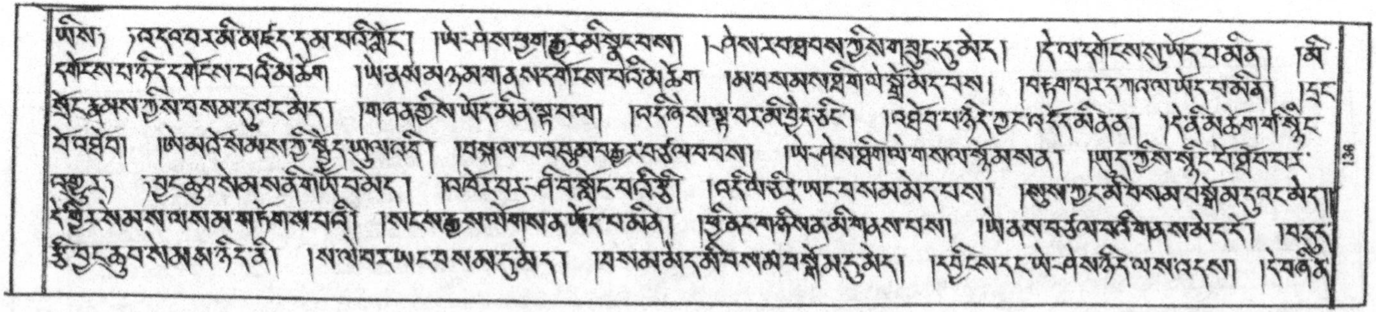

137

༄༅། །བསམ་མེད་སྙིང་པོ་ལ། །ཅིར་ཡང་མ་བསམ་མཉམ་བཞག་པ། །དེ་བཞིན་ཉིད་དུ་གནས་པ་དེ། །དེ་ནི་བསམ་མེད་སྙིང་པོའི་མཆོག །བསམ་
པར་བྱ་བ་གང་ཟག་མེད། །སྟོང་པ་ཉིད་དང་ཆོས་ཀྱི་དབྱིངས། །རང་རིག་སྙིང་པོ་དེ་བཞིན་ཉིད། །ཅིར་ཡང་མི་གཡོ་ཀློང་ནས་བཙལ། །བྱང་ཆུབ་འདོད་པའི་ཐབས་ཆེན་
ནི། །ལུང་བསྟན་མི་འགྱུར་བསྟན་དུ་མེད། །ཡང་དག་སངས་རྒྱས་དེ་ཉིད་ལ་ནས། །སྤྲུལ་པ་པོ་ཡང་སྟོང་སངས་རྒྱས། །རྣ་ཞིང་དམ་པར་མི་འགྱུར་བའི། །དེ་ལ་ཚེ་སྐྱི་
སྙིང་པོ་ཡོད། །མཁས་སོ་ལ་མི་མཐོང་ལྷུང་དེའི་ལམ། །འཕགས་པ་རྣམས་ཀྱི་ཡོངས་ནས་གནས། །སྤྲུལ་བསྟོད་ལ་གཟུང་འཛིན་ལ་མཁའ་དང་པ། །སྙིང་མེད་སངས་རྒྱས་ཁང་དེ་ར་
པའི་ཐབས། །ཡེ་ཤེས་སྒྲོན་ཡང་ས་ཆེན་པོའི་ཡུལ། །ཕྱིན་ཀ་ན་ཀྱི་མཆོག་ཏུ་བསྔགས། །ཞེས་གསུངས་སོ། །རྡོ་རྗེ་སེམས་དཔའ་ནམ་མཁའ་ཆེ་རྒྱལ་
པོ་རྒྱས་པའི་རྒྱུད་ལས། བསམ་སྒྲུབ་ལ་ས་འདས་པའི་ལེའུ་སྟེ་དགུ་པའོ།། །།དེ་ནས་ཡང་བཅོམ་ལྡན་འདས་ཀྱིས་ཆོས་ཐམས་
ཅད་རང་བཞིན་གྱིས་རྣམ་པར་དག་པའི་ཏིང་ངེ་འཛིན་ལ་སྙོམས་པར་ཞུགས་ནས་ཚིག་འདུ་བརྗོད་པ་འདི་བརྗོད་དོ། །དཀའ་ཐུབ་རྟགས་བསྐྱལ་བའི་ཡིད་བྱུང་མི་

138

དགོས། །ཚོགས་པས་གཅུ་ལ་བསྒོམ་པ་འཁྲུལ་པའི་ལམ། །གཞན་ནས་བཙལ་བས་ཐོབ་རེ་འཁྲུལ་པའི་ཆོས། །སངས་རྒྱས་གཞན་ནས་ཐོབ་རེ་ཉེར་བའི་ལམ།
ཀུན་རྫོབ་བཅོས་ལ་སྤྱོད་པ་རྟོགས་པའི་རྒྱུན། །དེ་ལྟའི་ཡུལ་ཅན་སངས་རྒྱས་མཐོང་བ་མེད། །ཡང་དག་བདེ་གཤེགས་ཅིར་ཡང་མི་དམིགས་པས། །སངས་རྒྱས་
སྟོན་པས་མིང་དུ་བཏགས་པས་བཞེར། །སྟོན་པས་བསྟན་པས་བྱང་ཆུབ་ལམ་མི་རྙེད། །མི་གནས་མི་དམིགས་སྤྲོས་འགག་མེད་པའི་དོན། །བརྗོད་ཅིང་དཔག་ཏུ་མེད་པ་
གསུང་དུ་འང་མེད། །སྟོན་པའི་ཞལ་ནས་གསུངས་ཞེས་བྱ་བ་འགའ། །ཡེ་མ་མཐོང་ཉིས་བགྲོད་པའི་རྒྱུ་ངེས་བྱང་ཆུབ་ལམ་མི་རྙེད། །མི་གཡོ་རང་བཞིན་གནས་པ་ལ་
སྣང་ཆེན་མ་བྱུང་ན། །རྟག་གསུམ་ནང་གི་ཁ་དར་ཆེ་བའི་གླ་གས་ཡོངས་མེད། །འཁྲུལ་རྟོགས་བསམ་ལ་རང་འཁྲུལ་པའི་རྒྱུན། །བཙལ་ནས་བྱང་ཆུབ་འདོད་པ་རྟོགས་པའི་
གཞི། །བདེ་བའི་མཆོག་ན་བསམ་རྟོགས་ཡུལ་དང་བྲལ། །བྱང་ཆུབ་འཁྲུལ་པ་ཡེ་ཧྲ་མ་ཆོས་ལ་ཟླ། །དེ་ལྟའི་ཡུལ་ཅན་སངས་རྒྱས་མཐོང་བ་མེད། །ཟད་མེད་མི་ཟད་
ཟད་མཐའ་མེད་པ་དེ། །ཅིར་ཡང་མི་སྤྲོ་ཅིར་ཡང་སྣང་བ་ལ། །འདུལ་བ་མ་དེ་རྗེར་བཏགས་པ་ཡིན་ནམ་ཞེར། །ཕྱིན་པའི་རིམ་པ་ཐུ་བ་ག་ཏིང་ཅན་མེད། །དགོན་མཆོག

ཕ

༄༅། །གསུམ་མེད་དབང་པོའི་སྤྱོད་ཡུལ་མིན། །གཟུགས་མེད་ཆོས་སྐུས་བ་ཤར་བ་གཏིང་མེད་ཀྱང་། །མེ་ལོང་ཆུ་ཟླ་བཞིན་དུ་ལྷ་ཚོགས་ཀྱིས། །
བ་ཤར་བ་ར་སྣང་ཞིང་ཐེག་པ་བསམ་མི་ཁྱབ། །བསམ་གཏན་ཏིང་འཛིན་ངོ་བོ་ལ་ཆགས་མི་སྲུང་། །ཡེ་རྫོགས་བྱང་ཆུབ་སེམས་ཀྱི་རང་བཞིན་དེ། །ཡེ་སངས་རྒྱས་པ་རང་གི་
སེམས་ཡིན་ཞིང་། །བྱང་ཆུབ་འབྱུང་བ་ཡི་རྣམ་ཆོས་ལ་ཟབ། །གསུར་རིང་དུ་རིག་པ་མ་ཤར་ན། །སྟོན་པས་བསྟན་པས་ཡི་གེ་རྟོག་པའི་རྒྱུན། །རྡོ་རྗེ་སེམས་དཔའ་
རང་གི་བྱང་ཆུབ་སེམས། །རྒྱལ་བ་སངས་རྒྱས་རྣམས་ཀྱི་གཞི་ཤེས་པ་མའི་འདི། །སྣང་དང་ཕྱི་རོལ་དོན་ལ་ཡང་མི་སྟེར། །སྟོན་པས་བསྟན་དུ་འདི་ཡི་མིང་མི་རྟེད། །འདི
ཞེས་བསྟན་དུ་གང་ཡང་འགྲུབ་པ་མེད། །བསྟན་པ་བར་གོ་བར་འགྱུར་མིན་གསུང་ཚིག་མིན། །སྐྱེ་ཤིང་འཕོ་བའི་ཆོས་མིན་གཅིག་ཕུར་སྣང་། །སྙིང་པོའི་རང་བཞིན་གནས་པ་
ཆོས་ཀྱི་སྐུ། །ཞེས་གསུངས་སོ། །རྡོ་རྗེ་སེམས་དཔའ་ནམ་མཁའ་ཆེ་རྒྱལ་པོ་རྒྱས་པའི་རྒྱུད་ལས། ། ཆོས་ཐམས་ཅད་རྣམ་པར་དག་པའི་ལེའུ་སྟེ་སྡུ་བཅུ་པའོ།།
༎དེ་ནས་བཅོམ་ལྡན་འདས་ཀྱིས་སྤྲོ་བ་མེད་པའི་ཏིང་ངེ་འཛིན་ལ་སྙོམས་པར་ཞུགས་ནས་ཚིག་དུ་བརྗོད་པ་འདི་བརྗོད་དོ། །མངོན་སུམ་ཀུན་ཏུ་མི་རྟོག

139

ཡང་ས་པའི་སྙིང་པོ་ལ། །གཟུང་བའི་ཡུལ་མེད་སེམས་ཀྱི་ཤེས་ཀྱང་མེད། །ཆོས་སྐུ་ཀུན་ཏུ་ཁྱབ་པས་བསྟན་པའི་ཚིག་མེད་དེ། །རང་བྱུང་མི་དམིགས་ཡུལ་ལ་ཇི་བཞིན་
གནས། །ངོ་མཚར་མཐོང་བའི་ཡུལ་མེད་དེ་ལ་མཐོང་བའི་མིག །རྣམ་པར་རྟོག་པ་མེད་པས་སྤྱོད་པའི་ཡུལ་ཡང་མེད། །སྐུ་ཉིད་སྐུ་རུ་སྣང་ཡང་ཡིན་ལུགས་མེད་པའི་སྐུ། །
མཐའ་ལ་མཚོན་དུ་མེད་པས་དབྱིངས་ལ་ཕྱི་བ་མེད། །ཆོས་འདི་ཡི་རི་ལ་ཉམས་ཕག་བསྟན་པ་དཀར་ཕྱི་སྒྲ་ཡང་མེད། །མཁའ་འདྲ་ཆོས་ཀྱི་དབྱིངས་ཏེ་དབྱེར་མེད་ཡེ་
ཤེས་བྲལ། །སྟོང་པའི་སྟོང་པ་ཡིན་ཏེ་སྟོང་པ་ཉིད་ཀྱང་མེད། །སྒོམ་པ་ཡིད་ཀྱིས་གཟུང་མེད་ཡུལ་མ་ཚལ་མཆུ་མེད།། སྤྱོད་པའི་རྗེས་སུ་རྟོག་པ་བཟང་བའི་གེགས། །མཐའ་ཅོལ་
བསམ་ཐར་པ་ར་འདོད་པ་བསྒྲུབ་པའི་ལས། །ཆོས་ཀྱི་སྙིང་པོ་གང་ཡང་དངོས་མིན་པས། །ཆགས་པའི་ཆེ་ལུགས་ལ་ཕྱག་རྒྱ་དང་གཞིས་འཆར། །སྒྲ་ངན་འདས་དང་འཁོར་བ་ལ་སྣ་
ཚོགས་པ། །ཡེ་ནས་དབྱེར་མེད་ཀྱི་ལ་འཁོར་གསུམ་དུ་འདུས། །མི་རྟོག་མདངས་མཉམ་པར་སྣང་བ་རྒྱས་ཚུལ་དུ། །མི་གཉིས་ཆོས་སྐུ་ཡེ་ནས་མ་གཡོས་ལས། །
ཆེ་བའི་ཡིན་ཏན་གཟུགས་ཀྱི་སྐུ་གཉིས་རྒྱས། །ཆོས་རྣམས་སྣ་ཚོགས་སྤྲུལ་འདས་འཁོར་བ། །དེ་ཡི་འཁོར་ཆེན་པོ་རྣམ་པ་གསུམ་དུ་བསྒོམ། །ཆོས་རྣམས་ཐམས

140

ཀ དོན་གཅིག

༄༅། །ཅིར་སྣང་མའི་རང་བཞིན་ནི། །རྒྱུ་ལྡན་རྩལ་དུ་སྣང་སྟོང་མི་དམིགས་ས་གནས། །མི་དམིགས་སར་དམིགས་པ་ཉིད་ན་སྣ་ཚོགས་སྣང་། །དེ་བཞིན་
གཤེགས་པར་ཡེ་ནས་ཀུན་མཉམ་ཉིད་པས། །སེམས་ཅན་བསད་པ་ཡེ་ནས་ནམ་མཁའ་ཉིད། །ཁམས་གསུམ་འཁྲུལ་བ་བསད་པ་ནམ་མཁར་ཞི། །ཀུན་འབྱུང་མི་
བསྐྱོད་རང་ལས་རྒྱས་ཞིང་དག་ཏུ། །རང་བཞིན་ཡོངས་ཀྱིས་དག་པ་རིགས་ཀྱི་མཆོག །སྐུ་གསུང་ཐུགས་ཀྱི་བདག་པོ་རྡོ་རྗེའི་སྐུ། །བདེ་གཤེགས་ངོ་བོ་ཉིད་གཙང་གསོས་མེད
པ། །རྒྱལ་མཆོག་འགྲུབ་འགྲུབ་རའི་དཔལ་ཐུབ་ཚོམ་མེད། །གཞན་གྱི་ཡུལ་མེད་སྙིང་པོའི་ཡུལ་མཆོག་འདི། །བསྟན་ཅིང་བརྗོད་པར་དཀའ་ལ་དམིགས་པ་སྤྱུ་རྩལ་ཙམ་མེད། །
ནམ་མཁའ་ཡིན་པས་བསམ་པས་བཞག་ཏུ་མེད། །ཤིན་ཏུ་སྤྲུར་བའི་བསམ་པས་བསྙག་པར་དཀའ། །ཉིན་མོ་ལས་ལྟ་ཉིད་ཡེ་ནས་སྙིང་པོའི་ཆོས། །སྙིང་པོའི་སྙིང་པོ་
ཡིན་ཏེ་ཆོས་ཀྱི་སྐུ། །ཡེ་ནས་རང་བཞིན་མེད་དེ་རང་བཞིན་གནས། །ཀུན་ནས་སེ་ཏུ་སྨྲེད་དེ་སྒྲུབ་ཤུ་བ་དྲུག་ཀུན་དང་བྲལ། །རྩལ་སྦྲན་གཅིག་ལ་རྩལ་ཤེ་རྒྱུགས་ལ་གང་བུའི་རྩལ། །
རྩལ་བསྒོམ་མི་འདར་དུས་བཞིར་མཐོང་བ་འང་འབྲུལ། །ངོ་མཚར་ཀུན་བསྒྲུབས་ཀུན་དང་ལྡན་པ་ཡིས། །མཐོང་བའི་ཡུལ་མེད་ཡེ་ནས་མཐོང་བའི་མིག །འབྱུང་བའི་

141

ནམ་ཁའི་རྣམ་གྲངས་མང་པོ་མེད། །སྙིང་པོའི་ཡུལ་ལ་ལྟ་མེད་པས་ཆོས་ཀྱི་སྐུ། །གང་ཡང་མེད་པས་རོ་འདི་བསྟན་པར་དཀའ། །འདི་འདྲའི་ཡུལ་ལ་ནི་སྤྲོས་བསམ་བརྗོད་
ལས་འདས། །ཞེས་གསུངས་སོ། །རྡོ་རྗེ་སེམས་དཔའ་ནམ་མཁའ་ཆེ་རྒྱལ་པོ་རྒྱས་པའི་རྒྱུད་ལས། ། བྱ་མེད་ལྷུན་གྱིས་རྫོགས་པའི་ལེའུ་སྟེ་བཅུ་གཅིག་པའོ།།
།།དེ་ནས་བཅོམ་ལྡན་འདས་ཀྱིས་མི་གཡོ་བའི་ཏིང་ངེ་འཛིན་ལ་སྙོམས་པར་ཞུགས་ནས་ཚེད་དུ་བརྗོད་པ་འདི་བརྗོད་དོ། །ཡུངས་སོ་ཆེའི
མི་འགྱུར་བདེ་བའི་གློང་། །ཡེ་ནས་གནས་སོ་སྲུས་ཀྱང་གཞོམ་དུ་མེད། །རྣམ་པ་རང་དག་གོ་ཅིས་ཀྱང་བསྒྲིབ་ཏུ་མེད། །གདོད་ནས་དག་པས་གཉེན་པོས་ཅི་ལ་སྦྱངས།།
རང་གི་སེམས་ལས་མ་གཏོགས་ཆོས་མེད་ཕྱིར། །རང་གི་སེམས་འདི་དེ་དག་རྣམས་དག་འགྱུར་ན། །ཉན་ཐོས་མཆོག་ཆེན་བསད་པ་རྒྱལ་བའི་ཐྲས། །སངས་རྒྱས་འབྲུམ
བསད་པ་འང་དྲུང་རྒྱུ་བ་ལམ། །མི་དམིགས་རང་བྱུང་ཡེ་ཤེས་འབུམ་ལ་རོལ། །མི་འགྱུར་སྙིང་པོ་ནམ་མཁའི་དབྱིངས་ལ་རོལ། །ཉན་ཐོས་བསྒྲལ་བ་མ་ཡིན་བདེ་བའི་མཆོག །
གང་ལ་འང་སྟོང་ལོན་མེད་པ་ཐར་པའི་ལམ། །འཛིན་རྟོག་སྦྱོང་བ་མེད་པ་ཚོས་ཀྱི་དབྱིངས། །རང་རིག་ཆེན་པོའི་གློང་དུ་ཡེ་ནས་དག་འགྱུར་ན། །སེམས་ཅན་ཉན་ཐོས་མཆོག་

142

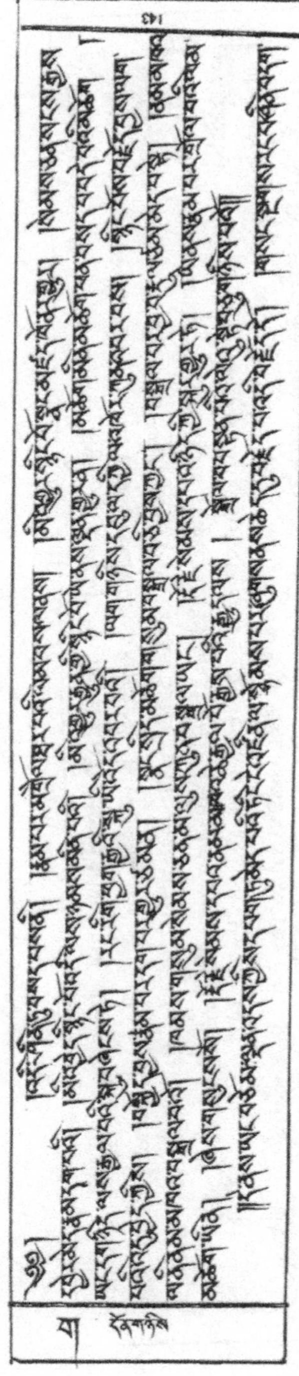

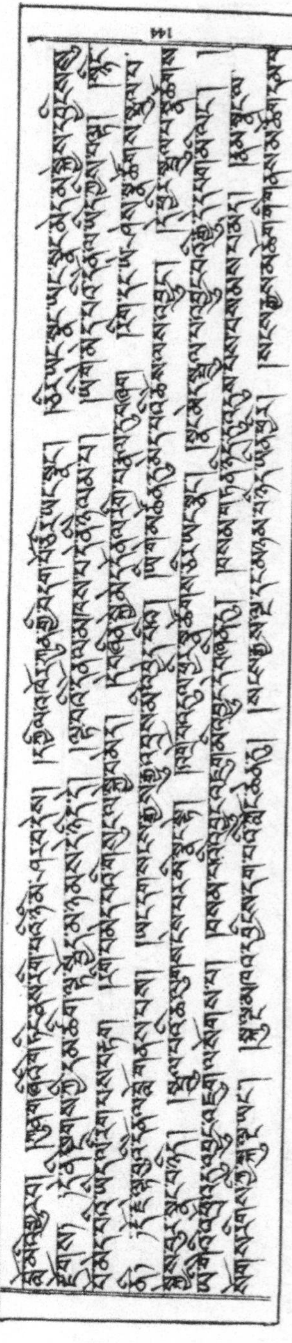

145

ཀ

༄༅། །ཧཱུྃ༔ ཐམས་ཅད་རྫོགས་ཡངས་པའི་ཀློང་ཡིན་ཕྱིར། །སྐུ་གཅིག་བསྒོམས་པས་རབ་འབྱིངས་ཀྱང་གསལ་བར་འགྱུར། །མི་འགྱུར་མི་ཤིགས་རྡོ་རྗེ་ནམ
མཁའི་ཀློང་། །ཐམས་ཅད་མ་ལུས་ལྷུན་གྱིས་རྫོགས་པའི་དཀྱིལ་འཁོར་ཆེ། །འཁོར་འདས་ཀུན་བསྐོར་སངས་རྒྱས་དེ་ལས་སྐུ་ཡང་འབར། །མི་འགྱུར་རང་རིག་ཅིར་ཡང་མི་འགྱུར
མཉམ་པའི་ངང་ལ་གནས་པ་སྟེ། །མི་དམིགས་པ་དང་སྒོམས་ཀློང་དེ་ར་རང་ངོ་བོ་མ་ཉམས་གཞག་ན། །སངས་རྒྱས་ཡང་དག་རྫོགས་པ་ཆེན་པོའི་མཆོག་དང་འདྲ་བར་སྟོན་པས
གསུངས། །ཞེས་གསུངས་སོ། །རྡོ་རྗེ་སེམས་དཔའ་ནམ་མཁའ་ཆེ་རྒྱལ་པོ་རྒྱལ་པའི་རྒྱུད་ལས། །ཐམས་ཅད་ཀློང་དུ་འགྱུར་བའི་ལེའུ་སྟེ་བཅུ་གསུམ་པའོ།།
།།དེ་ནས་བཅོམ་ལྡན་འདས་ཀྱིས་བཅུ་ལ་དུ་མེད་པའི་ཏིང་ངེ་འཛིན་ལ་སྙོམས་པར་ཞུགས་ནས་ཆེད་དུ་བརྗོད་པ་འདི་བརྗོད་དོ། །ཅིར་ཡང་མི་སྣང་གསལ
བ་ནམ་མཁའི་ངོ་བོ་ཉིད། །དེ་བཞིན་བདེ་ཆེན་སྤྲོས་བྲལ་ནམ་མཁའི་ངོ་བོ་ཉིད་འདི་ནི། །ཅིར་ཡང་མི་དམིགས་སྣང་མེད་ཆོས་ཉིད་ལ། །བསྒོམ་པ་ཡིད་ལ་མི་འགྱུར་མ་བཅོས་ལ
གཞག་ན་བསྒོམ། །ཉན་ཐོས་རང་རྒྱལ་མདོ་སྡེ་ནང་གཟུགས་སྣང་བར་འདོད་པ་དེ་དང་བཞི། །ཀྲི་ཡ་ཨ་ནུ་ཡ་སོགས་བསྐྱེད་རྫོགས་རྣམས་པར་འགྲོལ་བ་འདོད་པས། །འཇིག་གི་སྡ…

146

ཚོགས་སུ་སྒྲུབས་སུ་རུང་བ་པར་ནི་བ་ཀུན་ལ་རྣམ་བཅོལ་བ་ན། །འཚོལ་བ་དེ་ལས་དེ་བཞིན་ཉིད་དང་གིས་གནས་པའི་རྟོགས་པའི་དོན་མི་འབྱུང་། །ཡང་དག་རང་བྱུང་ཅི་ཡང་མི་ཚལ་བ
སངས་རྒྱས་དེ་དང་ལམ་རིང་འགྱུར། །ཤེས་རབ་ཐབས་མེད་ཞིག་ནས་ལྷག་མཐོང་མཉམ་སྒོམས་ཤིང་། །ཕྱིན་རིང་ཀ་འབས་དོན་ལ་བཙལ་ནས་རེག་པ་འདེད་པས། །
ཉན་ཐོས་བྱང་ཆུབ་སེམས་དཔས་བཙལ་བས་ཉམས། །གསང་བ་རྣམ་པ་བཞི་སྐུ་ར་སྤྱོད་ཕྱག་རྒྱའི་ཆ་ར་བབ་འདེ་དེ་དབང་མཆོག་གི་སྒྲོན། །བདེ་མཆོག་དེ་ནི་གང་ལ་འང་ཆགས་པ
མེད༑ ༑དེ་བཞིན་ཉིད་ལ་ཆགས་པ་གནས་ཀུན་ལ་རོལ་པ་བདེ་བའི་ལམ། །མཆོག་གི་སྤྱོད་པ་དེ་ལ་གང་འགོག་ཐར་པའི་ལམ་མཆོག་ཉིད། །ཁམས་གསུམ་མ་ལུས
ཡོངས་སུ་རྣམ་གྲོལ་བས། །སངས་རྒྱས་སྐུ་ཉིད་རྟོགས་སྣང་སྲིད་རྒྱུ་ཡིས་བཏབ། །མི་འགྱུར་ཀུན་ཏུ་བཟང་པོ་ཐུགས་སུ་ཆུད་པའི་ངང་ཉིད་ཀྱིས། །ཡེ་ཤེས་ཆེས་ཀྱི
དབྱིངས་ལ་ཡིད་ལ་འཁོར་བ་འང་རོལ་པའི་ཕྱིར། །ཡེ་ནས་ཀུན་བཟང་ངེས་དེ་ར་བ་བས་མེད་བ་རྣམ་གཡོ་གཉིས་ཀྱི་ས་ཞི། །གང་ལ་འདོད་ཆགས་དང་འཛིན་ངོ་བོ་མི
གནས༑ ༑མི་རྟག་མི་ཆགས་མི་གནས་པ་ཡང་གྲོལ། །དེ་ཉིད་སྤྲོད་པ་ར་ཀྱི་ཡང་ཞུམ་ལྷ་སུམ་ཚོགས་ཀྱི་མེད་པའོ། །གསུམ་རང་རིག་གློད་ནས་ཤར་བར་མ་འགྱུར

ཁ

༄༅། །ཀ༽ ༼ཚིག་དང་ཡི་གེ་མཚན་པ་འདི་ཡིས་དོན་མི་རྙེད། །ནུབ་པས་མ་ཉན་ཅིང་ཤེས་པ་ཤུས་མི་ཆོད་པས། །ལྷུ་ཡི་དབང་པོས་བརྗོད་དུ་རྒྱལ
ཙམ་མེད། །ཁམས་གསུམ་ལས་འདས་ནོར་བུ་རིན་པོ་ཆེ། །གང་ནས་བཙལ་ཀྱང་རྙེད་པར་མི་འགྱུར་ཏེ། །ཚིག་ཏུ་བརྗོད་པའི་ཚེ་ཤེས་ཙམ་ཡང་མེད་པའི་ཕྱིར། །
འདི་ཞེས་བསྒོམ་པ་བལྟ་རུ་རྡུལ་ཙམ་མེད། །ཅེས་གསུངས་སོ། །རྡོ་རྗེ་སེམས་དཔའ་ནམ་མཁའ་ཆེ་རྒྱལ་པོ་རྒྱས་པའི་རྒྱུད་ལས། །བཅོལ་བ་དང་བྲལ
བའི་ལེའུ་སྟེ་བཅུ་བཞི་པའོ།། ||དེ་ནས་བཅོམ་ལྡན་འདས་ཀྱིས་གཡོ་བ་མེད་པའི་ཏིང་ངེ་འཛིན་ལ་སྙོམས་པར་ཞུགས་ནས་ཚིག་ཏུ་བརྗོད་པའི
བརྗོད་དོ། །བྱང་ཆུབ་སེམས་ཀྱི་ངང་བཞིན་ཀུན་བཟང་ལ། །སྣང་སྲིད་སྣོད་བཅུད་ཚོགས་ཉིད་རང་བཞིན་ཏེ། །མ་ཡལ་མ་ཞི་རང་བཞིན་ཞི་བ་མེད། །ཆོས་རྣམས་ཐམས
ཅད་མ་ཡལ་མ་ཞི་བར། །རང་བཞིན་གསལ་ཏེ་ངོ་བོ་གཡོས་པ་མེད། །ཆོས་ཉིད་རང་བཞིན་སྤྲོས་མེད་ཞི་བ་སྟེ། །མ་ཡལ་མ་ཞི་རང་བཞིན་སྤྲོས་པ་མེད། །རང་བྱུང་ཡེ
ཤེས་མ་བསྒྲིབ་གསལ་བ་དེ། །མ་འགགས་མ་ཡལ་མ་ཞི་ཞི་བ་མེད། །སྟོན་པ་ཀུན་ཏུ་བཟང་པོར་ཉིད་དོ། །ཐམས་ཅད་བྱང་ཆུབ་སེམས་ལས་གཡོས་པ་མེད། །རང

147

བྱུང་ཡེ་ཤེས་རྒྱུ་རྐྱེན་མེད་པ་དེ། །རྒྱུ་དང་འབྲས་བུ་ཀུན་ལས་ཤིན་ཏུ་རྒྱལ། །རྒྱུ་འབྲས་ལྡོག་པ་ཅན་ལ་ཤིན་ཏུ་གསང་། །སེམས་ཉིད་མ་འགགས་གནས་མམ་བའི་དབྱིངས
ནས་རྒྱལ། །རྒྱུ་འབྲས་ཅན་ལ་མི་སྣང་ཤིན་ཏུ་གསང་། །མ་སྐྱེས་རྡོ་རྗེ་ཆོས་ཀྱི་དབྱིངས་ནས་རྒྱལ། །རྒྱུ་འབྲས་ཅན་ལ་མི་སྣང་ཤིན་ཏུ་གསང་། །སྣང་སྲིད་སྣོད་བཅུད
མ་བཅོས་ཆེ་བ་ཉིད་རྒྱལ། །རྒྱུ་འབྲས་ཅན་ལ་མི་སྣང་ཤིན་ཏུ་གསང་། །ནམ་མཁའ་ཁབ་སྐུ་མི་རྒྱུར་སྣང་བ་ལྔ། །བྱང་ཆུབ་སེམས་ཀྱི་ངོ་བོར་ཤིན་ཏུ་རྒྱལ། །རྒྱུ་འབྲས
ཅན་ལ་མི་སྣང་ཤིན་ཏུ་གསང་། །ཁམས་གསུམ་ཏུ་གསུམ་སྒྲ་གསུང་ཐུགས་གསུམ་རྒྱལ། །རྒྱུ་འབྲས་ཅན་ལ་མི་སྣང་ཤིན་ཏུ་གསང་། །རང་བཞིན་གསལ་ལ་ཏེ་ངོ་བོ་གཡོས
པ་མེད། ༼གཡོས་མེད་ངང་ལ་རྒྱུ་འབྲས་སྤྲུལ་བྱེད་པ། །དེ་ནི་ང་ཡི་ལུང་མིན་འདི་ལུང་ཡིན། །ང་ནི་དོན་དང་པ་མེད་པས་ཀུན་གྲུབ་སྟེ། །མི་འདོད་འདོད་པ་མེད་པར
རང་བཞིན་འགྲུབ། །འགྲུབ་ཙམ་ཙམ་བྱ་བང་ཡིས་སྨྲས་པ་མེད། །རྒྱུ་འབྲས་སྒྲུབ་པ་དེ་དག་རྣམས་ཀྱི་ཚིག་ཏུ་ཡིན། །ང་ཡི་སྒྲ་དང་སྐྱུར་པ་དགྲ་རྒྱུ་ཆེ། །ཡོད་དང་མེད་དང་གྲུབ
དང་མ་གྲུབ་དང་། །སྒྲ་དང་སྐྱུར་བ་བཏགས་པ་ཐམས་ཅད་ཀུན། །མི་རྟོག་ལས་ཅི་མི་ཉམ་པ་ཉིད་དུ་གནས། །མཉམ་པ་ཉིད་ལས་མ་གཏོགས་དགོངས་པ་ནི། །མང

148

༄༅། །རྒྱས་ཀུན་གྱི་མེས་པོ་ངས་མ་གསུངས། །ཞེས་གསུངས་སོ། །རྡོ་རྗེ་སེམས་དཔའ་ནམ་མཁའ་ཆེ་རྒྱལ་པོ་རྒྱས་པའི་རྒྱུད་ལས། །ཆོས་ཉམས
གཡོས་པ་མེད་པའི་ལེའུ་སྟེ་བཅོ་ལྔ་པའོ།། །།དེ་ནས་བཅོམ་ལྡན་འདས་ཀྱིས་མི་རྟོག་མི་གཡོས་པའི་ཏིང་ངེ་འཛིན་ལ་སྙོམས་པར་ཞུགས་ནས་ཚིག་ཏུ
བརྗོད་པ་འདི་བརྗོད་དོ། །སངས་རྒྱས་ཀུན་གྱི་སྐུ་གསུང་ཐུགས་རང་ཉིད། །སེམས་ཅན་རྣམས་ཀྱི་ལུས་ངག་ཡིད་གསུམ་ལ། །བཟང་ངན་ཆེ་ཆུང་ཁྱད་པར་ཡོང་མ་གསུངས
མ་གསུངས་སངས་རྒྱས་དགོངས་པ་ཀུན་མི་སྟོན། །གསུངས་པ་ཐམས་ཅད་ང་ཡི་ངོ་བོ་གསུངས། །ང་ཡི་ངོ་བོ་ཆོས་ཉམས་ཐམས་ཅད་ཡིན། །རང་བཞིན་ཉམ་དགས་ཉམ
པའི་རྒྱལ་པོ་དེ། །མི་འགྱུར་རང་བཞིན་ཆགས་པ་ཀུན་དང་བྲལ། །གཟུང་བའི་ཡུལ་མེད་སེམས་ཀྱི་གནས་ཀྱང་མེད། །རང་གི་སེམས་ནི་ནམ་མཁའི་རང་བཞིན་ཏེ། །
མཐའ་ལ་ལྷུག་པ་མེད་པས་དབྱིངས་ལ་གྲི་བ་མེད། །རང་སེམས་ནམ་མཁའི་རང་བཞིན་ནི་དམི་རིགས། །ཆོས་ཀྱི་རང་བཞིན་ཀུན་ཀྱང་དེ་ལྟ་སྟེ། །ཇི་བཞིན་པ་ལས་ཀུན
ཀྱང་དག་ཡོས་པ་མེད། །ཆོས་ཀྱི་རོལ་པ་དེ་ང་འཛིན་ཚ་བྱས་ཀྱང་། །ཇི་བཞིན་པ་ལ་དོ་བོ་འགྱུར་བ་མེད། །འགྱུར་མེད་ལྷུག་པའི་སྟོབས་ཚིག་ཆེ་རབ་འབྱུང་བ། །ཏིང་འཛིན་གཅིག

149

གསེར་འོད་པོ་རབ་ལྷག་མ་མེད། །སྣ་ཡང་རྗེ་བཞིན་པ་ལ་འགྱུར་བ་མེད། །རང་བཞིན་ཆེ་བའི་ཡུལ་ལ་རང་བཞིན་གནས། །རང་བཞིན་མ་བཅོས་པ་ཡི་མིང་ཡིན་ལ། །ཆེས
མ་བཅོས་པ་ལ་ཆེ་ཞེས་བརྗོད། །དེ་ལ་མ་ངེན་སུམ་མཐོང་བར་སྨྲ་འདོད་པར། །འདོད་པ་དེ་ནི་ཆགས་པའི་གནས་ཡིན་ཏེ། །དེ་ལ་མི་རྟོག་མཉམ་པའི་དགོངས་པ་མེད། །
ཆོས་ཉིད་རང་བཞིན་ཡེ་ནས་གནས་པ་ལ། །ང་བཙལ་བ་སམ་པ་སྤྱོད་སྒྲུབ་བྱེད་པ་ནི། །རང་སེམས་གཞན་དུ་ཚོལ་བར་བྱེད་པ་ཡིན། །དེ་ཡིས་ཆོས་ཀྱི་དབྱིངས་དང་ནམ
མཁའི་ཁམས། །ཁམས་གསུམ་གནས་དང་སྲིད་པའི་ཚིག་བ་ཤིག་ཀྱང་། །རང་སེམས་རང་བཞིན་གནས་པར་མི་རྟོགས། །མི་རྟོག་ཆོས་ཉིད་མཉམ་པ་ཉིད་དུ་མཉམ། །
མཉམ་པས་ཆོས་དང་ཆོས་མིན་གཅིག་ཀྱང་མེད། །སེམས་ཅན་རྒྱུ་མེད་སངས་རྒྱས་འབྲས་བུ་མེད། །རྒྱུ་འབྲས་སྟོན་པའི་སྟོན་པ་ཉིད་ཀྱང་ཆེར། །དེ་བས་ང་ལས་བྱུང་བའི
ཆོས་མཉམ་པས། །ང་ལས་བྱུང་བ་བཟང་ངན་མེད་མཉམ་གཅིག །ཅེས་གསུངས་སོ། །རྡོ་རྗེ་སེམས་དཔའ་ནམ་མཁའ་ཆེ་རྒྱལ་པོ་རྒྱས་པའི་རྒྱུད་ལས། །མཉམ་པ་ཉིད
ཀྱི་ལེའུ་སྟེ་བཅུ་དྲུག་པའོ།། །།དེ་ནས་བཅོམ་ལྡན་འདས་ཀྱིས་མི་འགྱུར་བའི་ཏིང་ངེ་འཛིན་ལ་སྙོམས་པར་ཞུགས་ནས་ཚིག་ཏུ་བརྗོད་པ་འདི་བརྗོད

150

ཤ

151

༄༅། །དེ་ ,ང་ཡི་ཆོས་ཉིད་དེ་བཞིན་ཉིད་གཅིག་ལ། །རྟོག་པར་བྱ་བའི་ཐབས་ནི་གཞི་མ་གྲུབ། །ལྟ་བའི་ཆོས་ཉིད་མཐོང་བའི་གཞི་མ་བྱེད། །དེས་ན་མི་མཐོང་
བར་བྱ་བའི་ཐབས་ཡིན་ནོ། །མ་སྐྱེས་དམིགས་པར་བྱ་བའི་ཡུལ་མེད་པས། །བལྟ་བས་དེ་བཞིན་ཉིད་ལ་མཐོང་བ་མེད། །དམ་ཚིག་རང་སྐྱོན་སེལ་བའི་གཞི་མ་བྱེད། །དེས་ནི
བར་ཆད་མེད་པའི་ཐབས་ཡིན་ནོ། །དེ་བཞིན་ཉིད་ལ་བསྲུང་བའི་ཡུལ་མེད་པས། །སྒྲུབ་པ་པས་དེ་བཞིན་ཉིད་ལ་འགྲུབ་པ་མེད། །ལས་ནི་གྲུབ་པར་བྱེད་པའི་གཞི་མ་བྱེད། །
རྩོལ་བས་འགྲུབ་པར་བྱེད་པའི་ཐབས་ཡིན་ནོ། །དེ་བཞིན་ཉིད་ལ་བཙལ་བའི་ཡུལ་མེད་པས། །དེ་བཞིན་ཉིད་ལ་ལས་ཀྱི་གྲུབ་པ་མེད། །ལམ་གྱིས་བགྲོད་པར་བྱེད་པའི
གཞི་མ་བྱེད། །དེ་ནི་གནས་སུ་ཕྱིན་པའི་ཐབས་ཡིན་ནོ། །དེ་བཞིན་ཉིད་ལ་ལམ་གྱིས་བགྲོད་མེད་ཕྱིར། །བགྲོད་པས་ཕྱིན་པ་དེ་བཞིན་ཉིད་མ་ཡིན། །ས་ནི་གནས་པར་བྱེད
པའི་གཞི་མ་བྱེད། །དེས་ནི་བགྲོད་མི་དགོས་པའི་ཐབས་ཡིན་ནོ། །དེ་བཞིན་ཉིད་ལ་ཐམས་ཅད་ཀུན་གནས་པས། །གནས་པར་བྱ་བའི་ས་ལ་སྤྱང་དུ་མེད། །ཡེ་ཤེས་རྟོགས
པར་བྱེད་པའི་གཞི་མ་བྱེད། །ཆོས་ཉིད་རིག་པར་བྱ་བའི་ཐབས་ཡིན་ནོ། །དེ་བཞིན་ཉིད་ལ་རྟོགས་པའི་ཡུལ་མེད་པས། །རང་བྱུང་ཡེ་ཤེས་ཡུལ་ལ་རྟོག་པ་མེད། །བྱང་ཆུབ

152

སེམས་ནི་ཆོས་ཀྱི་གཞི་ཡིན་པས། །ཐེག་པ་སོ་སོའི་ལྟ་སྤྱོད་རྟག་རྟག་གིས། །ལྟ་སྤྱོད་གཞི་མི་རྟག་ལ་བཙལ་བྱས་ཀྱང་། །དེ་བཞིན་ཉིད་ལ་བཙལ་བའི་ཡུལ་མེད་པས།
བཙལ་བས་དེ་བཞིན་ཉིད་ལ་བཅོས་པའི་ཕྱིར། །རང་སེམས་གཞི་མའི་བཅོས་མེད་དང་མི་འཕྲད། །ཅེས་གསུངས་སོ། །རྡོ་རྗེ་སེམས་དཔའ་ནམ་མཁའ་ཆེ་རྒྱལ
པོ་རྒྱས་པའི་རྒྱུད་ལས། །གཞི་མ་ཀུན་ཏུ་བཟང་པོ་ཡིན་པར་བསྟན་པའི་ལེའུ་སྟེ་བཅུ་བདུན་པའོ།། ||དེ་ནས་བཅོམ་ལྡན་འདས་ཀྱིས་བྱ
བ་མེད་པའི་ངང་ངམ་བརྗེན་ལ་སྙོམས་པར་ཞུགས་ནས་ཆེད་དུ་བརྗོད་པ་འདི་བརྗོད་དོ། །ལྟ་བ་བསྒོམ་དུ་མེད་ཅེས་བསྟན་པ་ནི། །ཆོས་ཀྱི་སྐུ་ན་སེམས་ལས་མེད་པའི
ཕྱིར། །རང་གིས་རང་ལ་བསྟན་དུ་མེད་པ་ནི། །རང་སེམས་ཡུལ་ཅན་ང་ཡིས་བསྟན་པ་མེད། །དེས་ན་ལྟ་བ་བསྒོམ་དུ་མེད་པ་ཡིན། །དམ་ཚིག་བསྲུང་དུ་མེད་པར་བསྟན
པ་ནི། །ཐམས་ཅད་ལྷུན་གྲུབ་བསྲུང་བའི་ཚིག་ལས་འདས། །བསྲུངས་པས་མི་ཐུབ་རང་གིས་མི་ཞིགས། །རང་བྱུང་ཡེ་ཤེས་ཡིན་པས་བསྲུང་དུ་མེད། །དེས་ན
དམ་ཚིག་བསྲུང་དུ་མེད་པ་ཡིན། །འཕྲིན་ལས་བཙལ་དུ་མེད་ཅེས་བསྟན་པ་ནི། །རྫོགས་ཆེན་རྒྱུ་འབྲས་ཡེ་ནས་འདས་པའི་ཕྱིར། །འཕྲིན་ལས་རྒྱུ་ལས་སྐྱེས་པས་ནམ་འགྲུབ

ཁ [illegible]

༄༅། །ཕྱག་རྡོར། །རྟོགས་ཆེན་འབྲས་བུ་འདོད་པ་མེད་པའི་ཕྱིར། །འབྲི་ཞིང་ལས་བཅོས་རྩ་མེད་ཅེས་བསྟན་པ་ཡིན། །ལམ་ལ་བགྲོད་དུ་མེད་ཅེས་བསྟན་པ
ནི། །དུས་གསུམ་སངས་རྒྱས་ཁམས་གསུམ་སེམས་ཅན་ལ། །བགྲོད་པས་བྱང་ཆུབ་སེམས་ཀྱི་ལམ་ལ་བགྲོད། །སེམས་སུ་སངས་རྒྱས་སེམས་ཅན་གཉིས་ལས
མེད། །དེས་ན་སེམས་ཀྱི་སེམས་ཀྱི་ལམ་མི་བགྲོད། །ས་ལ་སྦྱང་དུ་མེད་ཅེས་བསྟན་པ་ནི། །ཆོས་ཉིད་བྱང་ཆུབ་སེམས་ཀྱི་ས་འདི་ལ། །སྦྱངས་པས་ཐོབ་པར་འདོད་པ་རྒྱུ
འབྲས་ཅན། །ཆོས་དབྱིངས་བྱང་ཆུབ་སེམས་ཀྱི་ས་འདི་ལ། །སྦྱང་བཅོས་ཁྲུས་བསྒྲུབ་པ་རང་ས་མ་བསྟན། །ཡེ་ཤེས་ཡུལ་ལ་མི་རྟོག་ཅེས་བསྟན་པ། །ཡུལ་དེ་ཡིན་ས
རང་བྱུང་ཡེ་ཤེས་ཏེ། །རང་བྱུང་ཡེ་ཤེས་ཡུལ་དང་བྲལ། །ཡེ་ཤེས་པ་ཉིད་ཡིན་ཡུལ་ལ་མ་ཆགས། །དུས་གསུམ་སངས་རྒྱས་ཐམས་ཅད་དང་། །ཁམས་གསུམ
སེམས་ཅན་ཐམས་ཅད་ཀུན། །སྙིང་ཆེན་སེམས་ཀྱི་གནས་དེ་ལ། །མི་གནས་པའི་གཅིག་ཏུ་མེད། །ཀུན་གྱི་གནས་དང་ས་ཡིན་ཏེ། །འདུ་འབྲལ་མེད་པ་རང་ཉིད
བཞུགས། །དེ་ལ་སྦྱང་ཞིང་བགྲོད་མི་དགོས། །དེ་ལ་སྦྱང་ཞིང་བགྲོད་རྒྱུ་རན། །རང་སེམས་དེ་ལ་འཚོལ་བ་སྟེ། །བཅོས་པས་རང་སེམས་འགྲོ་ས་མི་འགྱུར། །ཅེས

153

གསུངས་སོ།། །རྡོ་རྗེ་སེམས་དཔའ་ནམ་མཁའ་ཆེ་རྒྱལ་པོ་རྒྱས་པའི་རྒྱུད་ལས། །བཅོས་པ་མེད་པར་བསྟན་པའི་ལེའུ་སྟེ་བཅོ་བརྒྱད་པའོ།།
༈ །དེ་ནས་བཅོམ་ལྡན་འདས་ཀྱིས་བྱ་མེད་རྟོགས་པའི་ཏིང་ངེ་འཛིན་ལ་སྙོམས་པར་ཞུགས་ནས་ཆེ་ངེར་དུ་བརྗོད་པ་འདི་བརྗོད་དོ། །བྱ་མེད་ཡུལ་ནི་མི་གནས་ནམ་མཁའ་འདྲ།།
མི་གནས་དམིགས་པའི་ཡུལ་མེད་མི་རྟོག་ཆེས་ཀྱི་ལམ། །བསྒོ་བའི་ཚ་ཤེས་སྤྲོ་མེད་ཡུལ་ལས་འབྱུང་བ་སྟེ། །རྟོག་སྒོམ་ཆོས་ཀྱི་སྐུ་ལ་ཕྱེད་པར་ནུས་མེད་པས། །
རང་བྱུང་ཡེ་ཤེས་ཀུན་ཏུ་རྟོགས་བཞིན་གནས། །བྱ་བྲལ་ཡུལ་ལ་མི་གནས་གཉེན་པོས་བཅོས་སུ་མེད། །ཡིན་ལག་ཆོས་ཀྱི་རང་བགེགས་སྙིང་པོ་ཡུལ་འཚོལ་ཞིང་། །རྣམ་པ
ཅིར་ཡང་མི་རྟོག་ཐབས་ཀྱིས་དེ་ལ་རོལ། །སྣང་བ་རང་བཞིན་འབྱུང་བས་ཆོས་སྐུ་གཞན་ནམ་མེད། །རྩལ་ལྡན་གཅིག་ལ་གཅེས་ཤིང་ཕྱོགས་ལྷུང་ཀུན་དང་བྲལ། །མི་གནས
དོན་ཉིད་ལེགས་པའི་ཡེ་ཤེས་རང་བྱུང་སྟེ། །མཐོང་སྣང་ཀུན་ཏུ་མི་རྟོག་ལེགས་པའི་སྙིང་པོ་ལ། །རྣམ་དག་ལམ་དུ་ཞུགས་ནས་མཉམ་ཉིད་པའི་རྒྱལ་པོ་ཐོབ། །མི་འགྱུར
འགྱུར་བ་མེད་པས་ཆགས་པའི་གནས་མེད་དེ། །དེ་བཞིན་ཉིད་ཀྱི་བྱུང་བའི་ཡུལ་མེད་སེམས་ཀྱི་གནས་ཀྱང་མེད། །མངོན་སུམ་མཐོང་བར་འདོད་པས་རྒྱུ་ལ་རྟག་ཏུ་བསྒོམ། །

154

པ རྡོ་ནམ་ཆེ

༄༅། །བསྒོམ་ཚིག་ལ་བརྟེན་པ་དེ་ལས་མ་ཉམས་པའི་དོན་མི་འབྱུང༌། །སྐུ་གཅིག་ཀུན་ཏུ་ཁྱབ་པས་བསྟན་པའི་ཆོས་མེད་དེ། །མཐའ་ལ་ཐུག་པ་མེད་པས
དབྱིངས་ལ་འགྲིབ་མེད། །ཆོས་ཀྱི་རོལ་པས་ཉམ་བག་ལྷག་པ་འཇིག་ནས་མེད་དེ། །རང་བྱུང་ཆེ་བའི་ཡུལ་ཡང་ཀུན་ཏུ་རྗེ་བཞིན་ཅི་གནས། །ངོ་མཚར་མཐོང་བའི་ཡུལ་མེད་དེ་ལ
མཐོང་བའི་མི་གི། །གང་ལ་གྲོལ་བར་མི་རིག་སབ་སྐྱེད་པ་ཀུན་དང་བྲལ། །ཆོས་དང་ཆོས་མིན་རྟག་ཏུ་འདྲེས་ཤར་དབྱེར་མེད་མཚུངས། །དོན་དམ་ཆོས་ཞེས་ལྷག་པའི
གནས་ཞེས་བ་ཤད་པ་མེད། །འཁྲུལ་དང་བྱང་ཆུབ་ལ་མར་རྟོགས་པ་ལས་གྲོལ་བ་མེད། །རང་བྱུང་ཡེ་ཤེས་ཉིད་ཀྱང་ཚིག་གི་མཐའ་དང་བྲལ། །ཡེ་ནས་གདངས་རྒྱལ་བ་དགོངས་ཉིད
མ་ཆེན་སྤྲུལ་མ་གནས་པ་ལ། །གྲིབ་མ་གཟུགས་ཀྱི་དཔེ་བཞིན་དེ་ལས་རྟོག་པ་འབྱུང༌། །མེད་དེ་མེད་པ་མ་ཡིན་མེད་པའི་སྣང་བ་འབྱུང༌། །སྟོང་དང་སྟོང་པ་མ་ཡིན་སྟོང་པའི
ཕྱུག་པ་གནས། །ནམ་མཁའི་རང་བཞིན་དེ་ལས་འབྱུང་བའི་དྲན་པ་སྤྲུ། །སྤྲུལ་ཟླ་ཞེ་པའི་ཡི་དེ་བའི་དོན་པ་མེད་པས་ལོན། །བཟང་བའི་ཡུལ་མེད་དེ་ལས་ཡེ་ཤེས
འབྱུང་བཙོམ། །སྟོན་ཀྱི་དྲང་སྲོང་རྗེས་སུ་ཆགས་པའི་འོད་ཀྱང་པ་རྩོག །རྣམ་རྟོག་འབར་བའི་གཏུང་བས་ཀུན་ཏུ་ཟིན་ཏ་རེ། །རང་བཞིན་ལ་མདང་ཞུགས་པས་ཐམས་ཅད

155

མཐེན་པ་མེད། །ཧེ་བཞིན་ཉིད་པ་ཤེས་རྣམ་རྟོག་དེ་གྲུབ་རྟོག་བསྒོམ་པ། །ཡ་དེ་བ་ཆེན་པོའ་དོར་བ་ལས་ཆགས་པའི་ཉིད་ཡིན་ཏེ། །མི་གཡོ་མཉམ་པར་གནས་པའི་སྣང་ཞེས་བསྟུས
ན། །མཐྲེ་རིས་བསྒྲོད་པའི་རྒྱུ་དེས་ཉེ་མིང་ཟིན་པར་འགྱུར། །ལམ་མེད་ལམ་དུ་ཞུགས་པ་བརྩམས་ཀྱི་ཉིད་ཚེབ། །སྤྲིན་པ་རང་དོར་བས་རིགས་སྒྲུ་གཞུ་སྐྱེས་པ་བདྲ། །ཧྲཱ
པར་ཡོ་ཁུ་བ་མེད་ངང་འཇིག་རྟེན་གསུམ་ལས་མི་འབྱུང་ཞིང་། །ས་སྟུ་རུ་བསྟོར་པའི་གནས་ཀྱང་བྱང་ཆུབ་ཐོབ་པ་ཡིན། །ཤེས་ཀྱུ་སྟུར་པའི་ཡེ་ཤེས་བསམ་པ་ཀུན་དང་བྲལ།
བ་ཤེས་རྒྱས་ཉིད་ཀུན་ལས་འབྱུང་བའི་ནོར་བུ་རིན་ཆེན་བཞིན། །དམིགས་པ་མེད་དབྱིངས་འགྱུར་བའི་གནས་ལ་མི་སྤྲོས་པར། །རང་གི་ངང་བཞིན་ལ་གསལ་བར་རབ་བསྟམས
ཅན་སྤྱོད། །བརྟགས་ནས་མེད་ལ་བཞག་ན་ལེགས་པའི་འབྱུང་བ་ཆེ། །འདོད་སྐུ་མི་སྣང་ཆགས་པའི་ཚེ་ལུགས་ཀུན་ལ་སྟོན། །བདག་དང་གཞན་དུ་བྲལ་བའི་སྟོན་མཐའ་ནི་ནི
ཆེན་མཛོད། །ཐམས་ཅད་སྒྲུབ་པའི་ཕྱུ་ཞེས་བ་དག་མེད་སྙིང་རྗེར་བསྟན། །ནང་ནས་མ་གཡོས་ནམ་ཏུ་བཅོལ་བའི་ཕྱུལ་མེད་དེ། །ཡུལ་གྱི་ཆགས་པ་ཡུལ་ལས་སྟོབ་པའི
དམིགས་པ་མེད། །མི་འབྱུང་མི་འཇིག་བདག་མེད་སྙིང་རྗེ་དེ་ཡིས་བའི། །གཞན་གྱི་ངོར་མིན་མི་ཤེང་ཡེ་ནས་གནས་པ་ཡིན། །བདེ་བ་འདོད་པས་བདེ་ལ་རྒྱུ་བ་ཀྱི་རྩེ་གས། །བདེ་བ

156

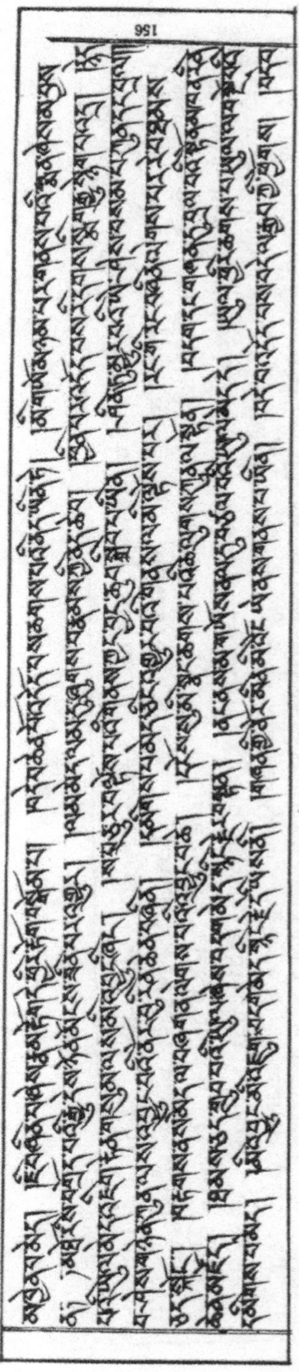

ཕ

༄༅། །ཟིན་ཏེ་བདེ་བས་བདེ་བ་ཚོལ། །བྱང་ཆུབ་འཁྲུལ་པ་ཡེ་རྗེ་མཆེས་ལ་ཟླ། །འདི་ལྟའི་ཡུལ་ཅན་སངས་རྒྱས་མཐོང་བ་མི་ཉི། །སངས་རྒྱས་མེད་པས
སངས་རྒྱས་མིང་ཡང་མེད། །སངས་རྒྱས་སྟོན་པས་མིང་དུ་བཏགས་པའོ། །སངས་རྒྱས་གཞན་ནས་འཐོབ་བྱེད་བོར་བའི་ལམ། །གཟུགས་ལ་མིང་ཆོས་སྐུ་ལས་བ་ཤར་བ་རྩལ
ཅམ་མེད། །ཟིན་དང་ཆགས་དང་བྲལ་དང་ནི། །ངོ་རྟོགས་པོ་མེད་དང་རྣམ་པར་སྤྲོང་། །རྡུ་ཉི་རྩེ་ཆེན་པོའི་ངང་བཞིན་པས། །བཟའ་བའི་ཐབས་ལ་རག་པ་མེད། །
ཡངས་སོ་ཆེ་འོ་ཆོས་ཆེན་པོ། །ཆུང་དུ་རྣམས་ཀྱི་གཉེན་པོ་ཡིན། །ཆེ་ལ་དམིགས་པའི་ཆེ་སྤྲུམ་ས་ནས། །ཆུང་ཆེ་རྣམས་དམིགས་དང་བྲལ། །གསུངས་སོ།
ངང་རྒྱལ་ལ་དམིགས་དང་སྤང་། །སྒྲ་མཁན་རི་མོའི་རྣམ་པ་བཞིན། །འབྱུང་འཇུག་ཡེ་ཤེས་བྱུང་རྒྱུ་གསལ་པའི། །དེ་ཡི་དབང་ལས་སྐྱེ་བར་འགྱུར། །ཀྱེ་དོན
ཐེག་པ་ཀུན་གྱི་རྒྱལ། །གདང་རྟོགས་ཞག་གི་རང་བཞིན་ཏེ། །འདོད་པ་མེད་ཅིང་ལེན་པ་མེད། །བྲོད་པ་རྡུལ་ཙམ་མི་སྐྱེད་དོ། །འབྱུང་ཆེན་ནམ་མཁར་ཐིམ་པ་བཞིན། །སྤྲོ
བ་མེད་ཅིང་བསྡུ་བ་མེད། །སྟོང་པར་མི་དགོས་བཟའ་བ་མེད། །རྒྱ་མཚོ་བཞིན་དུ་ཡེ་གནས་ལ། །ཆོས་རྣམས་སྣ་ཚོགས་འབྱུང་བར་བྱེད། །ཡོན་ཏན་ནམ་མཁའི

157

མཐའ་དང་མཉམ། །འབྱུ་བའི་གནས་སུ་ངེས་པ་མེད། །བྱང་ཆུབ་སྙིང་པོ་རི་མ་ཐག །ཏིང་འཛིན་རྒྱལ་པོ་ཆེན་པོར་འབྱུང་། །སྣང་བ་རྒྱ་མཚོ་ཆེན་པོ་བཞིན། །མི་རྟོག་གནས
མཁའི་མཐའ་ལྟར་ཡངས། །ཀུན་ཏུ་བཟང་པོའི་སྤྱོད་ཡུལ་ལ། །སྐྱེ་ཤི་འཕོ་བའི་ཆོས་མེད་དེ། །རྒྱུ་རྐྱེན་ཡན་ལག་ལྷ་བུ་གཉིས་པོ། །སྐྱུར་པ་རབ་འདས་བཅད་ཀ
པ་ཡིན། །འཁྲུལ་པ་རྣམས་ཀྱི་སྒོ་ཙམ་དུ། །མཁས་པས་དེ་བཞིན་ཞེས་པར་བྱས། །འགྲོ་བ་རྒྱུད་དྲུག་སྣང་བ་ཡང་། །དང་པོའི་ཡས་མ་དུ་ཞེས་པར་བྱ། །ཉོད
སྤྱོད་སྒྲིང་རྗེས་བསྟན་པས་ན། །གང་དུ་དགའ་བར་བྱང་ཆུབ་སྤྱོད། །ཞེན་པ་སྤྲད་འཚོང་མཚམས་མེད་པ། །ཐོན་མ་ཕྲ་འཛིག་རྟེན་ཚུངས། །ཡོངས་སུ་རྫོགས་པ་བཅོས
ཀྱི་རྩ། །བདེ་བ་ཆེ་ལས་གཞན་མེད་དོ། །ཡང་ཆོས་ཐམས་ཅད་དེ་བས་ན། །ཆོས་ཀྱི་རང་བཞིན་དེ་ཡིན་པས། །ཆོས་ཀྱི་ཆོས་ཉིད་བཅོལ་བ་དང་། །ནམ་མཁའ་ནམ
མཁའ་བཅོལ་བ་དང་། །གཞན་ལ་བཞེལ་པའི་ཆོས་རྣམས་ནི། །སེམས་མི་གསོད་པ་དང་འདྲ་སྟེ། །ཞིན་ཏུ་དཀའ་བའི་ལམ་བྱེད་པའོ། །རྣམ་པར་མི་རྟོག་སྙིང་པོ་འདི། །
ཡོངས་ཀྱི་རྒྱུད་ལ་སྨྲས་པ་མེད། །མི་ཤེས་བྱང་ཆུབ་སྤྱོད་རྣམས་ལ། །རྣམ་པ་ཀུན་ཏུ་རང་བཞིན་གནས། །ཞེས་གསུངས་སོ། །རྡོ་རྗེ་སེམས་དཔའ་ནམ་མཁའ་ཆེ་རྒྱལ་པོ…

158

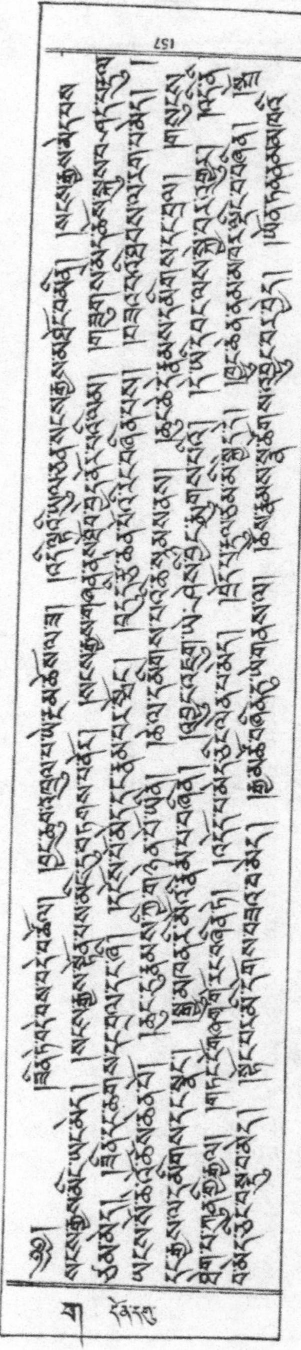

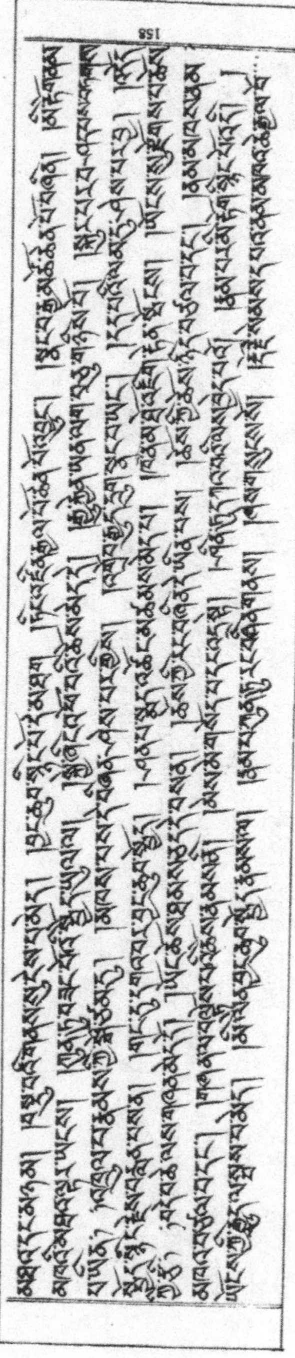

ཀ

159

༄༅། །རྒྱལ་པོའི་རྒྱུད་ལས། ། ཀུ་མེད་རྟོགས་པ་པའི་གནས་ཡུལ་མེད་ཀྱི་ལེའུ་སྟེ་བཅུ་དགུ་པའོ།། །།དེ་ནས་བཅོམ
ལྡན་འདས་ཀྱིས་བྱ་བ་མེད་པའི་ཏིང་ངེ་འཛིན་ལ་སྙོམས་པར་ཞུགས་ནས་ཆེད་དུ་བརྗོད་པ་འདི་བརྗོད་དོ། །ཆོས་རྣམས་ཐམས་ཅད་ངང་ལས་བྱུང་བས་ན། །རྗེ་ཉིད་སྣང
པའི་ཆོས་རྣམས་ཐམས་ཅད་ཀུན། །ཡེ་ནས་རྣམ་པར་གྲོལ་བས་ཀྱི་ངང་དུ་བསྟན། །ཕྱི་དང་ནང་གསུམ་ཡིན་ནས་ཆོས་ཀྱི་དབྱིངས། །ཡེ་ནས་རྣམ་པར་དག་པའི་སྤྱོད་ཡུལ
ལ། ;སངས་རྒྱས་དང་ནི་སེམས་ཅན་གཉིས་སུ་མེད། །ལམ་དང་གཉེན་པོས་བཅོས་སུ་ག་ལ་ཡོད། །བསྒྲུབ་མེད་རྩོལ་སྒྲུབ་སྒོམ་པ་མེད་པས་ན། །ཀུ་མེད་ལྷུན
རྫོགས་སྣང་མ་ངེར་སྣང་ན། །རྟོག་སྤྱོད་རྣམ་རྟོག་གཉིས་མེད་ཆོས་དབྱིངས་ལ། །ཞིག་རྟོག་ཕྱིས་པའི་སྤྱོད་པ་ཅི་ཞིག་བསྒྲུ། །འཁྲུལ་པ་མཚོར་པའི་སེམས་དུ་བསྟན་པ་ཡང་།།
གང་དུ་བསྟན་པའི་ལམ་ཆེན་དེ་ལ་སེམས་གཉིས་པས། །མཉམ་པར་ཞེས་པ་སངས་རྒྱས་ཀུན་ཏུ་རྗེ། །ང་དང་བདག་ཏུ་བསྟན་པ་སུ་སྟོན་ཅས་འཁྲུལ་པའི་ཐམ། །ཕྱིན་པའི
ཡུལ་མེད་རྟོགས་པ་འདི་དུས་མེད་པས། །ཆོས་ཉིད་ཆོས་ཚོལ་རྣ་དབར་གལ་འཁྱུར། །ཚོད་མ་རམ་སྒྱུར་སློབ་དཔོན་སྐྱ་འུག་ཏྲ་ཡིས་བྱུང་། །བསྟན་དང་ལ་མཚོར་རྟོག་པ་བྲིན

160

དང་། །དེ་བས་གསེར་ལ་ནག་རྒྱུར་བ་དང་བ་ཀྱི། །སྨོན་པར་ཆེན་ཡང་དག་སྟོན་པའི་རིན་ཆེན་དེ། །མི་ནུབ་དར་བ་གཏུ་མེད་པས་བསྐྱུ་བར་འདོས། །ཞེས་གསུངས་སོ། །ཧེ་ཧེ
སེམས་དཔའ་ནམ་མཁའ་ཆེ་རྒྱལ་པོ་རྒྱས་པའི་རྒྱུད་ལས། ། ཀུ་བྱེད་རྣམས་དག་དབྱིངས་ཀྱི་ལེའུ་སྟེ་ཉི་ཤུ་པའོ།། །།དེ་ནས་བཅོམ་ལྡན་འདས
ཀྱིས་རྟོགས་པ་ལྷུན་གྲུབ་ཀྱི་ཏིང་ངེ་འཛིན་ལ་སྙོམས་པར་ཞུགས་ནས་ཆེད་དུ་བརྗོད་པ་འདི་བརྗོད་དོ། །སྣ་ཚོགས་རང་བཞིན་མི་གཉིས་ཏེ། །ཆ་ཤས་ཉིད་དུ་སྤྲོས་པ་དང་བྲལ། །ཧེ
བཞིན་པ་ཞེས་མི་རྟོག་ཀྱང་། །རྣམ་པར་སྣང་མཛད་ཀུན་ཏུ་བཟང་། །རྩེ་བས་ཟུལ་བའི་ནང་སྣང་ངེས་ཏེ། །ལྷུན་གྱིས་གནས་པས་བཅས་པ་ཡིན། །ཞེས་གསུངས་སོ། །ཧེ་ཧེ
སེམས་དཔའ་ནམ་མཁའ་ཆེ་རྒྱལ་པོ་རྒྱས་པའི་རྒྱུད་ལས། ། ཀུ་མེད་རྟོགས་པ་ལྷུན་གྱིས་གྲུབ་པའི་ལེའུ་སྟེ་ཉི་ཤུ་རྩ་གཅིག་པའོ།། །།དེ་ནས་བཅོམ་ལྡན
འདས་ཀྱིས་མ་སྐྱེས་པའི་ཏིང་ངེ་འཛིན་ལ་སྙོམས་པར་ཞུགས་ནས་ཆེད་དུ་བརྗོད་པ་འདི་བརྗོད་དོ། །བསམ་པའ་དབས་བརྗོད་དུ་མེད་པའི་ཀྱང་རྒྱུ་མེད་མས། །རྟོན་པའི་ཀླུང་ནས་བསྒྱུར
པའི་ཀུན་ཀྱིས་མ་བསྟགས་པ། །ཆོས་ཀྱི་སྐུ་ཡང་ཁྱུ་ང་བས་ཁ་ཚམ་ད་ཕ་ལ་ཉིད་ཏུ་ཉིད། །ཐུ་བྲལ་ལྷུན་རྟོགས་བདེ་བའི་སྐུ་བ་ལ་གནས། །རྒྱལ་བ་མི་མས་ཀུན་ལས་སྒྲུབ་པ་ཆེ

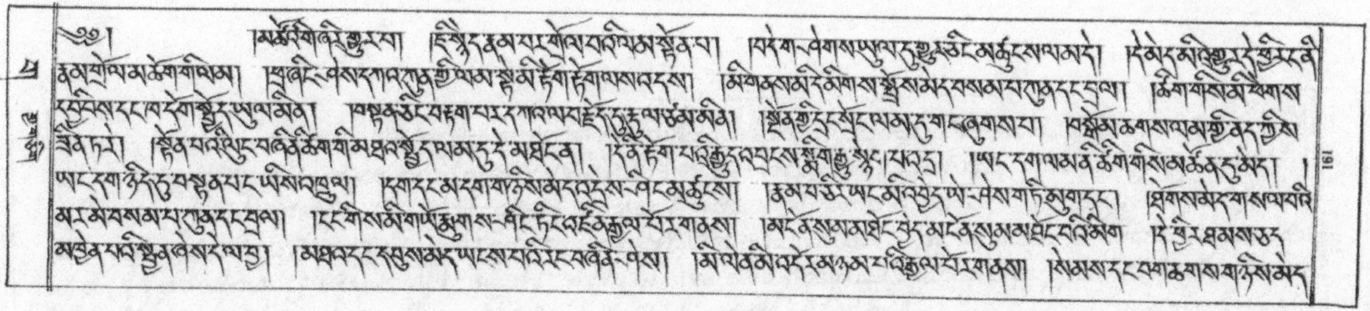

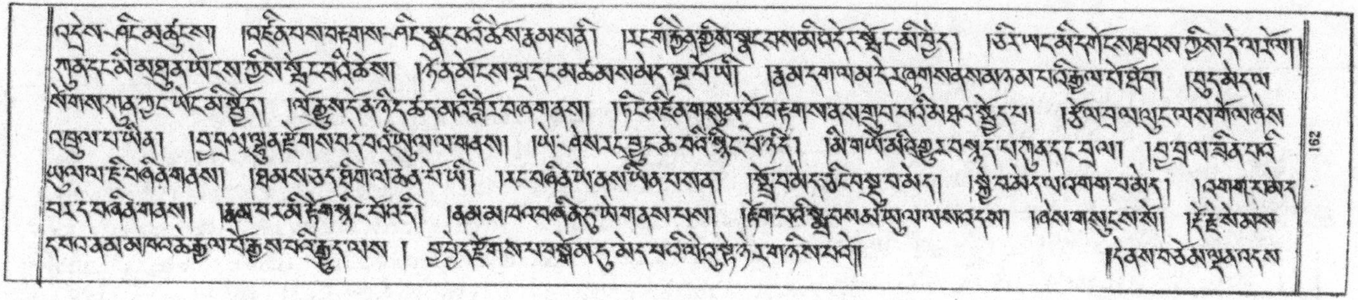

191

192

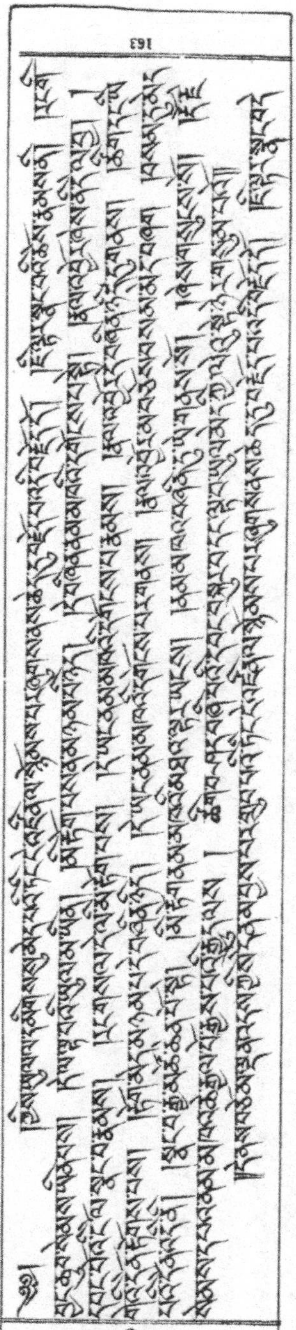

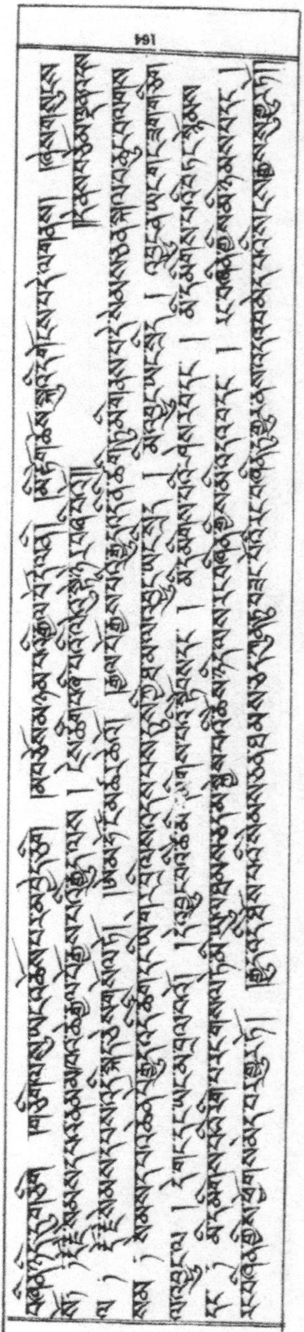

ཀ ཐལ་འགྱུར

༄༅། །རྒྱུད་འདི་ཐོས་པའི་ཡིད་རང་གྲོལ་ཡེ་ཤེས་སུ་གྱུར་ནས། །གཉིས་སུ་མེད་པ་མཐའ་ཅལ་བའི་ཁྲིག་ལེ་རྒྱུར་ཏོ། །རྡོ་རྗེ་སེམས་དཔའ་ལ་སོགས་པའི

འཁོར་རྣམས་རྗེས་སུ་ཡི་རང་ངོ་། །རྒྱུད་ཡོངས་སུ་གཏད་པའི་ལེའུ་སྟེ་ཉེར་ལྔ་པའོ།། ||རྒྱལ་པོ་རྒྱས་རྒྱུད་སྙིང་པོ་རང་གྲོལ་པའོ། །རྫོགས་སོ།།

||༄། ||༄ཀ་ར་སྐད་དུ། བཛྲ་སཏྭ་མ་ཧཱ་ཏནྟྲ་ནཱ་མ། བོད་སྐད་དུ། རྡོ་རྗེ་སེམས་དཔའ་ནམ་མཁའ་ཆེ་རྒྱུད་ཅེས་བྱ་བ།

དཔལ་རྡོ་རྗེ་སེམས་དཔའ་ལ་ཕྱག་འཚལ་ལོ། །འདི་སྐད་བདག་གིས་ཐོས་པ་དུས་གཅིག་ན། བཅོམ་ལྡན་འདས་དེ་བཞིན་གཤེགས་པ་ཀུན་ཏུ་བཟང་པོ་སྐུ་མདོག་ནམ་མཁའ་ལྟ་བུ་མེད

པ། ནམ་པར་ཐར་པའི་དབུག་སུམ་དང་ལྡན་པ། ཕྱག་རྒྱ་གིས་ནི་རྒྱན་པོ་ཆེའི་ངང་བ་ར་བ་བྱུར་བརྒྱད་པའི་རྫོན་པ་སྤྱི། སྐུ་ཀུན་ཏུ་བཟང་མོ་དང་གཉིས་སུ་མེད

པར་འཁྱིལ་གི་ནམ་མཁའ་མཐའ་དང་དབུས་མེད་པ་སུམ་ཅུ་གཞལ་ཡས་ཁང་ན། །གདན་ཟླ་བ་ཉི་མ་ལ་སོགས་པའི་སྟེང་ན་པདྨ་དང་ཉི་ཟླ་བསྟན་པའི་གདན་ལ། །རྡོ་རྗེ་སེམས

དཔའ་ལ་སོགས་པའི་དེ་བཞིན་གཤེགས་པ་རྣམ་པར་སྣང་མཛད་དང་། དཀོན་མཆོག་འབྱུང་གནས་དང་། སྣང་བ་མཐའ་ཡས་དང་། དོན་ཡོད་གྲུབ་པ་ལ་སོགས་པ

165

THE TANTRA OF VAJRASATTVA'S MAGNIFICENT SKY

From the mTshams brag Edition of the rNying ma rGyud 'bum

Volume Three, pages 165-191.

ཀ ཀུན་འདུས

༄༅། །རྒྱུད་འདི་ཐོས་པའི་ཡིད་རང་བྱུང་ལ་ཤེས་སུ་བཅུ་ར་ནས། གཉིས་སུ་མེད་པ་མཐའ་ཅ་ལ་བའི་ཕྲིག་ལ་རྫོགས་ར་ཏོ། །རྡོ་རྗེ་སེམས་དཔའ་ལ་སོགས་པའི
འཁོར་རྣམས་རྗེས་སུ་རང་ངོ། །རྒྱུད་ཡོངས་སུ་གཏད་པའི་ལེའུ་སྟེ་ཉི་ཤུ་པའོ།། །།རྒྱལ་པོ་རྒྱས་རྒྱུད་སྙིང་པོ་རབ་འབྱུང་བའོ། །རྫོགས་སོ།།
༄། །རྒྱ་གར་སྐད་དུ། བཛྲ་ཧ་ག་ས་མེ་མ་ཧཱ་ཏནྟྲ་ནཱ་མ། བོད་སྐད་དུ། རྡོ་རྗེ་སེམས་དཔའ་ནམ་མཁའ་ཆེའི་རྒྱུད་ཅེས་བྱ་བ།
དཔལ་རྡོ་རྗེ་སེམས་དཔའ་ལ་ཕྱག་འཚལ་ལོ། །འདི་སྐད་བདག་གིས་ཐོས་པ་དུས་གཅིག་ན། བཅོམ་ལྡན་འདས་དེ་བཞིན་གཤེགས་པ་ཀུན་ཏུ་བཟང་པོ་སྐུ་མདུན་རང་རྒྱ་བ་མེད
པ ; རྣམ་པར་ཐར་པའི་དབྱིངས་གསུམ་དང་ལྡན་པ། ཕྱག་རྒྱ་གིས་ཐེར་སྤྲིན་ནང་པོ་ཆེ་འོད་འབར་བ་བྱུང་བ་རྒྱུད་པའི་རྡོ་ན་པ་སྟོ། སྐུ་མ་ཀུན་ཏུ་བཟང་མོ་དང་གཉིས་སུ་མེད
པ་ར་ལོག་གི་ནི་གནས་མཐའ་དང་དབུས་མེད་པ་ཡུམ་གྱི་གཞལ་ཡས་ཁང་ན། གདན་སྣང་པོ་ཆེ་ལ་སོགས་པའི་སྟེང་ན་པདྨ་དང་ཉི་ཟླ་བ་སྤྲས་པའི་གདན་ལ། རྡོ་རྗེ་སེམས
དཔའ་ལ་སོགས་པའི་དེ་བཞིན་གཤེགས་པ་རྣམ་པར་སྣང་མཛད་དང་། དཀོན་མཆོག་འབྱུང་གནས་དང་། སྣང་བ་མཐའ་ཡས་དང་། དོན་ཡོད་གྲུབ་པ་ལ་སོགས་པ

165

བཙུན་མོ་དང་བཅས་པ་དང་། འཁོར་གྱི་བྱང་ཆུབ་སེམས་དཔའ་སའི་སྙིང་པོ་དང་། ནམ་མཁའི་སྙིང་པོ་དང་། འཇིག་རྟེན་དབང་ཕྱུག་དང་། ཕྱག་ན་རྡོ་རྗེ་ལ་སོགས་པ
བཙུན་མོ་དང་བཅས་པ་དང་། བྱང་ཆུབ་སེམས་དཔའ་བྱམས་པ་དང་། ཀུན་ཏུ་བཟང་པོ་དང་། སྒྲིབ་པ་རྣམ་པར་སེལ་བ་དང་། འཇམ་པའི་དབྱངས་ལ་སོགས་པ
བཙུན་མོ་དང་བཅས་པ་དང་། གཞན་ཡང་ཁྲོ་བོ་ཆེན་པོ་གཤིན་རྗེ་གཤེད་པོ་དང་། སྟོབས་པོ་ཆེ་དང་། རྟ་མགྲིན་དང་། བདུད་རྩི་འཁྱིལ་པ་ལ་སོགས་པ་བཙུན་མོ
དང་བཅས་པ་དང་ཐབས་ཅིག་ཏུ་བཞུགས་སོ། །གླེང་གཞིའི་ལེའུ་སྟེ་དང་པོའོ།། །།དེ་ནས་རྡོ་རྗེ་སེམས་དཔའ་ལ་སོགས་པའི་དེ་བཞིན
གཤེགས་པ་ཐམས་ཅད་ཀྱིས། བཅོམ་ལྡན་འདས་དེ་བཞིན་གཤེགས་པ་ཀུན་ཏུ་བཟང་པོ་ལ་འདི་སྐད་ཅེས་གསོལ་ཏོ། །བཅོམ་ལྡན་འདས་ཀུན་ཏུ་བཟང
པོ ; བདག་ཉིད་ཆེན་པོ་ལྷུན་གྱིས་གྲུབ་པའི་དཀྱིལ་འཁོར་རྡོ་རྗེ་ལྟར་བསྐྱོད་པ་ལགས། གནས་ནི་ཇི་ལྟར་བསྐྱེད་པ་ལགས། ཞེས་གསོལ་པ་དང་། བཅོམ་ལྡན་འདས
དེ་བཞིན་གཤེགས་པ་ཀུན་ཏུ་བཟང་པོས་བཀའ་སྩལ་པ། རྡོ་རྗེ་སེམས་དཔའ་ལ་སོགས་པ་འཁོར་གྱི་དེ་བཞིན་གཤེགས་པ་རྣམས་ཉོན་ཅིག །བདག་ཉིད་ཆེན་པོ་ལྷུན་གྱིས

166

ཡ ཀླུ་ཤི

༄༅། །སྒྲུབ་པའི་གནས་ཞི། །སྣ་ཚོགས་ཐིག་མ་གཅིག་གི་མཐོང་ཚིག་ལ་ཕྱུ་མཆོག་མ་ཆར་དག་པ་འགྲིབ་ཞལ་ཡས་ཁང་དུ་བསྟན་དོ། །དེ་ལ་བདག་ཉིད་ཆེན་པོ་ལྷུན་གྱིས
གྲུབ་པའི་དཀྱིལ་འཁོར་ལ་གཉིས་ཏེ། །དཀྱིལ་འཁོར་དུ་ལྷུན་གྱིས་གྲུབ་པའི་དཀྱིལ་འཁོར་དང་། །བདག་ཉིད་ཆེན་པོ་ལུས་ཀྱི་དཀྱིལ་འཁོར་རོ། །སྙིང་པོ་བསྡུས་པའི་ལེའུ་སྟེ་གཉིས
པའོ།། །།དེ་ནས་ཡང་རྡོ་རྗེ་སེམས་དཔའ་ལ་སོགས་པ་དེ་བཞིན་གཤེགས་པ་ཐམས་ཅད་ཀྱིས། །བཅོམ་ལྡན་འདས་དེ་བཞིན་གཤེགས་པ་ཀུན་ཏུ
བཟང་པོ་ལ་འདི་སྐད་ཅེས་གསོལ་ཏོ། །བཅོམ་ལྡན་འདས་དེ་བཞིན་གཤེགས་པ་ཀུན་ཏུ་བཟང་པོ། །བདག་ཉིད་ཆེན་པོ་ལྷུན་གྱིས་གྲུབ་པའི་དཀྱིལ་འཁོར་ཇི་ལྟར་ལགས། །
དེ་བཞིན་གཤེགས་པ་ཀུན་ཏུ་བཟང་པོ། །བདག་ཉིད་ཆེན་པོ་ལུས་ཀྱི་དཀྱིལ་འཁོར་ཇི་ལྟར་ལགས། །ཞེས་གསོལ་པ་དང་། །བཅོམ་ལྡན་འདས་དེ་བཞིན་གཤེགས་པ་ཀུན་ཏུ
བཟང་པོས་བཀའ་སྩལ་པ། །བཅོམ་ལྡན་འདས་རྡོ་རྗེ་སེམས་དཔའ་ལ་སོགས་པ་འཁོར་གྱི་དེ་བཞིན་གཤེགས་པ་ཐམས་ཅད་ཉོན་ཅིག །རིག་པའི་སྐད་ཅིག་མ་དེ་ཉིད་ལ་རིགས་ལྔ
དང་། །རིགས་ཀྱི་ཡུམ་ལྔ་དང་། །སེམས་དཔའ་བརྒྱད་དང་། །སེམས་མ་བརྒྱད་དང་། །ཁྲོ་བོ་དང་ཁྲོ་མོ་བརྒྱད་དུ་གསལ་བར་རྫོགས་པ་ཉིད་དོ། །བདག་ཉིད་ཆེན་པོ་ལུས

167

ཀྱི་དཀྱིལ་འཁོར་ནི། །ལྷ་རྣམས་སྐུ་ནམ་མཁའ་ལ་གསལ་བར་རྫོགས་པ་སྟེ། །བདག་ཉིད་ཆེན་པོ་ལྷུན་གྱིས་གྲུབ་པའི་དཀྱིལ་འཁོར་རོ། །བདག་ཉིད་ཆེན་པོ་ལྷུན་གྱིས་གྲུབ་པའི་དཀྱིལ
འཁོར་གྱི་ལེའུ་སྟེ་གསུམ་པའོ།། །།དེ་ནས་ཡང་བཅོམ་ལྡན་འདས་འཁོར་གྱི་དེ་བཞིན་གཤེགས་པ་ཐམས་ཅད་ཀྱིས། །བཅོམ་ལྡན་འདས་དེ་བཞིན་གཤེགས་
པ་ཀུན་ཏུ་བཟང་པོ་ལ་འདི་སྐད་ཅེས་གསོལ་ཏོ། །བཅོམ་ལྡན་འདས་དེ་བཞིན་གཤེགས་པ་ཀུན་ཏུ་བཟང་པོ། །ལུས་ཀྱི་ལྷ་རྣམས་ཇི་ལྟར་ལགས། །ཞེས་པ་དང་། །བཅོམ་ལྡན་
འདས་དེ་བཞིན་གཤེགས་པ་ཀུན་ཏུ་བཟང་པོས་བཀའ་སྩལ་པ། །བཅོམ་ལྡན་འདས་འཁོར་གྱི་དེ་བཞིན་གཤེགས་པ་ཐམས་ཅད་ཉོན་ཅིག །ལུས་ཀྱི་ལྷ་རྣམས་ནི། །རྩ་མདུད
ཟེར་ལྡན་པ་ལས་བཞི་དང་སོ་ང་རྒ་རེ་བ་སྐྱོལ། །ཡིད་ཆེན་ལྷ་དང་སྟོབས་ལྷ་ལྔ། །སྟོབས་ལྷ་ཐྭ་ཡང་ཡང་གནས་པ་སྟེ། །གཅིག་ནི་ཡིད་ལྷ་ཀུན་ཏུ་བཟང་། །མིག་ལྷ་གཉིས་དང་ལྷ
ལྷ་གཉིས། །སྣ་ལྷ་གཉིས་དང་སྤྱི་ལྷ་གཉིས། །རྣམ་ཤེས་བཞི་ཡི་ལྷ་བཞི་དང་། །དབང་པོ་བཞི་ཡི་ལྷ་བཞི་སྟེ། །རྣམ་ཤེས་བཞི་ཡི་ཡུལ་ལྷ་རྣམས། །ལྷ་རྣམས་གཞིར
གནས་ཚད་ནི། །དེ་ལ་ཏུས་བཞི་ལྷ་མོ་བཞི། །སྒོ་མ་ར་ལྷ་རྣམས་སྲིད་པར་ཆགས། །སྲིད་པ་གནས་དང་ཆགས་པ་དང་། །ཆད་ལྟ་བ་ཉི་འཛིན་པའི་ལྷ། །ཞིག་པས

168

ཕ

169

༄༅། །སྒོམས་པ་རྒྱུར་བའི་རྩ། །དུས་བཞི་ལྷ་མོའི་རྩ་རུ་ཤེས། །སྲིད་པ་སྤྲུར་ཚེ་རིག་པར་ཤེས། །དེ་ནས་དབང་པོ་ཡང་གའི་རྩ། །རིག་བྲུ་དྲི་མ་ཚན
ཉིད་གང་ཡིན་ཤེས། །དེ་ནི་ཕྱུགས་ཀྱི་དབང་པོ་རྩ། །རིག་བྲུ་རང་གི་ངོ་བོ་ཉིད། །ཕྱུགས་ཀྱི་རྩ་རུ་ཤེས་པར་བྱ། །ཉམས་སུ་སྐྱོང་བའི་མཚན་ཉིད་དེ། །ཕྱུལ་དང་པོ་རྣམ
ཤེས་གསུམ། །འདུས་པ་ལས་ནི་འབྱུང་བའི་རྩ། །རྩ་རྣམས་མས་མ་ཕྱུགས་སུ་རྟོགས་པས། །བདག་ཏུ་བཏགས་པ་མ་ཡིན་དང་། །དག་པ་ར་བཏགས་པ་མ་ཡིན་དང་། །
ཆད་པ་ར་བཏགས་པ་མ་ཡིན་དང་། །མཚན་མ་ར་བཏགས་པ་མ་ཡིན་པ། །དེ་ནི་ཕྱུགས་ཀྱི་རྩ་རྣམས་ཡིན། །རྩ་ཡི་ལེའུ་སྟེ་བཞི་པའོ།། །།དེ
ནས་ཡང་བཅོམ་ལྡན་འདས་དེ་བཞིན་གཤེགས་པ་ཐམས་ཅད་ཀྱིས་གསོལ་པ། བཅོམ་ལྡན་འདས་དེ་བཞིན་གཤེགས་པ་ཀུན་ཏུ་བཟང་པོ། རྩ་དེ་རྣམས་ཀྱུ་ལ་ཧཱི་ལྷ་རིག་རྣམ
པ་ལ་གནས། ཞེས་གསོལ་པ་དང་། བཅོམ་ལྡན་འདས་ཀྱིས་ལན་བཏབ་པ། དེ་བཞིན་གཤེགས་པ་ཐམས་ཅད་ཉན་ཅིག །སྙིང་དཀར་རྩ་ནི་སྒྲིལ་མ་ལ། །ཨ་དང་ཧཱུྃ། བདེ
ཆེན་རྩ་ཡི་རྩུལ་ལ་གནས། །སྲོག་པ་རྩ་ནི་སྒྲིལ་མ་ལ། །མི་བསྐྱོད་རྩ་དང་ཀུན་བཟང་རྩ། །ཐོད་དང་སྐུ་རུ་ཤེས་པར་བྱ། །རྩ་གཉིས་པ་ཡི་རང་བཞིན་དེ། །རྡོ་རྗེ་ཕྱིར

170

ཀྱི་རིམ་པ་སྒྲུབ་མ། །ཀུན་ཏུ་བཟང་པོའི་རྩ་རུ་ཤེས་བྱ། །དེ་ཡང་སྤྲ་དང་ཨ་རུ་བཏགས། །རྒྱ་སྐམས་པ་བཞི་ནི་ཏ་དང་། །ཀ་དང་ན་ཧྲི་ཧྲི་དང་། །ཝ་ཀ་བ་ཞི་ན་ཊཱ་ཤེས་པར་བྱ། །
ཀ་ཁ་དང་ཙ་ཤ་ལྷ་དང་། །པ་ཕ་དང་ནི་ཤུ་བརྗོད། །མི་རྩ་གཉིས་དང་སྣ་རྩ་གཉིས། །ལྕེ་རྩ་གཉིས་དང་རྣ་རྩ་གཉིས། །རྣམ་ཤེས་བཞི་དང་དབང་པོ་ལ་བྱུགས་ཙ་ནས་པ།
མིག་དང་རྣ་བ་སྣ་དང་ལྕེ། །དབང་པོ་བཞི་ཡི་རྩ་ལ་ནི། །ཙ་ཚ་ཛ་ཛྷ་བཞི་དང་ནི། །ཡ་ར་དང་ནི་ཤ་ལ་བཞི། །གསང་བའི་དབང་པོ་ཡང་གའི་རྩ། །ང་ཉ་ཎ་ཨ་བཞི་དང་
ནི། །ཀྵ་ཤ་ས་ཧ་བཞི་པོ་དང་། །དེ་རིག་ཁ་རོག་སྤྱིབས་ཀྱི་རྩུལ། །རྩ་རྣམས་ཡི་གེའི་རྩུལ་དུ་གནས་པའི་ལེའུ་སྟེ་ལྔ་པའོ།། །།དེ་ནས་ཡང་
འཁོར་ཀྱི་བཅོམ་ལྡན་འདས་དེ་བཞིན་གཤེགས་པ་ཐམས་ཅད་ཀྱིས། བཅོམ་ལྡན་འདས་དེ་བཞིན་གཤེགས་པ་ཀུན་ཏུ་བཟང་པོ་ལ་གསོལ་པ། བཅོམ་ལྡན་འདས་དེ་བཞིན
གཤེགས་པ་ཀུན་ཏུ་བཟང་པོ། སེམས་ཅན་ཐམས་ཅད་ཀྱི་རང་བཞིན་ཧི་ལྟ་བུར་གནས་པ་ལགས། ཞེས་གསོལ་པ་དང་། བཅོམ་ལྡན་འདས་དེ་བཞིན་གཤེགས་པ
ཀུན་ཏུ་བཟང་པོས་བཀའ་སྩལ་པ། བཅོམ་ལྡན་འདས་འཁོར་ཀྱི་དེ་བཞིན་གཤེགས་པ་ཐམས་ཅད་ཉོན་ཅིག །འབྱུང་བ་ཆེན་པོ་བཅོམ་ལྡན་འདས། །རྒྱུ་པ་ར་གནས་པས།

ཁ ཨ་ཧཱུྃ

༄༅། །བཅོམ་ལྡན་འདས། །འགྲོ་བ་ཀུན་ལ་རང་བཞིན་གནས། །ཡེ་ནས་རྒྱལ་བའི་རིགས་ཀྱི་ལམ་ཡིན་ནོ་ཞེས། །སྤྲིན་ཅི་ལྟོས་དུ་རྣམས་བདག་གིས་ཀྱང་། །
གྲོལ་བར་འདོད་རྒྱུད་གཞན་ལ་ས་མེད། །རང་བཞིན་ཉིད་ཀྱིས་གནས་པའི་ལེའུ་སྟེ་དྲུག་པའོ།། །དེ་ནས་ཡང་འཁོར་རྣམས་ཀྱི་དེ་བཞིན་གཤེགས་པ
རྣམས་ཀྱིས། བཅོམ་ལྡན་འདས་དེ་བཞིན་གཤེགས་པ་ཀུན་ཏུ་བཟང་པོ་ལ་གསོལ་པ། བཅོམ་ལྡན་འདས་དེ་བཞིན་གཤེགས་པ་ཀུན་ཏུ་བཟང་པོ། རྫོགས་པ
ཆེན་པོའི་དོན་མཐར་ཕྱིན་གང་གིས་རྟོགས་པར་བགྱི། དེ་བཞིན་གཤེགས་པ་ཀུན་ཏུ་བཟང་པོས་བཀའ་སྩལ་པ། བཅོམ་ལྡན་འདས་འཁོར་གྱི་དེ་བཞིན་གཤེགས་པ་རྣམས
ཉེ་ཅིག །རྟོག་མེད་མཉམ་ཉིད་ཆོས་ཀྱི་སྐུ། །ཆོས་སྐུ་ནམ་མཁའ་ལྟ་བུ་ལས། །འཕྲུལ་ཆེན་ལྷ་བུའི་སྐུ་རུ་བཞེངས་པ། །གཟུང་བ་མ་ཆགས་ཆུ་ཟླ་འདྲ། །ཐབས་དང་ཤེས
རབ་ཟུང་གཉིས་ལ། །ཨཱ་ལི་ཀཱ་ལི་ཡི་གེ་གསལ། །འདི་རུ་ལོ་བཞི་ཡང་གསལ་བ་ལས། །གཉིས་སུ་མེད་པ་རྒྱུ་ར་པ་ལས། །ཀུན་ཏུ་བཟང་པོའི་ངོ་ལ་པ་ཡིས། །ཨཱ་ལི
ཀཱ་ལི་སྲབ་དུ་བསྡུན། །དེ་ནི་ཡང་དག་མཛོད་པའི་དྲུ། །པད་དང་ཨ་ནུ་ལ་གསུམ་པ་བཞིན། །འདི་ཡི་དོན་ཡོངས་ཀྱི་སྤྱི་ཡུ་ལ། །སངས་རྒྱས་གསུང་གི་ཐབ་མོ་འབྱུང་། །

171

ཡེ་མཐོང་ངེས་རྒྱས་སྐྱེ་དགུ་ཡང་འདི། །བཙལ་བས་རྙེད་པར་གནས་མེད་དོ། །རྟག་གི་ཆོས་བཞིན་མི་འགྱུར་བས། །ལྷུན་ངེས་པས་ནམ་མཁའ་བསྐྱེགས་པ
བཞིན། །གོང་ནས་གོང་དུ་ཚངས་པའི་ལམ། །བྲུབ་ལ་ཆོས་དང་མཐུན་པ་མིན། །ཅི་སྙིང་ལམ་ལས་བགྲོ་འགྱུར་ན། །ནམ་མཁའི་མཐའ་དང་ཞེན་འགྲིབ་པ་མེད།།
མངོན་པར་བྱང་ཆུབ་པའི་ལེའུ་སྟེ་བདུན་པའོ།། །དེ་ནས་ཡང་བཅོམ་ལྡན་འདས་འཁོར་རྣམས་ཀྱི་དེ་བཞིན་གཤེགས་པ་རྣམས་ཀྱིས་གསོལ
བ། བཅོམ་ལྡན་འདས་དེ་བཞིན་གཤེགས་པ་ཀུན་ཏུ་བཟང་པོ། ཀུན་ཏུ་བཟང་པོའི་དོན་པ་ལས། །རྫོགས་པ་ཆེན་པོ་ཇི་ལྟར་འབྱུང་། །ཞེས་གསོལ་པ་དང་། །
བཅོམ་ལྡན་འདས་ཀུན་ཏུ་བཟང་པོས་བཀའ་སྩལ་པ། ཅི་ར་ཡང་མི་གནས་མི་རྟོག་པ། །ཨཱ་ལི་ཀཱ་ལི་ལས་འབྱུང་བ། །དེ་ལྟར་དེ་བཞིན་དེ་ཡི་ཕྱིར། །དེ་ལ་དེ་བསྟན
དེ་ཡང་སྟོན། །དེ་ནི་སྙིང་པོ་དེ་བས་ན། །དེ་ལས་དེ་འབྱུང་ངོ་མཚར་ཆེ། །སྟོན་ཀྱི་དེ་དང་དེ་ལྟའོ་དེ། །དེ་བཞིན་དེ་ཡི་གནས་སུ་ཆེ། །དེ་ལྟར་དེ་ཡིས་ལམ་འདྲ
བར། །དེ་ནི་དེ་ཡི་རང་བཞིན་ནོ། །དེ་དང་འདྲ་བ་ཡོངས་ཀྱི་ལམ། །སྣང་བ་ལས་འབྱུང་རྟེན་དང་བཅས། །ཀུན་གྱི་མཉམ་ཉིད་ཡིན་པ་ལ། །རྟོགས་ས་བུ་བསྟན་པས

172

༄༅། །མཐོང་བ་མེད། །གདོད་ནས་རང་བཞིན་རྣམ་པར་དག །ཡོངས་སུ་རྫོགས་པའི་ལེའུ་སྟེ་བརྒྱད་པའོ།། །།དེ་ནས
ཡང་ཁྱབ་འཁོར་གྱི་དེ་བཞིན་གཤེགས་པ་རྣམས་ཀྱིས་གསོལ་པ། བཅོམ་ལྡན་འདས་དེ་བཞིན་གཤེགས་པ་ཀུན་ཏུ་བཟང་པོ། །གདོད་མ་ནས་རང་བཞིན་གྱིས་རྣམ་པར
དག་པ་ལ། །ཐབས་ཤེས་རབ་ལ་བརྟེན་པ་རྫོ་སྐུར་ལགས། །བཅོམ་ལྡན་འདས་ཀུན་ཏུ་བཟང་པོས་བཀའ་སྩལ་པ། བཅོམ་ལྡན་འདས་ཁྱབ་འཁོར་གྱི་དེ་བཞིན་གཤེགས
པ་རྣམས་ཉོན་ཅིག །ཆེ་བའི་ཡེ་ཤེས་རྟོགས་དཀའ་བ། །ཤེས་རབ་ཐབས་ལ་བརྟེན་པས་འགྲུབ། །མི་འཚམ་གཞན་ལ་བསྟན་འདྲ་ཡང་། །མངོན་སུམ་བདེ་བ་རང་
ལས་འབྱུང་། །རང་བཞིན་ཆེ་བ་ལ་གནས་པའི་ལེའུ་སྟེ་དགུ་པའོ།། །།དེ་ནས་ཡང་འཁོར་གྱི་དེ་བཞིན་གཤེགས་པ་རྣམས་ཀྱིས་གསོལ་པ།
བཅོམ་ལྡན་འདས་དེ་བཞིན་གཤེགས་པ་ཀུན་ཏུ་བཟང་པོ་རྫོགས་པ་སྤྲོ་བཙོལ་དང་བྲལ་བའི་དོན་རྫོ་སྐུར་ལགས། བཅོམ་ལྡན་འདས་དེ་བཞིན་གཤེགས་པ་ཀུན་ཏུ
བཟང་པོས་བཀའ་སྩལ་པ། འཁོར་གྱི་དེ་བཞིན་གཤེགས་པ་རྣམས་ཉོན་ཅིག །བཅོམ་ལྡན་འདས་འཁོར་གྱི་དེ་བཞིན་གཤེགས་པ་རྣམས། རྫོགས་པ་ཆེན་པོ 173

སྤྲོ་བཙོལ་དང་བྲལ་བའི་དོན་ཅན། དབྱིངས་ཉིད་གདིང་མཐའ་མེད་པ་ནས། ཡིད་རང་བྱུང་གི་ཡེ་ཤེས་ཆེན་པོ་བཙོལ་བ་མེད་པར་ཡོ་ཉིད་རང་ཤར་བ་སྟེ་གདོད
མནས་རྩོལ་སེམས་དང་བྲལ་བའི་དོན་ནོ། །བཅོམ་ལྡན་འདས་འཁོར་གྱི་དེ་བཞིན་གཤེགས་པ་རྣམས་ཀྱིས་ཡང་གསོལ་པ། རྫོགས་པ་ཆེན་པོ་ཡི་རྩོལ་སེམས
དང་བྲལ་བ་ལགས་ན། བཅོམ་ལྡན་འདས་དེ་བཞིན་གཤེགས་པ་ཀུན་ཏུ་བཟང་པོ། སངས་རྒྱས་ཀྱི་ཆེ་བའི་ཡོན་ཏན་སྟོབས་དང་། མི་འཇིགས་པ་དང་།
མཚན་དང་། དཔེ་བྱད་རྒྱུ་ཅི་ལས་བྱུང་ལགས། བཅོམ་ལྡན་འདས་དེ་བཞིན་གཤེགས་པ་ཀུན་ཏུ་བཟང་པོས་བཀའ་སྩལ་པ། བཅོམ་ལྡན་འདས་འཁོར་གྱི
དེ་བཞིན་གཤེགས་པ་རྣམས། སངས་རྒྱས་ཀྱི་ཆེ་བའི་ཡོན་ཏན་སྟོབས་དང་མི་འཇིགས་པ་ལ་སོགས་པ་ནི། ཐེག་པ་འོག་མ་པའི་སྣང་བས་དེ་ཉིད་གཏིང་། རྫོགས་པ
ཆེན་པོ་སྤྲོ་བཙོལ་དང་བྲལ་བ་དེ་ཉིད་སྤྲོ་བཙོལ་སྤྲོ་བའི་དཀའ་བསླས་མེད་པར་རྫོགས་པ་ཆེན་པོའི་དོན་རྟོགས་མ་ཐག་ཏུ། སྤྲོ་བཙོལ་དང་བྲལ་བའི་རྫོགས་པ་ཆེན་པོ་རང་ལས
བྱུང་དེ; ཞེས་བཀའ་སྩལ་ཏོ། །ཡང་འཁོར་གྱི་དེ་བཞིན་གཤེགས་པ་རྣམས་ཀྱིས་གསོལ་པ། བཅོམ་ལྡན་འདས་རྫོགས་པ་ཆེན་པོའི་དོན་དེ། མ་རྟོགས་པའི 174

ཕྲ ཨ་བཅུ

༄༅། །རྣལ་འབྱོར་ཀྱིས་བསྒོམ་ན་ཇི་ལྟར་བསྒོམ། བཅོམ་ལྡན་འདས་ཀྱིས་བཀའ་སྩལ་པ། འཁོར་གྱི་དེ་བཞིན་གཤེགས་པ་རྣམས། རྟོགས་
པ་ཆེན་པོའི་དོན་མ་འདྲེས་པའི་རྣལ་འབྱོར་པས་བསྒོམ་ན་ཆོས་ཉིད་གདོད་མ་ནས་མ་སྐྱེས་པ་ལ་རང་གི་བློ་མ་སྐྱེས་པ་བཞག་ནས་བསྒོམ་པ་ཡིན་ནོ། །ཡང་འཁོར་གྱི་
དེ་བཞིན་གཤེགས་པ་རྣམས་ཀྱིས་གསོལ་པ། བཅོམ་ལྡན་འདས་ཆོས་ཉིད་མ་སྐྱེས་པར་བཞག་པ་ལས། ཆོ་འཕྲུལ་ཆེན་པོ་སྟོབས་དང་མི་འཇིགས་པ་ལ་
སོགས་པ་ཇི་ལྟར་འབྱུང་བ་ལགས། ཞེས་གསོལ་པ་དང་། བཅོམ་ལྡན་འདས་ཀྱིས་བཀའ་སྩལ་པ། ཆོ་འཕྲུལ་ཆེན་པོ་དཀའ་བ་མེད། །ཡོན་ཏན་ཀུན་དང་
སྟོབས་ཀྱི་རྣམས། །ཇི་བཞིན་རྟོགས་པ་སྲ་བ་ཡིས། །དེ་མ་ཐག་ཏུ་རང་ལས་འབྱུང་། །སྣང་བ་མེད་པའི་ཆོས་ཉིད་ལ། །མ་བཅོས་བཞག་ནས་བསྒོམ་པ་ཡིན། །དེ་དང་
དེ་ནི་རྣམ་བཅུ་ཡིན། །དེ་ལས་དེ་བཞིན་དེ་མི་འབྱུང་། །གྲུབ་ཚུལ་དང་གྲོལ་བའི་ལེའུ་སྟེ་བཅུ་པའོ།། ||བཅོམ་ལྡན་འདས་ལ། འཁོར
ཀྱི་དེ་བཞིན་གཤེགས་པ་རྣམས་ཀྱིས་གསོལ་པ། བཅོམ་ལྡན་འདས་དེ་བཞིན་གཤེགས་པ་ཀུན་ཏུ་བཟང་པོ། ཆོས་ཉིད་རང་བཞིན་གྱིས་གནས་པའི་དོན་ཇི་ལྟར

175

ལགས། ཞེས་གསོལ་པ་དང་། བཅོམ་ལྡན་འདས་ཀྱིས་བཀའ་སྩལ་པ། འཁོར་གྱི་དེ་བཞིན་གཤེགས་པ་རྣམས། ཆོས་ཉིད་རང་བཞིན་གྱིས་གནས་པ་ནི། རྡོ་རྗེ
སེམས་དཔའ་ནམ་མཁའ་ཆེ། །ཀུན་བཟང་ཡངས་པ་ཆོས་ཀྱི་དབྱིངས། །རྣམ་དག་ལམ་ཆེན་ཀུན་གྲོལ་ཕྱིར། །མི་སྐྱེ་མི་འགག་གཅིག་ཅར་མི་དགོངས། །སྤྲུལ་པས་བསམ་དོན
ཉིད་རྣམ་སྣང་ཕྱིར། །སྙིང་རྗེ་ཆེན་པོ་ཅི་ཡང་མི་མཛད། །ཆེ་བ་ཆེ་བའི་ཐབས་མེད་ཉིད། །ཡོན་ཏན་ཅིར་ཡང་བརྟགས་པ་མེད། །དོན་རྣམས་ཇི་བཞིན་མི་བསྒྱུར་དེ། །གྲུབ
མེད་པས་གྲོལ་བར་དགྲོལ། །རང་བྱུང་ཡེ་ཤེས་བཅོས་མེད་པས། །གྲོལ་ནས་གྲོལ་བའི་ལམ་ཡང་སྟོན། །ཆོས་ཉིད་རང་བཞིན་གྱིས་གནས་པའི་ལེའུ་སྟེ་བཅུ་གཅིག
པའོ།། །།ཡང་འཁོར་གྱི་དེ་བཞིན་གཤེགས་པ་རྣམས་ཀྱིས་གསོལ་པ། བཅོམ་ལྡན་འདས་དེ་བཞིན་གཤེགས་པ་ཀུན་ཏུ་བཟང་པོ། རང་གི
བྱང་ཆུབ་ཀྱི་སེམས་བརྗོད་པ་དང་བྲལ་བའི་དོན་ཇི་ལྟར་ལགས། ཞེས་གསོལ་པ་དང་། འཁོར་གྱི་དེ་བཞིན་གཤེགས་པ་རྣམས་ལ་བཀའ་སྩལ་པ། རང་གི་བྱང་ཆུབ
ཀྱི་སེམས་བརྗོད་པ་དང་བྲལ་བ་ནི། ཀུན་གཞིའི་ཆོས་ཉིད་གདོད་མ་ནས་མ་སྐྱེས་པ་སྟེ། མཚོན་དུ་གསང་བའི་ཆོས་ཉིད་དེ། །རྣ་དབང་གཞན་ལ་ཐོས་མི་འགྱུར། །

176

ཕ

༄༅། །དེ་བཞིན་ཉི་ཤུ་ཡི་དབང་པོས་ཀྱང་། །དེ་ལ་བརྗོད་དུ་རྣ་བ་ཙམ་མེད། །ཅེས་བཀའ་སྩལ་ཏོ། །རང་གི་བྱང་ཆུབ་ཀྱི་སེམས་བརྗོད་པ་དང་བྲལ་
བའི་ལེའུ་སྟེ་བཅུ་གཉིས་པའོ༎ ༎ཡང་འོག་མིན་གྱི་དེ་བཞིན་གཤེགས་པ་ཐམས་ཅད་ཀྱིས་གསོལ་པ། བཅོམ་ལྡན་འདས་དེ་བཞིན་གཤེགས་
པ་ཀུན་ཏུ་བཟང་པོ། རང་གི་བྱང་ཆུབ་ཀྱི་སེམས་དེ་ལས་ཀྱིས་འཚོལ་བ་ལ་ཡགས་སམ། མི་འཚོལ་བ་ལ་ཡགས། ཞེས་གསོལ་པ་དང་། བཅོམ་ལྡན་འདས་ཀྱིས་
བཀའ་སྩལ་པ། འགྲོ་བའི་སྡུག་བསྔལ་བྱང་ཆུབ་སེམས། །ཀུན་ཏུ་རྒྱུ་བ་པས་རྣམ་པར་རོལ། །དེ་ལ་བསྐྱེད་པ་མེད་པ་ཞིག་ཏུ། །ནམ་མཁའི་མཐའ་དང་མཉམ
པར་གནས། །བྱེད་པར་རྩེ་ར་ཡིང་མཚུངས་པ་ལ། །ལས་སོ་ཞེ་སའི་རྣམ་པར་བཏགས། །ཅི་སྟེ་ལས་ཀྱི་དབང་གྱུར་ན། །རང་བྱུང་ཡེ་ཤེས་ཡོད་མ་ཡིན། །རྒྱུ
ཉིད་རྡོ་རྗེ་ཆེན་དང་འདྲ། །མ་སྐྱེས་པས་ན་འཇིག་པ་མེད། །གདོད་ནས་སྙིང་པོ་བྱང་ཆུབ་ལ། །རྩོལ་བའི་བསམ་པས་དབྱིངས་མི་བསྐྱོད། །བྱང་ཆུབ་ཀྱི་སེམས་འགྲོ
བ་ལ་ལས་ཀྱིས་མི་འཚོལ་བའི་ལེའུ་སྟེ་བཅུ་གསུམ་པའོ༎ ༎ཡང་འོག་མིན་གྱི་དེ་བཞིན་གཤེགས་པ་ཐམས་ཅད་ཀྱིས་གསོལ་པ། བཅོམ་ལྡན་

177

འདས་དེ་བཞིན་གཤེགས་པ་ཀུན་ཏུ་བཟང་པོ། བྱང་ཆུབ་ཀྱི་སེམས་རྩོལ་སེམས་དང་བྲལ་བ་དེ་རུ་བ་འཛོག་པ་དང་སྒོམ་ལམ་གནས་ལ་ཡགས་སམ། ཞེས་གསོལ
པ་དང་། བཅོམ་ལྡན་འདས་ཀྱིས་བཀའ་སྩལ་པ། ཡོན་ཏན་ཆེན་པོའི་སེམས་མ་གཏན་ཞིག །ཐམས་མ་གཏན་ཉིད་པས་བསམ་ཏུ་མེད། །མཐའ་བས་མཐས་མ་སྦྱང་ངས
ཆོས་བཞིན་ཏུ། །རྣམ་རྟོག་ཉིད་ལས་ཡེ་ཤེས་སྐྱེ། །འཕྲ་བའི་བློ་མི་རྣམ་ཅན་བཏགས་ཤིང་། །སེམས་ཀྱི་དོན་པས་ལམ་མཚོལ་ཞིང་། །དགོན་པའི་རྒྱུད་དུ་དབེན
འཛིན་ཞིང་། །ཁ་ཏག་སན་རྣམ་པར་རྟོག་འབྱུང་བར་སྒོམ། །རྒྱུ་དང་འབྲས་བུ་རམ་མིང་བཏགས་ཤིང་། །དགེ་སྡིག་གཉིས་ཀ་རྣམ་པར་སེལ། །འཇིག་རྟེན་འདི་ད་ལ་འབྱུང
ངོ་ཞེས། །སྣང་དེ་རང་གྲོལ་བ་མཆོག་ཏུ་བསྐྱེད། །ཅེས་བཀའ་སྩལ་ཏོ། །བྱང་ཆུབ་ཀྱི་སེམས་རྩོལ་སེམས་དང་བྲལ་བའི་ལེའུ་སྟེ་བཅུ་བཞི་པའོ༎
༎ཡང་འོག་མིན་གྱི་དེ་བཞིན་གཤེགས་པ་ཐམས་ཅད་ཀྱིས་གསོལ་པ། བཅོམ་ལྡན་འདས་དེ་བཞིན་གཤེགས་པ་ཀུན་ཏུ་བཟང་པོ། བྱང་ཆུབ་ཀྱི་སེམས
རྩོལ་སེམས་དང་བྲལ་བ། བསམ་ཏུ་མེད་པ་དེ་ཉིད་གཉིས་སུ་མེད་པའི་སྒྲིབ་དང་བྲལ་བ་ལ་ཡགས་སམ་མ་ཡགས། ཞེས་གསོལ་པ་དང་། བཅོམ་ལྡན་འདས

178

ཀ།

༄༅། །ཀྱིས་བཀའ་སྩལ་པ། ཆགས་དང་མཆམས་མཆོག་གི་ཡུམ། །སྒྱུ་མ་བཞིན་ཏེ་བྲག་ཆ་འདྲ། །བདེ་དང་སྡུག་བསྔལ་རྒྱུ་མཚན་ཞེས།
བཅོམ་ལྡན་འདས་ཀྱིས་བཀའ་སྩལ་ཏོ། །བྱང་ཆུབ་ཀྱི་སེམས་གཉིས་སུ་མེད་པའི་སྒྲོན་དང་སྒྲོལ་བའི་ལེའུ་སྟེ་བཅོ་ལྔ་པའོ།།
ཡང་འཁོར་ཀྱི་དེ་བཞིན་གཤེགས་པ་རྣམས་ཀྱིས་གསོལ་པ། བཅོམ་ལྡན་འདས་དེ་བཞིན་གཤེགས་པ་ཀུན་ཏུ་བཟང་པོ། བྱང་ཆུབ་ཀྱི་སེམས་བདག་ཉིད་
ཆེན་པོ་དེ། རང་ལས་ཡེ་ཤེས་བྱུང་བ་ལགས་སམ་མ་ལགས། ཞེས་གསོལ་པ་དང་། བཅོམ་ལྡན་འདས་ཀྱིས་བཀའ་སྩལ་པ། འདོད་ཆགས་ཞེ་སྡང་
གཏི་མུག་ཀྱང་། །བྱང་ཆུབ་ཆེན་པོའི་ལམ་ལས་བྱུང་། །ཀུན་སྤྱོད་ཡོན་ཏན་རྣམ་ལྔ་ཡང་། །ཆོས་ཉིད་མཉམ་ཉིད་ཀྱི་རྒྱན། །ཅེས་བཀའ་སྩལ་ཏོ། །ཡེ་
ཤེས་ཆེན་པོ་རང་ལས་བྱུང་བའི་ལེའུ་སྟེ་བཅུ་དྲུག་པའོ།། ||ཡང་འཁོར་ཀྱི་དེ་བཞིན་གཤེགས་པ་རྣམས་ཀྱིས་གསོལ་པ། བཅོམ་ལྡན་
འདས་དེ་བཞིན་གཤེགས་པ་ཀུན་ཏུ་བཟང་པོ། ཐབས་དང་ཤེས་རབ་གཉིས་སུ་མེད་པའི་ལྟ་བ་དང་། ཡོངས་སུ་རྫོགས་པའི་དགོངས་པའི་དོན་ཇི་ལྟ་བུ་ལགས།

179

ཞེས་གསོལ་པ་དང་། བཅོམ་ལྡན་འདས་ཀྱིས་བཀའ་སྩལ་པ། ནམ་མཁའི་རྟོག་པ་སྐྱེ་མེད་ཅིང་། །རྟོག་པ་དེ་ཉིད་ནམ་མཁའ་འདྲ། །མ་ཆགས་ནམ་མཁའ་སྤྱོད་
ལགས། །སང་རྡོ་ཆེན་པོ་ནམ་མཁའ་ལ་བྱུང་། །ཞེས་བཀའ་སྩལ་ཏོ། །ཡོངས་སུ་རྫོགས་པ་དང་སྦྱོར་ཐབས་ཀྱི་ལེའུ་སྟེ་བཅུ་བདུན་པའོ།།
ཡང་འཁོར་ཀྱི་དེ་བཞིན་གཤེགས་པ་རྣམས་ཀྱིས་གསོལ་པ། བཅོམ་ལྡན་འདས་དེ་བཞིན་གཤེགས་པ་ཀུན་ཏུ་བཟང་པོ། ཐབས་དང་ཤེས་རབ་ཀྱི་སྦྱོར་སྒྲོལ་བ་ཆགས་པ
དང་བྲལ་བ་ལགས་སམ་མ་ལགས། ཞེས་གསོལ་པ་དང་། བཅོམ་ལྡན་འདས་ཀྱིས་བཀའ་སྩལ་པ། དཔའ་བོ་དེ་དང་སྒྱུ་མའི་བདེ། །མ་རྟོགས་སྒྱུ་མ་པ་དང་རྒྱུ་བ་ལ
འབྱུང་། །དེ་ཡང་རྣམ་པའི་སྒྲོན་ཡིན་པས། །དེ་ལ་བརྟེན་པ་རབ་མི་འགྱུར། །ཞེས་བཀའ་སྩལ་ཏོ། །ཆགས་པ་དང་བྲལ་བའི་ལེའུ་སྟེ་བཅོ་བརྒྱད་པའོ།།
||ཡང་འཁོར་ཀྱི་དེ་བཞིན་གཤེགས་པ་རྣམས་ཀྱིས་གསོལ་པ། བཅོམ་ལྡན་འདས་དེ་བཞིན་གཤེགས་པ་ཀུན་ཏུ་བཟང་པོ། ཆགས་པ་དང་བྲལ་བའི་
བྱང་ཆུབ་ཀྱི་སེམས་དེ་གདོད་མ་ནས་ཚད་ཀྱི་སྙིང་པོ་ལ་རང་བཞིན་གྱིས་གནས་པ་ལགས་སམ་མ་ལགས། ཞེས་གསོལ་པ་དང་། བཅོམ་ལྡན་འདས་ཀྱིས་བཀའ

180

ཁ

181

༄༅། །སྤྲུལ་པ ༑ དུས་གསུམ་གཅིག་སྟེ་ཁྱད་པར་མེད། །སྔོན་མེད་ཕྱིས་མེད་གདོད་ནས་འབྱུང་། །ཆོས་སྐུ་ལྷུན་གྲུབ་པས་གཅིག་པའི་ཕྱིར། །ཆེ
པས་ཆེན་པོ་རང་བཞིན་གནས། །ཞེས་བཀའ་སྩལ་ཏོ། །ཀ་དག་ནམ་མཁའ་ཆེ་བའི་སྙིང་པོ་རང་བཞིན་གྱིས་གནས་པའི་ལེའུ་སྟེ་བཅུ་དགུ་པའོ།། ༎
ཡང་འཁོར་ཀྱི་དེ་བཞིན་གཤེགས་པ་རྣམས་ཀྱིས་གསོལ་པ ། བཅོམ་ལྡན་འདས་དེ་བཞིན་གཤེགས་པ་ཀུན་ཏུ་བཟང་པོ ། རང་བཞིན་གྱིས་གདོད་མ་ནས་མ་སྐྱེས་པའི་བྱང་
ཆུབ་ཀྱི་སེམས་དེ་སྟོན་པ་ལམ་དང་བྲལ་བ་ལ་ལགས་སམ་མ་ལགས ། ཞེས་གསོལ་པ་དང་ ། བཅོམ་ལྡན་འདས་ཀྱིས་བཀའ་སྩལ་པ ། སྲིད་པ་གསུམ་ན་སྐྱེ་རབ་ཡང་།།
མིང་ཙམ་སྒྱུ་མ་ར་སྣང་བ་སྟེ། །འཁོར་ལོས་སྒྱུར་བའི་གནས་ཆེན་ཡང་། །སྒྱུ་མ་སྤྲུལ་པའི་བསྟི་གནས་ཡིན། །རྣམ་སྤྱོད་དུས་ལ་བལྟོས་པ་རྣམས་ཀྱིས། །དུས་འདི་འབྱུང་
བར་མི་འགྱུར་ཏེ། །བྱ་བྲལ་སྟོན་པ་སྤྱོད་པས་ན། །སྟོང་པའི་མཚན་ཉིད་གསུངས་པ་བཞིན། །ཞེས་བཀའ་སྩལ་ཏོ། །ཀུན་ཏུ་སྟོན་ལམ་དང་བྲལ་བའི་ལེའུ་སྟེ་ཉི་ཤུ
པའོ།། ༎ཡང་འཁོར་ཀྱི་དེ་བཞིན་གཤེགས་པ་རྣམས་ཀྱིས་གསོལ་པ ། བཅོམ་ལྡན་འདས་དེ་བཞིན་གཤེགས་པ་ཀུན་ཏུ་བཟང་པོ ། བྱང་

182

ཆུབ་ཀྱི་སེམས་སྟོན་པ་ལམ་དང་བྲལ་བ་དེ་ལ ། ལྷུང་བ་སྤྱོད་པ་མཆིས་སམ་མ་མཆིས ། ཞེས་གསོལ་པ་དང་ ། བཅོམ་ལྡན་འདས་ཀྱིས་བཀའ་སྩལ་པ ། གཅིག་སྟེ
རྣམ་པ་ཡོངས་ཀྱི་མེད། །རྣལ་འབྱོར་ནམ་མཁའ་བྱ་ལམ་གནས། །མ་བྱུང་མ་སྤྲུལ་སྙིང་པོ་ལ། །སྒྲ་བདགས་ཚིག་ཀུན་གང་ལ་ཡོད། །ཕྱི་ནང་གཉིས་ཀ་ཀྱི་ཉིད་དང་། །
ཐམས་མེད་འདི་ཆ་ཤེས་རྟོགས་པ་སྤྲུལ་མེད། །སྲིད་པའི་མིང་ཙམ་ལོག་པའི་སྟོབས། །དེ་བས་ཏིང་འཛིན་མཉམ་དང་བྲལ། །དེ་ལ་ཕྲ་ཚིག་ལྟ་ཡི་དང་། །རང་བཞིན་ལྷུང་པོ་ཁམས
བཞིན་གནས། །དུས་གསུམ་དེ་དང་མི་འབྲལ་བས། །ཕྲ་ཚིག་མིང་དུ་བཏགས་པ་མེད། །ཡེ་ཤེས་ཆེན་པོའི་ཐིག་ལེའོ། །ཞེས་བཀའ་སྩལ་ཏོ། །བྱང་ཆུབ་ཀྱི་སེམས་ལ
ལྷུང་བ་སྤྱོད་དུ་མེད་པའི་ལེའུ་སྟེ་ཉི་ཤུ་གཅིག་པའོ།། ༎ཡང་འཁོར་ཀྱི་དེ་བཞིན་གཤེགས་པ་རྣམས་ཀྱིས་གསོལ་པ ། བཅོམ་ལྡན་འདས་དེ་
བཞིན་གཤེགས་པ་ཀུན་ཏུ་བཟང་པོ ། བྱང་ཆུབ་ཀྱི་སེམས་མཉམ་པ་ཉིད་ལ་དབང་བསྒྱུར་དུ་མཆིས་སམ་མ་མཆིས ། ཞེས་གསོལ་པ་དང་ ། བཅོམ་ལྡན་འདས་ཀྱིས
བཀའ་སྩལ་པ ། མི་གཡོ་བ་ནི་སྐུ་ཡི་རྒྱ། །མི་བསྐྱོད་པ་ནི་ཡེ་ཤེས་ཏེ། །མི་ལྡན་པས་ན་བདག་མེད་ཅིང་། །མི་བདེ་ཚིག་བྲལ་མཉམ་ཉིད་དོ། །གང་དང་གང་གི་ཡུལ

ཕ

༄༅། །དེ་ཡང་། ཀུན་འབོལ་ཀུན་རྫོགས་རང་བདག་ལས་བྱུང་། །འདི་ལ་སྤྲོས་པའི་མཐུད་མེད། །ཅེས་བཀའ་བསྩལ་ཏོ། །མཉམ་པ་ཉིད་ལ་དབང་བསྒྱུར་
དུ་མེད་པའི་ལེའུ་སྟེ་ཉི་ཤུ་གཉིས་པའོ།། །།ཡང་འཁོར་གྱི་དེ་བཞིན་གཤེགས་པ་རྣམས་ཀྱིས་གསོལ་པ། བཅོམ་ལྡན་འདས་དེ་བཞིན་
གཤེགས་པ་ཀུན་ཏུ་བཟང་པོ། བྱང་ཆུབ་ཀྱི་སེམས་མཉམ་པ་ཉིད་ལ་དབང་བསྒྱུར་དུ་མཚུངས་སམ་མི་མཚུངས་པ་ལགས། སྤྱོད་ལེན་མཚུངས་སམ་མི་མཚུངས།
ཞེས་གསོལ་པ་དང་། བཅོམ་ལྡན་འདས་ཀྱིས་བཀའ་བསྩལ་པ། འདི་ལ་སྤང་བསྒྲུབ་དག་ཤུལ་གྱིས། །གནས་པ་རབ་འབྱུང་བའི་གཞི་མེད་དེ། །ཀ་དག་པ་ར་ཞི
ནམ་ལྡན་ན། །སྒྱུ་མ་བདེ་བ་བསྒྲུབ་པར་འདོད། །དེ་ཡང་འཛིན་པའི་སྒྲིབ་ཡིན་ཏེ། །རང་བཞིན་གཅིག་ཏུ་མ་ངེས་པས། །ཇི་ལྟར་བལྟས་པ་དེ་ལྟར་སྣང་། །སྣང་
འདོད་སྟེ་ལ་སེམས་སོ་བདེ་བ་ཡང་། །དེ་ནི་སྒྲིབ་པའི་སྒྲིབ་ཆེན་ཡིན། །བྱང་ཆུབ་ཡན་ལག་ཀུན་གྱི་སྒོ། །ཚུལ་ཁྲིམས་བསྒོམས་པས་ཆུ་ཀླུ་བཞིན། །མཆགས་མ་མགོས་ལ་འབྱུང་
འཁྲུར་ཡང་། །བསྒོམས་པས་བསྒྲིབས་པའི་སྒྲོར་ལྟ་བཞིན། །དེ་ཡི་སྐབས་སོར་ཕྲེ་གཉེར་ཆ་ཕྱུགས་ཀྱི། །ཕྲེ་བདག་ཆེན་པོ་འདི་གླུགས་པས་བསྒྱུར་ནས། །ཤི་ཤི་མ་དོན་དུ་ཐུར་ན

183

ཡང་། །ཞི་བ་དེ་ཉིད་མཐོང་བ་མིན། །ཏ་ལའི་མགོ་བོ་བཅད་པ་དང་། །ས་བོན་མེ་ཡིས་བསྲེགས་པ་ཡང་། །དེ་ཡི་རང་དུ་མི་འགྱུར་ཏེ། །རྣམ་གྲངས་བསྐལ་བརྒྱ་སྟོང་
མཐའ་ཡས་པ། །གང་ལྟར་བསྒྲིད་ཀྱང་མི་རྟོགས་སྐྱོ། །མཚན་མ་མེད་པའི་རང་བཞིན་ན། །བསྒོམ་གནས་དེ་ལས་འབྱུང་མི་འགྱུར། །ཞེས་བཀའ་བསྩལ་ཏོ། །བྱང་
ཆུབ་མཉམ་པ་ཉིད་ལ་སྤྱོད་ལེན་མེད་པའི་ལེའུ་སྟེ་ཉི་ཤུ་གསུམ་པའོ།། །།ཡང་འཁོར་གྱི་དེ་བཞིན་གཤེགས་པ་རྣམས་ཀྱིས་གསོལ
པ། བཅོམ་ལྡན་འདས་དེ་བཞིན་གཤེགས་པ་ཀུན་ཏུ་བཟང་པོ། བྱང་ཆུབ་ཀྱི་སེམས་སྤྱོད་ལེན་མེད་པ་ལ་བདེ་བ་ཆེན་པོ་ཐོབ་པར་བྱ་བའི་ཐབས་མཆིས
སམ་མི་མཆིས། ཞེས་གསོལ་པ་དང་། བཅོམ་ལྡན་འདས་ཀྱིས་བཀའ་བསྩལ་པ། གྲོང་ཁྱེར་འདི་ལ་གནས་པ་ཡི། །རྣལ་འབྱོར་དེ་ཉིད་སྐལ་བ་བཟང་།
བདག་དང་གཞན་དུ་མི་འཕྱེད་པས། །སྒྱུ་མ་ལྟ་བུ་ཀླུ་བ་ལ་ཡོལ། །ཞེས་བཀའ་བསྩལ་ཏོ། །བྱང་ཆུབ་ཀྱི་སེམས་སྤྱོད་ལེན་མེད་པ་ལས། །སྒྱུ་མ་ཚོམ་དུ
བདེ་བ་ཆེན་པོ་ཐོབ་པར་བྱ་བའི་ཐབས་བསྟན་པའི་ལེའུ་སྟེ། ཉི་ཤུ་བཞི་པའོ།། །།ཡང་འཁོར་གྱི་དེ་བཞིན་གཤེགས་པ་རྣམས་ཀྱིས་གསོལ

184

ཕ སོ་གསུམ

༄༅། །ཕ ༈ བཅོམ་ལྡན་འདས་ཀུན་ཏུ་བཟང་པོ ། སྐུ་མ་ཚམ་དུ་བདེ་བ་ཆེན་པོ་སྤྲོས་པར་བྱ་བའི་ཐབས་ལ་མཆིས་པན ། འགྲོ་བ་ཐམས་ཅད་ལ་རང་བཞིན་
གྱིས་སངས་རྒྱས་པ་མཆིས་སམ ། ཞེས་གསོལ་པ་དང་ ། རྡ་གཞུ་ཞིན་ཀྱིས་བཀའ་སྩལ་པ ། གསོ་བའི་ཡུལ་ན་བདེ་བ་ཆེ། །འདི་ཉིད་རྣམ་དག་འཛེག་རྟེན་ཡིན། །དེ་
ལ་རྫོགས་ཀྱི་འོད་འདུས་པས། །ཕྱོགས་བཞི་མཚམས་དང་སྟེང་འོག་འགྲུབ། །མ་ངེས་འཇའ་འཚོན་ཁ་དོག་ལས། །ཐིགས་ཀྱི་ཕྱུང་པར་མཐོང་ཏུ་སྣང་། །དེ་བཞིན་གཡོ་
རྟུལ་མི་གཡོ་བར། །འབྱུང་བ་ལྔ་ལས་གཙོ་ཆེན་ཡིན། །ཞེས་བཀའ་སྩལ་ཏོ། །འགྲོ་བ་ཐམས་ཅད་རང་བཞིན་གྱིས་སངས་རྒྱས་པའི་ལེའུ་སྟེ༔ ཉི་ཤུ་པའོ།།
།།ཡང་ཕྱིར་ཀྱི་དེ་བཞིན་གཤེགས་པ་རྣམས་ཀྱིས་ཡང་གསོལ་པ ། བཅོམ་ལྡན་འདས་དེ་བཞིན་གཤེགས་པ་ཀུན་ཏུ་བཟང་པོ ། འགྲོ་
བ་ཐམས་ཅད་རང་བཞིན་གྱིས་སངས་རྒྱས་པ་ལ ། ཚོགས་དབུལ་བ་དང་རང་བཞིན་གྱིས་ཡོངས་སུ་རྫོགས་པ་མཆིས་སམ་མ་མཆིས ། ཞེས་གསོལ་པ་དང་ །
བཅོམ་ལྡན་འདས་ཀྱིས་བཀའ་སྩལ་པ ། འདས་དང་མ་བྱོན་ད་ལྟར་གྱི། །ཐ་སྙད་མིང་ལ་མི་གནས་ཏེ། །སྤྱི་ལྷག་ག་མེད་པ་རྣམ་བརྟགས་ན། །འདི་ནི་དུས་གསུམ

185

ཆེན་པོར་སྨྲེར། །མཉམ་པའི་རིག་པ་ལས་བཀོད་པ་མེད། །གཅིག་པའི་ཕྱོགས་སུ་བསྡོད་དང་བྲལ། །ཚོགས་ཀྱི་རྒྱུན་དུ་དགྲམ་པ་ཡང་། །རང་བཞིན་གནས་པས་འདྲིམ་པ
མེད༔ ༑ལྷུན་གྱིས་གནས་པས་མི་བསྐྱོད་ཤིང་། །གདོད་ནས་དག་པས་བདུད་རྩི་ཡིན། །འདུ་བྱེད་བཅུ་གཉིས་ཕྱུང་པར་ཏུ། །རང་བཞིན་ལྷུན་གྱིས་གྲུབ་པ་ལ། །སྐུ་གསུམ
ཡེ་ཤེས་ཤར་བས་ན། །ལྷག་པའི་བསམ་པས་གཟུང་དུ་མེད། །ཅེས་བཀའ་སྩལ་ཏོ། །ཚོགས་རང་བཞིན་གྱིས་ལྷུན་གྱིས་གྲུབ་པ་དང་ཡོངས་སུ་རྫོགས་པར་བསྟན
པའི་ལེའུ་སྟེ༔ ཉི་ཤུ་གཅིག་པའོ།། ||འཁོར་ཀྱི་དེ་བཞིན་གཤེགས་པ་རྣམས་ཀྱིས་ཡང་གསོལ་བ ། བཅོམ་ལྡན་འདས་དེ་བཞིན་གཤེགས
པ་ཀུན་ཏུ་བཟང་པོ ། ཚོགས་ཀྱི་བདག་པོ་དང་རྒྱན་རང་བཞིན་གྱིས་གྲུབ་པར་གནས་པ་མཆིས་སམ་མ་མཆིས ། ཞེས་གསོལ་པ་དང་ ། བཅོམ་ལྡན་འདས་ཀྱིས
བཀའ་སྩལ་པ ། ཡིད་ཀྱི་བསམ་པ་ཡོན་བདག་སྟེ། །བཀླུབས་པའི་སྟོབས་ནི་བཀྲམ་པའོ། །མཐོང་བ་རྒྱུར་པ་དངོས་རྒྱུར་ལ། །དེ་ནི་མཉམ་གཞག་རྫོགས་པའོ། །
ཡུད་ཙམ་བསྒྲུང་བས་སྒྱུར་བ་ཡིན། །དགའ་བར་འགྱུར་པས་དམ་ཚིག་སྟེ། །ཐབས་ཀྱི་གར་བསྒྱུར་བསྐྱོད་པ་ཡིས། །གཉིས་མེད་སྦྱོར་བས་ཕྱུལ་བ་ཡིན། །ཅེས

186

པ སོ་བཞི

༄༅། །བཀའ་རྩལ་ལ་ཏོ། །ཚོགས་ཀྱི་བདག་པོ་དང་རྒྱན་རང་བཞིན་གྱིས་ལྷུན་གྱིས་གྲུབ་པ་ར་བསྟན་པའི་ལེའུ་སྟེ་ཉི་ཤུ་བདུན་པའོ།།
།།འཁོར་གྱི་དེ་བཞིན་གཤེགས་པ་ཐམས་ཅད་ཀྱིས་ཡང་གསོལ་པ། བཅོམ་ལྡན་འདས་དེ་བཞིན་གཤེགས་པ་ཀུན་ཏུ་བཟང་པོ། གདོད་མ་ལ་སོགས་པའི
ལས་རྒྱ་མཚོ་ལ་མཉམ་པར་གཞག་པ་ས་གྲུབ་པ་མཆིས་སམ་མ་མཆིས། ཞེས་གསོལ་པ་དང་། བཅོམ་ལྡན་འདས་ཀྱིས་བཀའ་རྩལ་པ། མི་གཡུང་བ་དོང
བས་གདོད་མ་ཡིན། །ཐུབ་མེད་པས་ལས་རྣམས་ཟིན། །མི་རྟོག་པ་ཡི་ཤེས་བགེགས་བལ་ལ་གནས། །མི་གསུང་མཉམ་བཞག་ལྷུགས་ཚིག་གོ །ཞེས
བཀའ་རྩལ་ལ་ཏོ། །གདོད་མ་ལ་སོགས་པའི་ལས་རྒྱ་མཚོ་དུ་མི་དགོས་པ་ར་མཉམ་པར་བཞག་པ་ས་འགྲུབ་པ་ར་བསྟན་པའི་ལེའུ་སྟེ་ཉི་ཤུ་བརྒྱད་པའོ།།
།།ཡང་འཁོར་གྱི་དེ་བཞིན་གཤེགས་པ་ཐམས་ཅད་ཀྱིས་གསོལ་པ། བཅོམ་ལྡན་འདས་དེ་བཞིན་གཤེགས་པ་ཀུན་ཏུ་བཟང་པོ།
གདོད་མ་ལ་སོགས་པའི་ལས་ཐུབ་པས་ཉེ་མོངས་པ་ར་འགྱུར་བ་མཆིས་སམ་མ་མཆིས། ཞེས་གསོལ་པ་དང་། བཅོམ་ལྡན་འདས་ཀྱིས་བཀའ་རྩལ་ 187

པ། བླ་མ་མཆོད་དང་གཏོང་བ་དང་། །དེ་བཞིན་བསོད་ནམས་ཐམས་ཅད་དང་། །མ་ཆགས་མི་གཡོ་ན་སེམས་ས་མེད་ན། །ཐུས་ན་འཆིང་བ་ཆེན་པོར
འགྱུར། ཞེས་བཀའ་རྩལ་ལ་ཏོ། །གདོད་མ་ལ་སོགས་པའི་ལས་ཐུས་ན་ཉེ་མོངས་འཆིང་བ་ཆེན་པོ་ར་བསྟན་པའི་ལེའུ་སྟེ་ཉི་ཤུ་དགུ་པའོ།།
།།ཡང་འཁོར་གྱི་དེ་བཞིན་གཤེགས་པ་ཐམས་ཅད་ཀྱིས་གསོལ་པ། བཅོམ་ལྡན་འདས་དེ་བཞིན་གཤེགས་པ་ཀུན་ཏུ་བཟང་པོ། རང་བཞིན
ལྷུན་གྱིས་གྲུབ་པ་ལ་ཐུགས་སམ། ཞེས་གསོལ་པ་དང་། བཅོམ་ལྡན་འདས་ཀྱིས་བཀའ་རྩལ་པ། དེ་ལ་དེ་ཐུར་སྒྲིབ་པ་ར་འགྱུར། །ཇི་ལྟར་དེ་ལ
རྟོགས་ན། །དེ་ལ་དེ་ཉིད་གྲུབ་པ་མེད། །ཅེས་བཀའ་རྩལ་ལ་ཏོ། །རང་བཞིན་ལྷུན་གྱིས་གནས་པའི་ལེའུ་སྟེ་སུམ་ཅུ་པའོ།།
།།འཁོར་གྱི་དེ་བཞིན་གཤེགས་པ་ཐམས་ཅད་ཀྱིས་ཡང་གསོལ་པ། བཅོམ་ལྡན་འདས་དེ་བཞིན་གཤེགས་པ་ཀུན་ཏུ་བཟང་པོ། རང་བཞིན་གྱིས་ལྷུན་གྱིས
གྲུབ་པ་མི་འགྱུར་བ་ར་གནས་པའི་དོན་རྟོ་ལྟར་འགྱུར་བ་ལགས། བཅོམ་ལྡན་འདས་ཀྱིས་བཀའ་རྩལ་པ། ལྷག་མ་མེད་པས་ཡོངས་སུ་རྫོགས། ། 188

ཁ

༄༅། །འཁྲུལ་བས་ཡིན་དྲང་པོར་གནས། །ནམ་མཁའ་བཞིན་དུ་མཉམ་འགྱུར་ཞིང་། །གཞན་ལས་སྒྲོ་བས་འགྱུར་ཆེས་མ་ཡིན། །མཚུངས་པ་མེད་
པའི་ཡེ་ཤེས་ཀྱི། །ལྷུན་གྱིས་གནས་པའི་བདེ་ཆེན་དེ། །ངང་གི་ཐུགས་ཡིས་རྟོགས་པ་ལས། །ཆོས་ཉིད་གཞན་ནས་འབྱུང་མི་འགྱུར། །སྤྲོ་ཞིང་དཀའ་ལ་སྤྱོད་ཀྱང་རང་དགའ། །
མངོན་སུམ་མི་གནས་ཀུན་ཏུ་ཁྱབ། །མངོན་སུམ་འདོད་ཞེས་པ་བརྟན་པ་རང་ནི། །རྡོ་རྗེ་སེམས་དཔས་མཚོན་དུ་མེད། །ཅེས་བཀའ་སྩལ་ཏོ། །ཆོས་ཉིད་ཀུན་ཏུ་མི་འགྱུར་
བར་བསྟན་པའི་ལེའུ་སྟེ་སུམ་ཅུ་གཅིག་པའོ།། །།འཁོར་གྱི་དེ་བཞིན་གཤེགས་པ་རྣམས་ཀྱིས་ཡང་གསོལ་པ། །བཅོམ་ལྡན་འདས་དེ་
བཞིན་གཤེགས་པ་ཀུན་ཏུ་བཟང་པོ། །རྣམ་པར་རྟོག་པའི་དགའ་བ་ལ་ཆགས་ནས་སྟོན་དུ་འགྱུར་བ་མཆིས་ལགས་སམ། །ཞེས་གསོལ་པ་དང་། །བཅོམ་ལྡན་འདས་ཀྱིས་
བཀའ་སྩལ་པ། །ངོ་མཚར་རྨད་བྱུང་རྟོགས་པ་འདི། །ཐུ་བྲལ་ཉམ་མཁའ་ཇི་བཞིན་ཏེ། །ཅིར་ཡང་མི་དམིགས་གདིང་ཕྱུག་ལས། །དེ་མ་ཐག་ཏུ་རང་ལས་འབྱུང་། །
འདོད་ཡོན་སེམས་ཅན་མཚུངས་པའི་ཡུལ། །འགྲོ་བ་ཀུན་ལ་རང་བཞིན་གནས། །ཕྲིས་པས་བསྐྱེད་པའི་འཁྲུལ་པའི་ཕྱིར། །སྣང་ཉིད་སྣང་བའི་ཚུལ་བ་བཞིན། །ཞེས་བཀའ་

189

སྩལ་ཏོ། །རྣམ་པར་རྟོག་པའི་དགའ་བ་ལ་ཆགས་ནས། །སྟོན་དུ་འགྱུར་བར་བསྟན་པའི་ལེའུ་སྟེ་སུམ་ཅུ་གཉིས་པའོ།། །།ཡང་འཁོར་གྱི་དེ་
བཞིན་གཤེགས་པ་རྣམས་ཀྱིས་གསོལ་པ། །བཅོམ་ལྡན་འདས་དེ་བཞིན་གཤེགས་པ་ཀུན་ཏུ་བཟང་པོ། །མཐོང་བའི་རྣལ་འབྱོར་པ་རྣམས་ཀྱིས་རྟོགས་པ་ཆེན་པོའི་
དོན་ཉམས་སུ་ཇི་ལྟར་བླང་བར་བགྱི། །ཞེས་གསོལ་པ་དང་། །བཅོམ་ལྡན་འདས་ཀྱིས་བཀའ་སྩལ་པ། །འཁོར་གྱི་དེ་བཞིན་གཤེགས་པ་རྣམས་ཉོན་ཅིག །མ་འདྲེ་
པའི་རྣལ་འབྱོར་པས་རྟོགས་པ་ཆེན་པོའི་དོན་ཉམས་སུ་འདི་ལྟར་བླང་བར་བྱའོ། །རྟོགས་པ་ཆེན་པོའི་དོན་ནི། །རྒྱུ་དང་། །རྐྱེན་དང་། །འབྲས་བུ་གང་ལ་ཡང་མི་
ལྟོས་ཏེ། ། ཡེ་ནས་ལྷུན་གྱིས་གྲུབ་པའི་ཆོས་ཉིད་ལ། །མ་བཅོས་མ་ཡེངས་པར་ནི་གནས་པར་བྱའོ། །དེ་ཉིད་མངོན་དུ་གྱུར་པ་སངས་རྒྱས་ཡིན། །རྟོགས་པ་
ཆེན་པོའི་ངང་བཞིན་ནི། །ཅི་ཡང་མི་དམིགས་གདིང་ཕྱུག་ཆེན་པོ་ལ། །མ་ཡེངས་བཏང་སྙོམས་ཆེན་པོར་གནས་པ་ལས། །དེ་མ་ཐག་ཏུ་སངས་རྒྱས་རང་ལས་
འབྱུང་། ། ཡུལ་དུ་སྣང་བ་མེད་པའི་ཆོས་ཉིད་ལ། །ཡེ་ཤེས་བཅལ་དུ་མེད་དེ་རྩོལ་སེམས་མེད། །དེ་ཡི་ངང་ལ་མ་ཡེངས་སྐྱོང་རིས་མཐོས། །དེ་ཉིད་འབྲས་

190

161

ཁ

༄༅། །སྐུ་ཆོས་ཀྱི་སྐུ། །བསམ་མེད་བརྗོད་བྲལ་བའི་ངང་ཉིད་ལ། །ཡེ་ཤེས་གདེང་རྫུམ་པ་བསམ་གྱིས་མཉམ་གཞག་ན། །སྤྲུལ་པ་མེད་པའི་ཕྲིན་ལས་ལྷུན་
གྱིས་གྲུབ། །མཆོད་པ་བཞི་རྣལ་འབྱོར་པས་རྟོགས་པ་ཆེན་པོའི་དོན་ཉམས་སུ་བླང་བར་བསྟན་པའི་ཡི་གེ་སྟེ་སུམ་ཅུ་གསུམ་པའོ།།
རྡོ་རྗེ་སེམས་དཔའ་ནམ་མཁའ་ཆེ་ཉིད་རྫོགས་སོ།། ༄། །རྒྱ་གར་སྐད་དུ། པོ་དྷི་ཙིཏྟ་ཀྲ་མ་དྷུ་བན་ཏི་ཁ་ས་མེ་ཨ་ཡ་ང་ཀ
ར་ཧ་ན་ཧ་ཏྲ་ཛྙ་ཏུ་མ། བོད་སྐད་དུ། བྱང་ཆུབ་ཀྱི་སེམས་རྟོགས་པ་ཆེན་པོ་ནམ་མཁའ་མཉམ་པ་ཀློང་གི་རྒྱུད་ཀྱི་རྒྱལ་པོ་ཞེས་བྱ་བ། བཅོམ་ལྡན་འདས་དཔལ་རྡོ་རྗེ་སེམས
དཔའ་ལ་ཕྱག་འཚལ་ལོ། །འདི་སྐད་བདག་གིས་ཐོས་པའི་དུས་གཅིག་ན། དེ་བཞིན་གཤེགས་པ་དགྲ་བཅོམ་པ་ཡང་དག་པར་རྫོགས་པའི་སངས་རྒྱས་བཅོམ
ལྡན་འདས་གསང་བའི་ལོངས་སྤྱོད་མཁའ་མཛོད་ཅིང་མི་ཟད་པ་ཆེན་པོ། ཆོས་ཐམས་ཅད་དང་གཉིས་སུ་མེད་པར་བཞུགས་པ། ནམ་མཁའ་ཉི་མ་ཟླ་འགྲས
པར་ལོངས་སྤྱོད་པ། སྐུ་གསུང་ཐུགས་ཀྱི་གསང་བ་རྡོ་རྗེ་ལྟར་ཟླུམ་པར་བསྒྲིལ་བ། ཁམས་གསུམ་པ་བདེ་བ་ཆེན་པོའི་གྲོང་དུ་ཤ་རཱ་བ་རི་མཆེད་པ། ནམ་པ་ཐམས་

ABOUT THE TRANSLATOR

Christopher Wilkinson began his career in Buddhist literature at the age of fifteen, taking refuge vows from his guru Dezhung Rinpoche. In that same year he began formal study of Tibetan language at the University of Washington under Geshe Ngawang Nornang and Turrell Wylie. He became a Buddhist monk, for three years, at the age of eighteen, living in the home of Dezhung Rinpoche while he continued his studies at the University of Washington. He graduated in 1980 with a B.A. degree in Asian Languages and Literature and another B.A. degree in Comparative Religion (College Honors, Magna Cum Laude, Phi Beta Kappa). After a two year tour of Buddhist pilgrimage sites throughout Asia he worked in refugee resettlement programs for five years in Seattle, Washington. He then proceeded to the University of Calgary for an M.A. in Buddhist Studies where he wrote a groundbreaking thesis on the Yangti transmission of the Great Perfection tradition titled "Clear Meaning: Studies on a Thirteenth Century rDzog chen Tantra." He proceeded to work on a critical edition of the Sanskrit text of the 20,000 line Perfection of Wisdom in Berkeley, California, followed by an intensive study of Burmese language in Hawaii. In 1990 he began three years' service as a visiting professor in English Literature in Sulawesi, Indonesia, exploring the remnants of the ancient Sri Vijaya Empire there. He worked as a research fellow for the Shelly and Donald Rubin Foundation for several years, playing a part in the early development of the Rubin Museum of Art. In the years that followed he became a Research Fellow at the Centre de Recherches sur les Civilisations de l'Asie Orientale, Collège de France, and taught at the University of Calgary as an Adjunct Professor for five years. He has published several volumes of translations of Tibetan literature, and is currently engaged in further translations of classic Buddhist literature.

---

[1] Mi nub rgyal mtshan nam mkha' che
[2] For an eight volume collection of just the works of Vairochana, see The Rgyud 'bum of Vairocana : A collection of Ancient Tantras and Esoteric Instructions compiled and translated by the 8th century Tibetan Master reproduced from the rare manuscript belonging to Tokden Rinpoche of Gangon by Tashi Y. Tashigangpa. Leh, Ladakh, 1971. 8 Volumes.
[3] Beyond Secret: The Upadesha of Vairochana on the Practice of the Great Perfection. http://www.amazon.com/Beyond-Secret-Upadesha-Vairochana-Perfection/dp/1503270041
[4] See Christopher Wilkinson: The *Mi nub rgyal mtshan Nam mkha' che* And *the Mahā Ākāśa Kārikās*: Origins and Authenticity. Revue d'Etudes Tibétaines *numéro vingt-quatre — Octobre 2012* Studies in the Sems sde tradition of rDzogs chen. Edited by Jean-Luc Achard. P. 21-81.
[5] Secret Wisdom: Three Root Tantras of the Great Perfection. P. 145-183. http://www.amazon.com/Secret-Wisdom-Three-Tantras-Perfection/dp/1501018698
[6] I am currently engaged in a study involving the Tantra for the Yogins and Tantra for the Yoginis, and hope to publish a translation in the near future.
[7] For a description of the categories of Tantra according to the New Schools see my translation of An Overview of Tantra by Sachen Kunga Nyingpo in An Overview of Tantra and Related Works, p. 11-36. http://www.amazon.com/Overview-Tantra-Related-Kongma-Series/dp/1500697966
[8] See Beyond Secret: The Upadesha of Vairochana on the Practice of the Great Perfection, p. 118.
[9] Ibid.
[10] rNying ma rgyud 'bum mTshams brag dgon kyi bri ma, National Library, Royal Government of Bhutan, Thimpu, 1982. 46 Vols.
[11] For a listing of the five Atiyogas, see my Secret Wisdom: Three Root Tantras of the Great Perfection, pages 148-150.
[12] sTong nyid dben pa
[13] Sadhana
[14] bDag nyid, Atmatā
[15] Kun bzang sems dpa'
[16] bDag, Atman
[17] bDag nyid chen po, Mahātman
[18] Byang chub sems rje btsan dam pa 'od 'phro ba'i rgyud
[19] rGyud kyi rgyal po mi nub rgyal mtshan rje btsan dam pa rdo rje 'od 'phro ba'i rgyud
[20] gZu bo chen po
[21] rNam par snang mdzad
[22] bLa
[23] The Sanskrit word for "body" or "embodiment" is used in the Tibetan text.
[24] dGyes pa
[25] dGes pa

[26] Thig le
[27] rTsa
[28] sKu lnga
[29] Rig 'dzin
[30] rGyud
[31] rDo rje 'dzin pa
[32] rDo rje 'chang
[33] Kun spyan sa
[34] Thig le
[35] bDag nyid, Ātmatā
[36] Rang rgyud
[37] 'Byung ba chen po
[38] bDag, Ātman
[39] Yi ge med pa
[40] Thod rgal
[41] Ga bur rong
[42] Ye ge med pa. This is the title of another Magnificent Sky Tantra translated in this volume.
[43] sKye ba med pa. This is the title of the Root Tantra of the Magnificent Sky, which I have translated in Secret Wisdom: Three Root Tantras of the Great Perfection.
[44] Ye nas sangs rgyas bdag nyid
[45] rNam par snang mdzad, Vairocana.
[46] Sems dpa' chen po'i rgyud
[47] Probably referring to gYu dra sNying po, the King of Tsawarong.
[48] bDag nyid chen po, Mahātman
[49] rTsa
[50] 'Byung ba chen po
[51] dGon pa'i rgyud
[52] gNyis su med pa, Advaita.
[53] The Sanskrit word for "Blessed One" is used here.
[54] 'Du byed

Made in the USA
Monee, IL
04 November 2024

69288618R10218